STUDS TERKEL

STUDS TERKEL

Politics, Culture, but Mostly Conversation

ALAN WIEDER

MONTHLY REVIEW PRESS
New York

Library of Congress Cataloging-in-Publication Data available from
the publisher—

ISBN: 978-1-58367-593-9 paper
ISBN: 978-1-58367-594-6 cloth

MONTHLY REVIEW PRESS, NEW YORK
www.monthlyreview.org

Typeset in Bulmer 11/14

5 4 3 2 1

Contents

This book is dedicated to Craig Kridel whose work with African American teachers in the South mirrors Studs' lifelong belief in conversation and democracy.

Acknowledgments

THIS PROJECT BEGAN IN MY HEAD over twenty years ago. As a university oral historian, it was Studs Terkel's books that made my work possible, credible in the academic setting that swept further and further into the world of empirical data. People's stories were not to be trusted, but Studs made them legitimate. Studs' radio interviews, available through the generosity of Tony Macaluso, Angela Schein, and their colleagues at WFMT, as well as Studs' numerous books, have been instrumental to my work. Tom Weinberg's videos of Studs at Media Burn and Transom's interviews were also invaluable. I am deeply indebted to the Chicago History Museum. Russell Lewis and Lesley Martin facilitated my access to the many boxes of Studs' yet to be catalogued public papers. In addition, I would be remiss if I didn't mention Tony Parker's book of interviews, *Studs Terkel: A Life in Words*, and the many articles that Chicago journalist Rick Kogan has scribed about Studs.

But since this book is more collage/oral history than biography, I want to express my gratitude to the people who kindly had conversations with me about their memories of Studs. Each person's name is listed in the bibliography and their words, which were transcribed thoughtfully by Amanda Steiger, are cited throughout the book. Studs worked at WFMT Radio for forty-five years, and his colleagues at the station, Lois Baum, Sydney Lewis, and Tony Judge, were always available for my many additional questions. Two other colleagues at the station, George Drury and Donald Tait, through the kindness of their hearts, sent me artifacts that brought greater understanding of Studs. Other individuals I interviewed, Pearl Hirshfield, Katrina vanden Huevel, Mark Larson, David Schwimmer, Prexy Nesbit, Victor Navasky, Peter Kuttner, Bernardine Dohrn, and Bill Ayers, introduced me to individuals who were part of Studs' life.

Some of the same people kindly read chapter drafts and others the entire manuscript. As with my prior book, Joanie Krug was with me through all thirty-plus drafts. Craig Kridel, Bill Ayers, Mark Larson, Tony Macaluso, and Paul Buhle provided feedback; and oral historian Ronald Grele judiciously reviewed the entire manuscript. At Monthly Review Press, Erica Biddle, Erin Clermont, and Michael Yates thoroughly and critically edited the entire manuscript. All of these readers have made *Studs Terkel: Politics, Culture, but Mostly Conversation* a better book.

As was the case with my previous Monthly Review book, the support of the people at the press was incomparable. Besides Michael Yates, appreciative thanks go to Susie Day and Martin Paddio. Tony Macaluso must again be acknowledged as it was he who provided the WFMT photographs that appear on the cover. And, of course, I am particularly thankful to Kevin Coval, whose poetry brings me both rage and smiles, and who is every bit as Chicago as Studs. I am also grateful that the book's afterword, a poem on Studs, was generously gifted by Haki Madhubuti. There are two others who must be again noted: Bill Ayers, who brought Chicago to me; and Joanie Krug, whose support and love was all-in throughout the project and beyond.

Foreword

STUDS TERKEL WAS AMERICA'S GREATEST LISTENER. he changed the way we listen & to who. he sat with thousands of people across the spectrum of existence & garnered a broader & broader notion of who the population was & what they dreamed of & feared. a true & radical democrat, not of the party, but of the social experiment, he celebrated the uncelebrated. a champion of the underdog. he would go to the story, the person, to the history, around us now & listen. he made oral history the new journalism, a people's journalism.

Studs was a Chicago centrist, who put on for theater groups & artists & writers & musicians from here. a megaphone for the raw talent & urban realists around him. a documenter of Chicago's Janus-head & broken heart. a white ally before the term. more than an ally, which connotes a static position of undoing or of not doing, an idleness. Studs was constant & constantly active & moving & speaking against the monolith. Studs was aligned with equity & racial justice & aware of his privilege, "I am furious at myself. they have suffered these humiliations, not I."

i have tears in my eyes after reading the conclusion to Alan Wieder's book *Studs Terkel: Politics, Culture, but Mostly Conversation.* Chicago misses Studs so much. so much right now. we are a city at war. a city that dehumanizes & criminalizes its young. that shoots them dead in the street and holds the evidence for 400 days to win a mayoral election. a city that pushes its poor to the fringes & cow tows to the millionaires. Studs would be pissed right now. he'd be raging on a stage or behind a microphone demanding justice. he'd be at the homes of the families who lost someone, comforting & hearing them, like he did with Mamie Till. he'd be in the streets along side the young Black & queer activists in organizations like BYP 100 & We Charge Genocide & Assata's Daughters, organizers who are making Chicago inhabitable for all bodies. Studs Terkel put his body where his politic was. in a moment of turmoil & twitter activism, Wieder's revelatory & beautiful biography of a Chicago/american hero is an essential reminder that our life is a collection of actions, of showing up & knowing people & knowing which side we fight on.

here is a blueprint of how to work in the world. a rigorous portrait of a rigorous life of intentionality & un-compromise. how refreshing & lovely to come to know the man behind the microphone. someone who spent years & years hearing & tributing the unheard, now has an appropriate & stunning tribute of his own in Wieder's prose.

this is not the portrait of the grandfather mascot the city can defang, which happens when some in city hall or mainstream cultural institutions utter the name Studs beneath glass chandeliers & neo-liberalism. nope. this is a portrait of the life of the firebrand, of Studs the radical, the red, the never no snitch, the radio man who loved Ida like he did the city, who loved the city like he did the people who made it great. Studs' social life & circle is a who's who of counter cultural makers, from Richard Wright to Mahalia Jackson to James Baldwin. his cipher, a stunning account of the american organic intellectual fabric of the last century. all in one man, one little jew, who i miss so much, who i shared a stage with at Steppenwolf speaking against endless war, who Rick Kogan introduced my work to & came back with a handwritten note that continues to be the apex of my literary accomplishments. i miss seeing & hearing Studs around the city, in his red socks, cracking a joke & coming back with a jab & upper cut at some threat to the dignity of a life.

i miss Studs so much. & yet here he is, in the mouths of the masses, he listens in the wind, at the water, in the streets to the people who demand this city/country be more & more just. Studs has influenced & given rise to the renegade journalist, the poets of portraiture & resistance. his ears open & giant but not a big as his heart, not as lovely as his ability to make so many feel seen & heard. Wieder's book makes the man flesh & bone. This is a tribute to one of the greatest men in the history of the greatest & most horrible of cities. Studs the mayor of the eternal saloon! Studs the great comrade & convener of the counter culture. Studs to save us all, to make us all more whole & human & holy. a mensch, a tzadik. Chicago's secular saint. read & listen & listen & listen & go forth & make the totality of the city/country seen. the whole & holy horror & hilarity. the whole Studs accounted for, wanted to account for, wanted the whispers from the margin to be as grand & grander than the pork-bellied bellows of the oligarch in the downtown hold. the masses are coming. Studs is listening, ready for the rumble.

— KEVIN COVAL
poet. Chicagoan, February 2016

Introduction

ONE OF THREE SONS OF IMMIGRANT JEWS from Bialystok, Poland, Louis "Studs" Terkel was born on May 16, 1912, in New York City. In 1922, Studs moved with his parents and his two brothers to Chicago, where he lived for the rest of his life. Actor, disc jockey, author, raconteur, husband and father, Studs is probably best known as host of the *The Studs Terkel Show* from 1952 to 1997 on Chicago's WFMT. The program earned him the title of "Mr. Chicago" and many people in the city have said they always knew it was between ten and eleven in the morning if they caught an earful of his radio program.

Studs has been described as "one of the greatest listeners of the twentieth century."[1] As an interviewer, Studs provided a microphone for the voiceless, or as he put it, "the uncelebrated." His friend, guerrilla journalist Jamie Kalven, describes Studs' gift as "a sense of people whose stories, whose character, whose presence, the changes they'd gone through, enlarged the sense of human possibilities. He was modeling a way of being in the world—a way of treating other people—a way of engaging with other people in conversation. I think what he did with a great deal of heart he embodied the possibilities of the conversational engagement of citizens."[2]

Studs lived through the Depression, was blacklisted during the McCarthy era, and often said that he never met a petition he didn't sign. He did his daily commute to his radio job at WFMT by bus and engaged his fellow passengers in his passion: conversation. This book proposes that his commitment to conversation was in effect a quest for social justice.

As will be discussed in detail, formative influences for his progressive politics and passion for discourse were the debates held in the lobby of his parents' rooming house, the Wells-Grand Hotel, and the legendary Bughouse Square debates at nearby Washington Square Park. Noted Chicago radical Franklin Rosemont, who with his wife, Penelope, helmed Charles H. Kerr Publishing—the nation's oldest labor press—once described Bughouse Square as "the most celebrated outdoor free-speech forum in the entire country, where leading soap-boxers harangued eager crowds that often numbered in the thousands."[3] Studs' distinct conversational style was established as he listened to these speakers, a diverse group of union members, non-union workers, Wobblies, immigrants, scabs, progressives, conservatives, and religionists. He learned the art of dialogue, but perhaps more importantly, he fine-tuned his capacity for listening.

Bill Ayers provides an apt description of Studs' unique ability and how it serves as an important connection between conversation and politics:

> An organizer takes on faith that if you knock on the door and somebody answers it, that person has a brain and an experience and a culture and a language that has to be taken into account. A good teacher does the same thing, and Studs did it every day with his radio show, with the interviews, with the books, and with the encounters on the bus. He always believed there was wisdom in the room.[4]

Studs emphasized that his method was to "listen, listen, listen."[5] He understood the importance of patience and was attuned to what is said in silence.

The day after his death, *The Guardian* ran a piece on Studs by Ed Vulliamy. In it, Vulliamy refers to Studs as "a master chronicler of American life."[6] Referring to the impact Studs' passionate listening had on his audience, Vulliamy writes: "As you listen, you know in your bones that each person has never told their story as cogently or as fully before and will never do so again, for that was Terkel's art. He was maestro of that most precious craft in the practice of both journalism and history: listening. He was the world's greatest—and loudest-mouthed—listener. He even called his 1973 autobiography *Talking to Myself*.[7]

Curiosity, interest, and knowing the potential of human beings were most valuable for Studs. He often asserted that there were no rules to conversation and that it was important to experiment. Studs viewed his conversations as exploration. He said of his approach, "I want them to talk about what they want to talk about in the way they want to talk about it, or not talk about it in the way they want to stay silent about it. I'll keep them to the theme—age or the Depression or work or whatever—but that's all."[8] The truth for the person Studs interviewed often proved to be as equally enlightening for the speaker as it was for Studs and his audiences.

How did Studs encourage these possibilities with his tape recorder? He spoke on the topic with Tony Parker: "It's exciting—and it's scary, it frightens you. It frightens the person you're going to interview too. Remember that. Where in the radio interview you start level in confidence, in knowing where you're going, in the one-to-one interview you start level in the unconfidence, in not knowing where you're going."[9] Studs went to great lengths to explain that on his radio program he was not interviewing people but rather having a conversation. He had great regard for the people who appeared on the show. He elaborated on the importance of respect in his conversation with Parker:

> What's the first thing I do? I pay him respect. And how do I do that? I pay him respect by reading his book—and if he's written others before this one, by reading those too, or at least I have a look at them. You'd be surprised how many people don't do that elementary thing. You can hear them on other talk shows, talking to authors whose books they haven't read! Can you believe that?[10]

The people Studs interviewed remember the experience well. They speak of his interview preparation and how they sometimes felt that Studs knew their work better than they did when they came to his program.

Victor Navasky, longtime editor of *The Nation* and author of various political and historical works such as *Naming Names,* visited *The Studs Terkel Show* numerous times. He recalls the experience of appearing on Studs' show during a book tour and discovering that Studs had underlined all the passages in his book that interested him with a yellow highlighter. He juxtaposes this to other promotional appearances on his tour, where it was clear the host had not read the book; they "hadn't done their homework."[11] He recounts his interview with Studs as follows:

> He starts in and he says listen to this, listen to this, it's page thirty-seven and he reads thirty-seven in a way that he reads all kinds of meaning that you didn't know were in there and it's a brilliant new insight that he credits you with. He knows the book inside out, and he can make references forward and backwards.[12]

Studs' approach was not the norm for most radio hosts. Yet he was astounded that this attention to his guests was seen as exemplary. He spoke about his approach to interviewing authors with fellow oral historian Ronald Grele:

> I go through it pretty thoroughly. . . . I don't memorize what I've read but I have an idea generally, and a phrase or two might come to mind. He says something and it reminds me of something I've read. I call it, "the phrase that explodes," whatever it might be.[13]

In conversation with author Denis Brian, for whom Studs was the subject of the last chapter of his book *Murderers and Other Friendly People: The Public and Private Worlds of Interviewers,* Studs explains:

> To me, interviewing is equivalent to being a craftsman or being a slovenly workman. You could not conceive of a carpenter coming to the house without his toolbox, could you? You couldn't think of an electrician coming without his fusebox. . . . I mean, do you say a carpenter is remarkable when he comes with his tools? Basically,

I must respect the person I'm interviewing: there's no point to it otherwise, life is much too short.[14]

His listeners' responsiveness to his approach eventually led to Studs writing his numerous oral histories.

Studs is celebrated for his oral histories, which he began writing in 1967 when he was fifty-five years old. An interview with a London theatre troupe, "The Establishment," inadvertently led to Studs writing his many books. One of the group's members, Eleanor Bron, who was friends with Lena Schiffrin, the wife of André Schiffrin, editor-in-chief of Pantheon Books, suggested that André contact Studs. Following Bron's suggestion, he read some of Studs' radio interviews that were published in *Perspective on Ideas and the Arts*. As Studs recalled, these were published transcripts of his conversations with Marlon Brando, C. P. Snow, and Bertrand Russell. André phoned Studs in 1965. He told Studs that Pantheon was producing Jan Myrdal's book *Report from a Chinese Village* and asked him to do an oral history of Chicago as an "American village." Studs was skeptical. Two years later, the book, *Division Street America*, was published. This project initiated Studs and André's long-term collaboration and deep friendship. While all of Studs' oral histories are commendable, his three most known titles are *Hard Times*, *Working*, and *"The Good War,"* an oral history of the Second World War for which he earned a Pulitzer Prize.

Interviewing people for his books, transcribing, and editing often occurred simultaneously. The oral history process actually began with selecting people with whom he would speak. Studs asserted that he was greatly influenced by the filmmaker Denis Mitchell who was "looking for the 'hurts' in people, the hurts."[15] He talked about his process with oral history scholar Ronald Grele, in an interview printed in Grele's book *Envelopes of Sound* (1981):

How do I select? Sometimes an individual—in that individual is more than one person, you know. In someone who might be the archetype, is the anti-archetype. . . . There has to be someone who, in his own way, has an articulateness but at the same time is not so atypical as to be so different.[16]

Studs' conversations with the individuals who appeared in his books propelled the process. Step two was the completion of a full transcript of each of the interviews. Studs often listened to the interview before he handed the tape to the transcriber.

The main transcribers over the years were three women Studs worked with at WFMT—Cathy Zmuda, Kathy Cowan, and Sydney Lewis. Studs would read and reread the transcript when the draft was delivered. Using a mining metaphor, Studs touched on his transcription process with Grele:

> I get sixty pages. Now then, I sift. This is the water, this is the dust. Out of the sixty pages—the essence: five–six pages, whatever. You get the truth and cut out the fact. I'm like the prospector, I'm cutting whatever they cut out . . . I can look for a form and that's part of it. And after the form you edit it again. And there is the book, you think. But there are still your own thoughts that have got to be put down; that's the Preface, Introduction. And finally it comes out. So I say it's prospecting for gold.[17]

Studs' process was a collaborative effort in the sense that he integrated Cathy, Kathy, or Sydney's ideas as well as André's and other editors. There was an ongoing flow—interviews were conducted while others were simultaneously being transcribed and revised.

As Studs was editing and re-editing the original transcripts, he was also crafting sections and the placement of particular oral histories within the book. He was in constant contact with André who would do the same editing at certain points in the process. The opening paragraph from a letter that Studs sent André as he was organizing *Hard Times* reveals their collaborative efforts: "Thought I would try to lay out a tentative framework—obviously, there is much repetitive stuff—much, much editing and cutting ahead—yet I thought I'd do it in this manner—so I can get a feel of the overall—I'm a gestalt man myself."[18]

André understood and honored Studs' work. "We really did get rid of all the extra stuff. The books were very clearly the delineation of what was the heart of each interview, and of course, that did not affect the content of the interview."[19]

Studs provided insights into turning his conversations into books in various interviews. He spoke about Senator Russell Long of Louisiana when he talked with Michael Lenehan about how he constructed his books:

> But generally speaking, I shift things around. An interview is not written in stone. You can adjust the sequences. But never altering the words—the words are the words of the person, that's clear. . . . See now there, you see, you gotta be as truthful as you possibly can. At the same time you don't want to embarrass the guy either. There's one guy who asked me—the only person in all the thousands I've done—asked if I'd change the grammar, and that was Russell Long, the son of Huey Long, he was a senator. And Russell Long said look, my English is not that great, I want you to—and I said don't worry about that, I will, I'd alter it, see. But you want that language. I wouldn't change goin' to going, or ain't to aren't.[20]

Russell Long's request transcended grammar. Always sensitive to respecting privacy, Studs was also careful throughout his process—conversation, transcribing, and constructing—of preventing embarrassment for anyone he interviewed. He invited five academic oral historians to his show in 1973 and ethics was one of the many issues that were discussed. At one point, after sharing two stories about struggling on whether or not to include certain oral histories, Studs concluded, "It is a question of not hurting people."[21]

Studs' technique in "prospecting" or "gold mining" transcends craft. His unspoken plea to the people he met—"Amaze me"—corresponds to his spirit of interest and curiosity. Kalven explains:

> I often think of Studs in conversation in a kind of musical con-text. His pleasure was in that syncopated moment where the cliché

would carry you in one direction, and there's some pleasure in the expectation of that, but then it goes in another direction and you go, that's just so pleasing. And I think he was looking for those moments.[22]

"Amaze me" might well have guided Studs toward authentic conversation—talk that included what Jacob Bronowski referred to as the "impertinent question," those questions that lead to people discovering their own deeper truths.

Studs' interviews, however, did not just provide a microphone for the voiceless. Instead, he taught interviewees as well as his listeners and readers that we were not impotent, that we had much to say, and that our voices and our actions, not a savior politician, could change the world.

Many of this book's insights into Studs come from people he knew throughout his life. *Studs Terkel: Politics, Culture, But Mostly Conversation* includes more than one hundred conversations with Studs' family members, friends, colleagues, comrades, and other people whose lives he touched. I also listened to his shows, watched videos of his talks, and watched documentaries on his life. I read and reread, sometimes many times, his books and countless articles. Tony Parker's book *Studs Terkel: A Life in Words* was especially helpful. Finally, there were the hundreds of articles written about Studs, interviews with Studs, and the numerous boxes of his papers in the archives of the Chicago Historical Museum.

Numerous times as I was interviewing people for this book, I was asked why I was writing about Studs. In actuality, I had been scripting Studs' story in my head for many years. Ten years after he published his first oral history, *Division Street: America*, I was completing an oral history for my doctoral dissertation. The year was 1977. Despite the fact that the academic world already had an Oral History Association—the organization was established one year before *Division Street: America* was published—I was convinced that the only reason I was encouraged to be an oral historian was the popularity of Studs' work. I still believe this to be true.

There is much that remains to be learned from Studs Terkel's life in 2016. Historian Michael Frisch reminds us: "The emphatic ear and the moral heart are what lifted Terkel's listening above the ordinary."[23] Studs taught us that we are more than we even realize. He taught us that we have power if we speak out and that, collectively, we have strength when we wed conversation and action. *Studs Terkel: Politics, Culture, but Mostly Conversation* is an attempt to introduce and include more people in Studs' dialogues.

1

From Bialystok to Chicago

STUDS TERKEL'S ASHES, BLENDED WITH those of his wife, Ida, are buried at Bughouse Square, the same place where Studs listened to political speeches as well as the words of "everyman" as a youth. After Terkel died on Halloween 2008, his son Dan and various family and friends fulfilled a request that he had made shortly following Ida's death in 1999. Studs told filmmaker Tom Weinberg in *Studs on a Soapbox*: "It's not as though she's here because she's not. Of course the spirit is so I have fresh daisies for her here. The urn is still here—the urn of her ashes. So when I kick off we'll mix the two ashes and spread them around Bughouse Square."[1]

Following Studs' death, friends planted a tree in his honor at Bughouse Square. Then, about a half-year later, Studs and Ida's combined ashes were buried under the tree. As Garry Wills stated, "He knew this was where he would be most at peace, and had asked that we bring him to this as his Chicago home."

From Bialystok to New York

Samuel and Anna Terkel, Studs' parents, married in 1898 and immigrated to the United States from Bialystok[2] during the first decade of the twentieth century. In 1903, Anna and Sam joined fellow Bialystok Jews who fled the Polish city for the United States, Argentina, Australia, South Africa, and Palestine. In spite of this global dispersion, in the early years of the twentieth century Bialystokers remained tightly bound by their allegiance to their community. Anna and Sam were no exception. They moved their family from 213 Avenue A on the Lower

East Side of Manhattan to Boston Road in the Bronx in order to live in a building with other Bialystok Jews.

Studs was Anna and Sam's third son, born in 1912. His older brothers, Meyer and Ben, were born in 1905 and 1907. As part of his recurrent shtick, Studs often said, "I came up the year the *Titanic* went down."[3] Memories of the first ten years of his life as a boy in New York are briefly documented in all of his memoirs as well as in the introduction to his oral history on death and dying, *Will the Circle Be Unbroken?* Besides describing images of his poor health as a young child due to his struggles with asthma, Studs reflects on his parents as well as his neighborhood. He recalls outings with his father to watch parades in Manhattan. He reminisces about sitting on his father's bed as they listened to music, politics, and baseball on the radio together.[4] "America's favorite pastime" was a passion he shared with both of his brothers. He writes emotionally of viewing photographs of his brothers in clothing designed and sewn by their father who was a tailor by trade.

Studs often refers to family photographs in his recollections of his early years. After viewing a picture of his family smiling, Studs admits to writer Tony Parker that his family life was anything but happy and that his parents' marriage was fraught with problems. Describing another image in his second memoir, *Touch and Go*, Studs writes: "Sam and Annie were creatures of different spheres whom some God of the perverse had blessed and cursed into union."[5]

He also reminisces about his brothers in *Touch and Go*. Of Ben, Studs writes: "There was a worldwide protest, no demonstrator more fervent and fiery than my brother, Ben, a flamboyant ten, displaying as many buttons as a cockney pearlie."[6] Studs views his brother Meyer as his first teacher. Meyer's son Sandy recounts that Meyer, who always called Studs "Louie," held his hand as they walked to the library to get Studs' first library card.[7] Recollections of his neighborhood in the Bronx are of Italian, Jewish, and Irish children intermingling. Studs recalls ethnic slurring among each of the groups dissipating in 1920 when in his words, "all the kids on the block became Irish."[8] This unity revolved around a Sinn Fein prison hunger strike. Studs' time as a boy in New York was brief. There are many more memories from his teenage years.

From New York to Chicago

When he was nine, Studs' family moved to Chicago. With the financial assistance of Anna's brother-in-law, Studs' parents were able to open a rooming house at the corner of Ashland Avenue and Flournoy Street, in a largely Italian neighborhood on the Near West Side of Chicago. The Terkels ran this rooming house together until they took over the Wells-Grand Hotel in Chicago's "Towertown" in 1925.

In his introduction to Frank O. Beck's *Hobohemia*, a radical history of 1920s–1930s Chicago, Franklin Rosemont describes Towertown as a "heady mix of radical politics and cultural nonconformity."[9] Towertown was home to the Radical Bookshop where Wobblies leader Big Bill Haywood and poet Carl Sandburg played chess. It was also the community of the Studio Players, Ben Reitman's Hobo College, the Dil Pickle Club, and of course the activities at Bughouse Square. These inhabitants all flavored Studs' youthful appreciation of conversation, learning, politics, and culture, which began during his teenage years in Chicago. He fondly recalls the influence of various teachers at McKinley High School. WFMT colleague Lois Baum expresses her amazement at the lucidity of Studs' memory. "He remembered his high school Latin lessons. I remember him quoting from them when he was ninety-six. He fondly remembered his teacher, her name, the books they read in class and how her lessons gave his life new meaning that evidently lasted all those years."[10]

At McKinley High School, Studs remembers the patient but bigoted algebra teacher who gave him copies of Henry Ford's anti-Semitic *Dearborn Independent* and the English teacher in whose class he read *Ivanhoe*, *The Ancient Mariner*, *Treasure Island*, and *Beowulf*. At his graduation, this teacher gifted Studs with a *Roget's Thesaurus* and Olive Schreiner's *Story of an African Farm*. The latter present always befuddled Studs. He talked about it in a 1979 interview with South African novelist Nadine Gordimer and they were both puzzled by the gift.

From a young age, Studs was an avid reader. He devoured the biographies of Rousseau, Voltaire, Jefferson, Paine, Gandhi, and other great thinkers. One of the Wells-Grand's occupants introduced him to the E. Haldeman-Julius *Little Blue Books* that were published in Girard, Kansas. Baum puts great emphasis on the importance of the humanities on Studs' life and work, and how this shaped his approach to conversation:

> Most of all I think he wanted to connect things, which is what the humanities do. . . . A news article about, say, the South Side of Chicago would remind him of a poem of Gwendolyn Brooks or a conversation with James Baldwin or an early Louie Armstrong recording—that kind of thing.[11]

Much of Studs' formative experiences with learning took place "in the world" and this also greatly shaped his approach. Studs credits his brother Meyer with introducing him to theater, books, and classical music. It was his brother Ben who first acquainted him with jazz. Together they frequented the Dreamland Ballroom, where the clientele was all white while the performers were all-black. At the time, impresario Paddy Harmon ran the club and the bandleader was Charles "Doc" Cook. Studs was energized and excited by the music.

Studs counts his father among his most influential teachers. In his writings, he repeatedly emphasizes his father's admiration for socialist labor leader Eugene V. Debs. Many years later, he recalled his father's knowledge of Debs' proclamation when he was sentenced to prison: "While there is a lower class I am in it; while there is a criminal element, I am of it; while there is a soul in prison, I am not free."[12]

He credits his mother as another life teacher. Although Studs viewed his mother as a harsh woman, he attributes some of his political foundations, especially about women and social class, to her. In *Touch and Go* he writes, "Annie was sympathetic to women who were in trouble. She was a crazy kind of feminist, a red-stocking feminist."[13] Elsewhere, he describes his mother as a tough woman, a hardworking woman in a man's world.[14] School and family, of course, helped shape Studs' worldviews. However, it appears that even in his youth, Studs welcomed the world as his teacher.

The Wells-Grand Hotel

The Wells-Grand lobby resonated with a colorful spirit. Card games, including cribbage, hearts, and pinochle, were played. All booze was welcome. Magazines such as *Judge*, *Life*, *Liberty*, and *Literary Digest* were in the lobby and Studs as well as the hotel's patrons read them and debated politics and culture. This early exposure to heady discussion and debate had a huge impact on Studs. He made an effort to get to know the people who inhabited the hotel lobby.

The Wells-Grand was a "men's hotel," kind of the opposite of a flophouse.[15] In Studs' memoir *Talking to Myself*, we are introduced to an old Wobblies' organizer, Sprague, and a dishwasher, "Civilization," whom Sprague and other people in the lobby endured. Civilization's real name was Joe Chch and Studs wrote that there were many other "Civilizations" on the streets of Chicago at the time. Chch sent letters that predictably went unanswered to politicians, athletes, performers, writers, and even Al Capone. His lectures left a lasting impression on Studs. In *Talking to Myself* he says, "His explanations, long, tortuous, and gnostic, are profoundly incomprehensible. It is a religious moment for all present."[16]

The lives of the men in his parents' hotel illustrated the humanity of workingmen—ordinary people, whom Studs referred to as "the uncelebrated." Roberta Lynch, currently Executive Director of AFSCME Council 31, the nation's largest public employees service union, says:

> One of the really amazing things about him was the tremendous respect that he had for working people, which you just didn't encounter very much in our culture. Many people who think they're liberal or progressive are actually contemptuous of or completely indifferent to working people, and Studs just recognized the incredible talent and intellect that is there in the ranks of any, almost any, group of workers that you could find.[17]

He was most intrigued by the debates between the Wobblies and what some of the tenants derogatorily referred to as "company men." The latter group argued that IWW stood for "I Won't Work."

Studs loved their discussions. He recounts them being "heated, full of four-letter words, but at the same time there was something exciting. There was argument, debate—and we hardly have that these days. We just sit there, paralyzed or catatonic, watching the TV."[18] As Paul Buhle writes in his introduction to *Wobblies! A Graphic History of the Industrial Workers of the World*, "The world of the Wobblies was one realized in its best moments by solidarity across race, ethnic, gender and nationality lines."[19] Throughout his life Studs upheld the Wobblies as a model for political action.

The Chicago that nurtured the young Studs Terkel was as Thomas Dyja, the author of *The Third Coast: When Chicago Built the American Dream*, notes, "America's biggest labor town, the birthplace of May Day, the eight-hour day, the Industrial Workers of the World, and the American Communist Party."[20] Perhaps more than any other, the period where he worked in his parents' hotel and visited nearby Bughouse Square represents Studs' enculturation into both political discussion and action.

The Depression

Studs' *Hard Times: An Oral History of the Great Depression* (1970) begins with a short essay, "A Personal Memoir (and parenthetical comment)." Revolving around memories of the patrons at the Wells-Grand Hotel, Studs discusses the Depression and the subsequent changes in people's lives, including their shame and humiliation. These are topics that Studs revisits in many of his books.

When the Depression hit in 1929, Studs recalls that his parents were generous toward their patrons. Regulars at the hotel were allowed to forgo their rent deadlines but the Wells-Grand and the Terkel family were also victims. In *Touch and Go*, Studs references the Depression as shaping not only his politics but also his life:

> I was there watching what hard times did to decent people. The great discovery is how they behaved during a specific issue, not what they were labeled. It was easy to call somebody a Commie, or

a Red, or a Fascist for that matter. It's how that person behaved at a certain moment that counted.[21]

In *Hard Times*, he explains that in the mid-1920s the hotel was at full occupancy and its guests were fully employed. He remembers the symbolism of seeing the Vacancy sign appear at the entrance of the Wells-Grand as the hotel's patrons faced unemployment. The Depression ultimately resulted in the hotel's closure.

Bughouse Square

Just as he viewed himself as an observer of the hotel lobby debates, Studs continued that role when visiting one of the favorite places in his life, Bughouse Square. Studs often spoke about how much he loved the speeches there and that he visited the park as often as possible from the late 1920s through the 1930s. In *Touch and Go* he writes, "Bughouse Square was much like London's Hyde Park, where free speech is the power and the glory. . . . In its heyday, during the 1920s and 1930s, there were five soapboxes on which the most celebrated speakers were allowed twenty minutes and then afforded the privilege of passing the hat."[22]

Bughouse Square was Studs' political link from adolescence to adulthood; the scene provided Studs with an introduction to anarchist, socialist, and communist oratory. Studs listened to radical labor organizer Lucy Parsons, the wife of Haymarket martyr Albert Parsons, and Ben Reitman, the "hobo doctor" who was Emma Goldman's comrade and lover, as well as many of the "uncelebrated," as they roared against the Haymarket Affair, American capitalism, and world imperialism. Many years later, reflecting on Haymarket, Studs' underlying theme regarding the event was political transformation. Not personally, but collectively, as he wrote and spoke on numerous occasions crediting the Haymarket martyrs with the eventual reality of the eight-hour workday.

The University and the Death of Sam Terkel

Although the University of Chicago became Studs' academic home in 1928, he was simultaneously observing life and politics at Bughouse

Square and he was still working with his parents at the Wells-Grand. In 1931, Sam Terkel died of heart disease at the age of fifty-four. Studs found his father on his deathbed and he shared his feelings in *Will the Circle Be Unbroken?*:

> My father's death, the first in our family, brought upon me a heartache that was too much to bear. . . . I was remarkably calm until, seated on the Grand Avenue streetcar the next day, heading nowhere in particular, I surprised myself by breaking into uncontrollable sobs. Embarrassed, seeking to stifle them, blubbering despite myself, I hurried toward the rear of the car, ready to hop off anywhere, just to escape my show of grief.[23]

Sam had been sick for many years and at times had been bedridden. Both Ben and Meyer, like their father, would die of heart attacks in their fifties. Studs worried about having a heart attack throughout his entire life.

By the time Studs completed his undergraduate degree at the University of Chicago in 1932, his family had lost the Wells-Grand. He entered law school in 1934. He never wrote about his years as an undergraduate student and his memories of law school were for the most part negative. Reading Studs' reflections on law school it appears that his classes were relegated to a lowly fourth place behind movies, baseball, and music. Studs viewed his exploration of black music as the highlight of his law school days at the University of Chicago. While waiting for a streetcar in what was then labeled the "Black Belt," he would buy used jazz and blues records, referred to then as "race records," a practice that continued when he became a disc jockey in the 1940s. This music spoke a new language for Studs—it wasn't the language of the "underdogs" who lived at the Wells-Grand Hotel, but nonetheless the language of the underdog. Chicago poet Haki Madhubuti recalls: "Very few people knew as much about black music as Studs, even black people."[24]

In the 1930s, Chicago was the most racially segregated city in the northern United States. Studs' law school class included only three women and one black student amid many young white men. Years later, he told Denis Brian: "I went to law school dreaming of Clarence Darrow and woke up to see Julius Hoffman.[25] You can imagine my astonishment."[26]

In a 2003 panel discussion, Studs spoke eloquently about his disdain for torts and courts.[27] Although Studs graduated from law school at the University of Chicago and was admitted into the Illinois State Bar Association,[28] he never had any intention of practicing. Instead, he actually applied for nine-to-five jobs and sought out various acting roles. His vanity and the aspect of Studs that was the "ham" received affirmation even during his school years. In 1933, wearing a gray fedora, his face donned the cover of *Official Detective*. There were radio soap opera gangster roles in Studs Terkel's future.

2

Work, Theater, Politics, and Most Importantly, Ida

BEGINNING IN 1934, THE YEAR HE GRADUATED from law school, Studs appeared in three bit roles at the Chicago Opera House. Recalling one of those early roles, Studs writes, "I doubt whether any member of the audience sees me. I am directly behind the knight, who may be Wilt Chamberlain."[1]

At the same time, Studs sought nine-to-five employment. Using his hotel experience, he began writing letters to apply for concierge jobs at upscale hotels throughout the world. Studs also applied for a job as a fingerprint classifier at the FBI in Washington. The initial interview was cordial, but he was not hired for the job. Studs was uncertain why. He thought his rejection might have occurred because he was Jewish. The answer emerged when he requested his FBI files and found that he had been besmirched by one of his professors. Many years later, Studs told his publisher André Schiffrin he was proud of the fact that Hoover had said, "He's not our kind of guy, not our kind of boy."[2]

Studs did secure a different position at the Federal Emergency Relief Administration (FERA) office in Chicago, doing statistical research on unemployment in Omaha. After a short period, he moved to New York and continued working for the same agency. He was able to attend the city's coveted theatrical productions, but after six months a higher paying position at the Treasury Department lured him to Washington.

Although Studs' stay in the nation's capital was brief, he made good friends and scored a role in the Washington Civic Theater Group's production of Sinclair Lewis's *It Can't Happen Here*. In it, Studs plays a handyman who transforms into a storm trooper. Of this role, Studs recalls:

> I've come across these nobodies in real life, who were just ordinary people, but they feel frustrated by something and they take it out on the wrong person. And I remember putting that uniform on, the Corpos uniform. And I'm addressing this audience. And I'll never forget the feeling of power, the power that I, a nobody, felt as a somebody. That's what Sinclair Lewis had in mind.[3]

Studs' analysis of his role in the play is something of a foreshadowing. He would tell the stories of "ordinary people" throughout the rest of his life.

During his short stints in New York and Washington, Studs remained a Chicagoan at heart. He returned home in 1938 and joined the Workers' Theater, which two years later became the Chicago Repertory Theater. A colleague from FERA, Charles DeSheim, introduced him to the group where they studied Stanislavski's *An Actor Prepares*. It was at the Chicago Repertory Theater where Louis Terkel acquired the nickname "Studs."[4] His fellow performers noticed him carrying James Farrell's *Studs Lonigan* books—thus the nickname. Some friends found the new name humorous as they viewed the character, Studs Lonigan, as a loser. However, it is easy to imagine that Farrell's depiction of Lonigan spurning societal mores was attractive to Louis Terkel.

Studs worked with the troupe during the prewar years and considered the experience a turning point in his life. His first role was as the taxi driver Joe Mitchell in Clifford Odets' *Waiting for Lefty*. By 1935, the show had become both the most widely performed and the most widely banned play in the United States. Besides theaters, the troupe performed in various alternative venues including union halls, soup kitchens, street demonstrations, taverns, and cultural centers. The audiences were filled with working people. Two high school–aged members of the group, Haskell Wexler and Nathan Davis, became

Studs' lifelong friends. Wexler, a radical filmmaker, who died in 2015 just before his ninety-third birthday, had one line in *Waiting for Lefty*. Years later when Nathan Davis was honored for his lifetime achievement with a Jeff Award Celebrating Excellence in Chicago Theater, Studs spoke about meeting the "kid." He said, "We needed a young kid, a juvenile. A kid comes in named Nate Davis out of nowhere. Reads for the part of this young, nineteen-year-old kid, and our director says, 'he's a natural.' That was his first time in the theater."[5]

In addition to his Chicago Repertory roles, Studs began playing gangsters in various radio soap operas. According to a 1992 biography, Studs' New York accent and *Official Detective* look made him a natural for roles as a criminal.[6] Studs was quick to remind interviewers that his work as a soap opera gangster was limited as his character always ended up either in prison or dead. Reminiscing, he explained that there were three types of gangsters: the bright gangster, the middle gangster, and the dumb gangster. His role was always the latter.[7]

Politics and Community

On May 30, 1937, Studs was deeply affected by the Memorial Day massacre of protesting Republic Steelworkers. Marching with their families, workers were attacked by the Chicago police who were, for all practical purposes, representing Republic Steel. While Studs was not at the demonstration when police shot and killed ten unarmed workers, one of his friends, Harry Harper, lost an eye in the melee.

The following day, alongside other members of the Chicago Repertory Theater, Studs paid homage to the fallen workers. He was infuriated to learn that most had been shot in the back. Studs and his fellow actors performed for their comrades at Sam's Place, the southeast Chicago watering hole that was home to the steelworkers. A week later he attended a massive rally at the Chicago Opera House where A. Philip Randolph and Carl Sandburg were among the speakers. In his book *Studs Terkel's Chicago*, Studs captures the mood: "The atmosphere at the Opera House was more highly charged than any I had ever experienced. I could sense the trembling indignation on the stage. You could taste the wrath of the audience."[8] The United States Senate investigated the killings, and it was the son of one of Sam Terkel's heroes, Robert La Follette, Jr., whose committee concluded that the police had acted criminally In addition, the findings of the committee helped elevate the place of trade unions in the American ethos—a response dear to Studs.

When the Chicago Repertory Theater disbanded at the beginning of the Second World War, Studs became involved in Franklin Delano Roosevelt's Works Progress Administration (WPA). He secured a place at the Illinois Writers' Project–Radio Division in 1936. He wrote a screenplay on Tecumseh as part of his application and was hired for a salary of eighty-four dollars a month. Writers' Projects throughout the country published state and regional guides that included culture, geography, food, and vivid descriptions of everyday life. With participants like Richard Wright, Saul Bellow, Ralph Ellison, Zora Neale Hurston, Claude McKay, Kenneth Patchen, Philip Rahv, Kenneth Rexroth, Harold Rosenberg, Margaret Walker, Frank Yerby, and Nelson Algren involved in the program nationally, the writing was superb.[-]

The radio division produced shows on great artists that were aired on WGN in Chicago. Studs worked directly with curators at the Art Institute of Chicago to devise topical discussions that might include commentary about Daumier, Van Gogh, Matisse, or Eakins.

While Studs wrote first drafts for his broadcasts at home, he took great joy in the collective-communal ethos of the radio division. He said of the experience: "We'd read it to our colleagues for their approval and our director's approval. Oh it was wonderful. We all liked each other very much and were rooting for each other. But we also criticized the work. There was a comradeship there. We knew we were in for something exciting at that moment."[9] Comradeship, community, and the uncelebrated were vital elements of Studs' time at the Writers' Project. Paraphrasing Albert Einstein, he emphasized the community aspect of the project in his interview with the *Soul of a People* filmmakers:

> He said the individual in a society such as ours feels he will lose individuality if he's part of something, say a union or a neighborhood. He'll lose individuality. On the contrary says Einstein. He

enriches his individuality. You don't live in a vacuum. You live in a world of others. And if you take part in it what you've discovered as you grow, you are enriched as a person, as an individual.[10]

Participation in the Writers' Project and his friendship with Nelson Algren continued to influence Studs' work his entire life. Bettina Drew's biography, *Nelson Algren: A Life on the Wild Side*, asserts that Algren encouraged Studs to pursue his second career as an author. In addition, Studs often referenced Algren's Writers' Project work managing oral history projects. Studs further acknowledged the influence of the Writers' Project in his conversations with the *Soul of a People* filmmakers: "Were it not for the Writers' Project, I doubt whether I'd have been doing this stuff or being even a writer."[11]

Ida

The most significant event in Studs' life was his marriage to Ida Goldberg on July 2, 1939. They first met at the Chicago Repertory Theater. Ida was a social worker and she had gone to the theater with a friend to attend an acting class. Studs described their initial encounter in each of his memoirs as well as *Will the Circle Be Unbroken?*. Both Studs and Ida reminisced about their courtship with Tony Parker. Ida recalled her first impression when she met Studs:

> I thought he looked like a hoodlum, and I wondered how he'd got into the place and what he was doing there. But he'd overheard us reading and talking about the play, and he came over and said he'd just been in New York and he'd seen it performed professionally, and he thought it was wonderful. So I thought, Well, the guy might look like a hood but he didn't talk like one.[12]

In their interview, Ida told Parker about their first date seeing the French film *Club des Femmes*. She recalled accompanying Studs to Russian movies and the two of them developing a private rapport: "In Russian films the hero and heroine didn't embrace, they shook hands on meeting or parting. So we used to do the same, like this—'Natasha!

Aloushka!' 'Ah Natasha! Ah Aloushka!' with a very hearty handshake to show affection."[13] Studs and Ida shared multiple common interests and loves—theater, politics, music—they sang the same songs.

After the couple married, Studs often talked about Ida being the primary breadwinner. Her job as a social worker brought in much more money than his salary from the Illinois Writers' Project and his bit acting roles. He loved to joke about marriage being a way to cancel his debts to Ida.

Ida Goldberg was the love of Studs Terkel's life and she felt likewise. "Being married to Louis has been a great thing in my life, and I've never thought I'd want to be married to anyone else. I just consider myself very lucky that we found each other, I really do."[14] Together, Studs and Ida were involved in various political causes. Throughout their lives, Studs always pointed out that Ida was the political activist. For example, shortly after they met she boycotted wearing silk stockings in response to Japan's colonialism in Asia. And it was Ida who insisted on the ironic quotation marks on the title for Studs' later book, *"The Good War."* They supported the Soviet-American Friendship Committee (SAFC) and the Anti-Fascist Committee (AFC). With SAFC, the mission was to promote an alliance with the Soviets. The Anti-Fascist Committee was Studs' introduction to the Spanish Civil War and to the Abraham Lincoln Brigade, progressive Americans who fought fascism in Spain prior to the Second World War.

They also participated in anti-lynching protests. The anti-lynching movement started in earnest in the late nineteenth century and its most well-known leader was Chicagoan Ida B. Wells. The National Association for the Advancement of Colored People (NAACP) led the movement in the early twentieth century. By the 1930s, socialist and communist organizations were also deeply involved in the fight against American white supremacy. For example, Communist Party affiliate the International Labor Defense (ILD) defended the Scottsboro Boys, the nine teenagers who were accused of rape in Alabama.

Haskell Wexler cites stories of Studs being furious after Mussolini gifted the city of Chicago with the Balbo Column during the World's Fair of 1933. It was a pillar from the archaeological site of an ancient

Roman temple. Seaplanes from Italy, led by Italian aviator Italo Balbo, delivered the column. Chicagoans were excited about the gift, including Wexler, and the city's mayor, Ed Kelly, even changed the name of Seventh Street to Balbo Drive.[15] Wexler recalls Studs' initial reaction:

> "'The, goddamn fascist! Goddamn fascist!' And I remember saying, 'Well, Studs, those are great planes! Look, they ran in the lake!' So I said, 'What is fascist?' So he says, 'Well look, kid.' He says, 'Fascist is when the government and the military and big business, they all get together and they get some joker like Mussolini to confuse the people full of bullshit, and they run the country. And that's what a fascist is.'"[16]

Despite the couple's antiwar political stance, Studs volunteered for the Air Force in 1941. He served for only a year. Studs was not eligible to participate in the war because his eardrums had been perforated since childhood. Just prior to leaving for basic training in Missouri, the Chicago Repertory Theater Group gave Studs a farewell party. He remembered that there was a big crowd and that Billie Holiday, who was performing at a nightclub nearby, appeared and sang a few songs.

After basic training, Studs served stints in Colorado, Miami, and North Carolina. During his time in Colorado, Studs was involved in some radio productions, but his superiors were suspicious. In *Touch and Go*, he writes about being called in by his commander: "The fact that Billie Holiday sang for me was held against me because the FBI hated her. As soon as she began performing 'Strange Fruit'[17] and singing at benefits for politically progressive causes, the FBI started tailing her."[18]

When Studs returned home to Chicago, he and Ida began to craft their lives together in earnest. Ida worked as a social worker; Studs continued to act and also began his involvement in radio as a disc jockey. Studs got to know Ida's sister Minsa, a dancer who studied with Martha Graham, wrote poetry, and was a choreographer throughout her life. Minsa was married to Italian artist Alberto Burri who was credited with helping to revive Italian art after the war. Burri worked with mundane materials such as burlap and wood, and his paintings were later exhibited at the Guggenheim Museum in New York, the Pompidou Center in Paris, and the Tate Gallery in London.

In turn, Ida was fated to experience Anna Terkel and the extended Terkel family. She talked with Studs about his Aunt Fanny, Sam Terkel's sister, referring to Anna: "My introduction to your aunt was a rather interesting one. The first thing Fanny said to me, she took me by the arm, and kissed me on the cheek, and she said, 'I want to tell you something. See that woman there? She killed my brother.'" [19]

Studs' long friendship with folk musician and activist Pete Seeger also began at this time. Their first encounter when Seeger's band visited Chicago in 1941 led to Studs, not for the first or last time, imposing on Ida. Seeger and his band, the Almanac Singers, included Woody Guthrie, Millard Lampell, and Lee Hayes. As Studs remembers, he sent the band to his apartment at two in the morning with a note to Ida that read: "These are good fellas. Put them up for the night." Their apartment was small and Ida would be getting up early for work, but this did not prevent Studs from intruding on his wife.

Pete Seeger often appeared on Studs' radio shows in the coming decades, and Studs helped nurture Seeger and blues artist Big Bill Broonzy's recording with Folkway Records. Seeger was a Harvard graduate whose name became synonymous with folk music. Yet he hated being referred to as a folksinger or a celebrity. Like Studs, Seeger believed in the "everyman": "This whole emphasis on who's important and who's not—we're all important, and the artist no more than anyone else. The goal isn't to be an Important Artist, a star, separate from everyone else. The goal is to get everyone to be an artist."[20] Pete's quote, of course, could be attributed to Studs. They were truly friends and comrades.

Radio Life

Through the efforts of politically progressive ad man Ed Gourfain, Studs became a radio fixture in Chicago throughout the 1940s. Gourfain was a benefactor of the Chicago Repertory Theater, and he respected and admired Studs. Even though Studs' politics often insulted his sponsors as well as the "Duke of Chicago," Colonel

McCormick, Gourfain always protected Studs. In 1944, a political acquaintance, Leo Lerner, hired Studs to do a weekly program for the Independent Voters of Illinois. The organization was referred to as a Communist front in Studs' FBI file. In reality, IVI was a progressive group in Chicago that opposed machine politics and promoted civil rights. The show was aired on WCFL, the radio station of the Chicago Federation of Labor.

In 1944 and 1945, IVI sponsored forty shows on WCFL. Studs worked as one of their scriptwriters as well as a presenter. In addition, he hosted a weekly news and commentary show. One particular episode focused on the Henry A. Wallace and Jesse Jones political debates. "Shall Plutocracy or the People Rule in the U.S. of A.?" was rerun twice on WCFL and reprinted in the *Federation News*. The most powerful program that Studs was involved in at WCFL was one he co-wrote and hosted with Louis Scofield in 1944. *The Progress of Labor* was a one-hour program that historian Nathan Godfried describes as a dramatization of "the historical development of the labor movement in America from the days of indentured servants to the present."[21] The program generated a positive response across the country. The following year Scofield and Studs collaborated on a show called *The Last Bomb* that dramatized the struggles of workers after the war. As the Cold War began, Scofield, who was under suspicion as a Soviet sympathizer, left the station. Soon after, because of his own progressive dispositions, Studs' work at WCFL also came to an end.

Beginning in 1945, most of Studs' time as a disc jockey was spent spinning records on WNER, Chicago's ABC-affiliated station. Among his multiple haunts were Stuart Brent's Seven Stairs Bookstore on Rush Street and the Concord Radio-Camera Shop in Bronzeville. It was at the latter that he acquired his records. He called his show *The Wax Museum*, because the old records were made with wax.

Due to Studs' initial radio success, the *Chicago Sun-Times* courted him to fill a position as a music critic at the newspaper. It was at this time that Studs first met Mahalia Jackson, initiating a strong friendship that would continue until she died in 1972. Many years later, onstage at Berkeley, Studs described his early days in radio to Harry Kreisler:

I became a rather eclectic disc jockey. I played operas. I played jazz—Louis Armstrong's "West End Blues." I might play an aria from *Fidelio* with Lotte Lehmann singing Leonore. And then follow with Woody Guthrie doing the Dust Bowl Ballads. That's when I first discovered Mahalia Jackson. I heard this voice . . . it was an Apollo record. It was called, "Move On Up a Little Higher," a gospel song, written for her by Professor Thomas A. Dorsey, a great songwriter who wrote "Precious Lord, Take My Hand," Martin Luther King's favorite song. I said, "This is a voice I've never heard before." So I played her a lot, and she used to give me credit as being the white disc jockey who enlightened the white world.[22]

Studs loved the diversity of his radio work. He loved discovery. He loved being amazed. One of the people who continually astonished him, and later would become a friend, was the "Poet Laureate" of radio, Norman Corwin.[23] On May 8, 1945, Studs and Ida tuned in to hear *On a Note of Triumph*, Norman Corwin's radio broadcast marking the end of the Second World War in Europe. It was the most listened-to radio drama in U.S. history. In an interview with Sydney Lewis, Studs reflected on Corwin's influence on his own work: "Norman Corwin elevated the word. He did scores of programs, one better than the other. But he wrote for the ear. And he was the master of it; I'd be remiss if I didn't mention Corwin as the bard of radio. He had a tremendous influence on my own work. The way he used words, the way they sounded."[24]

American Racism

In 1946, Ida and Studs' son Dan was born. Studs assumed the traditional American male role in child rearing, thus the early raising of Dan fell more to Ida. As he became more well known in Chicago as both a disc jockey and actor, Studs also worked with colleagues and comrades in the struggle to end white supremacy in the United States. He stayed abreast of those southerners, black and white, who maintained the fight against segregation and oppression, honoring both their shrewd intelligence and bravery. It was at Orchestra Hall in Chicago where Studs befriended one such person, Virginia Durr,[25] who was speaking along with Mary McLeod Bethune[26] on an anti-segregation program. When Studs introduced himself to Durr, she thanked him but then gave him a hundred leaflets with the command, "Now dear, you better hurry outside, pass those out quickly because Dr. Bethune and I will be at the African Episcopal church in two hours."[27]

In 1948, Ida and Studs became heavily involved in the presidential candidacy of Henry Wallace. Wallace's platform advocated universal health care and the end of segregation. Wallace had been FDR's Secretary of Agriculture in 1933. He became vice president in 1940. However, both Republicans and Democrats viewed him as too progressive and Harry Truman was instead selected to be vice president in 1944. As Chicago politico Don Rose pointed out, "Studs was a third-party guy."[28]

Studs worked with friends Algren, South Side activist Timuel Black, recent medical school graduate Quentin Young, and many other supporters on the Wallace campaign. At one of the rallies, at which Studs was the master of ceremonies, Zero Mostel did a routine on J. Edgar Hoover saying, "Who's going to investigate the man who investigates the man who investigates me?"[29] A Detroit friend, Lew Franks, asked Studs to co-produce an NBC special for Wallace's campaign. His co-producer was the musicologist Alan Lomax. The show included two voices, Henry Wallace and Paul Robeson. Studs' most powerful memory was of the awed crowd outside the studio when Robeson appeared. Studs greatly admired Wallace, but it was Robeson he most remembered from that evening. Speaking personally about American racism, Robeson reflected on his father and sang the provocative song "Scandalize My Name." Unfortunately, the event and the dialogue on racism it highlighted did not lead to Wallace's election.

That same year Paul Robeson turned fifty. He had already been called before the House Un-American Activities Committee (HUAC), yet, or maybe due to this, his birthday was celebrated throughout the world. Studs emceed the celebration at the Chicago Civic Opera House. Both Robeson and Lena Horne sang at the party. When Studs'

FBI files were released, he felt proud that one of the reasons cited for his blacklisting was his association with Robeson. Ardent in vocal support of the Abraham Lincoln Brigade in the 1930s, fighting for civil rights, and supporting the Soviet Union in the 1940s, Robeson overtly represented Studs' political views.

Also in 1948 Studs and Win Stracke toured with Big Bill Broonzy. Still spinning records as a disc jockey, Studs mixed folk music with jazz, blues, and even gospel. Their two-week tour of the Midwest was called *I Come for to Sing*. Broonzy sang country blues as well as folk music and ballads. Ten days into their road trip, they were on the way to a performance at Purdue University in West Lafayette, Indiana, and stopped at a tavern for food and drink. Bill Broonzy was leery, anticipating racism. He told the others to go in by themselves and to bring him a ham sandwich. Studs was incensed. In *Talking to Myself* he writes: "Bill had cast no more than a casual, almost imperceptible glance that way. How does he know? How dare he jump to such conclusions? These are, after all, hardworking guys, decent men."[30] The group convinced Broonzy to join them. As they walked up to the bar to place their orders there was silence until the bartender spoke, "I can serve three of you gentlemen."[31] In this instance, although Studs writes about many other racist occasions—he emphasizes Big Bill's ability to never get humiliated despite how demeaning the circumstances may be—Bill Broonzy became one of Studs Terkel's teachers.[32] He and Studs were friends throughout the 1940s and 1950s and he appeared on Studs' WFMT show various times until his death in 1958.

As the 1940s came to a close, life was exciting for Studs. He was well known as both a radio personality and a politico in Chicago, and was expected to have a show as television readied to debut in the city, joining broadcasts that originated in New York and Los Angeles. When Studs reflected on the decade, he described how his affiliation with progressive organizations and his talks at political rallies had a great effect on his life in the 1950s as he launched his television show, *Studs' Place*.

3

Television, the Blacklist, and WFMT

WITH *STUDS' PLACE*, STUDS TERKEL was caught in the late 1940s–early 1950s wave of what became known as the "Chicago School of Television." Shows were shot locally on a low budget, improvised rather than based on a script, broadcast live, and tended to push the boundaries of contemporary televised fare. Three programs in particular exemplify this trend: Burr Tillstrom's puppet show *Kukla, Fran, and Ollie*; the musical variety show *Garroway at Large*; and the dramatic series *Studs' Place*.

Studs' Place first aired in 1949. The show started as a sketch on the variety show *Saturday Night Square* in which Studs played a bartender. In *Touch and Go*, Studs writes:

> *Studs' Place* was a revolutionary program; we were pioneers. Remember, this was 1949, and TV was a brand-new medium. The radio had brought hearing a voice into your home, but seeing someone, the visual aspect, this was brand new. . . . Working in TV at that time, it was frontier country, you could do anything—your impulses could be expressed and nobody was there to stop it. The reverse of what TV has become today.[1]

Set in a small greasy spoon diner, Studs' character was the "everyman" proprietor. The other recurring cast members were the waitress, played by Beverly Younger, and the diner's regulars, played by Chet Roble and Win Stracke. For Studs, the show was "an arena in which dreams and realities of 'ordinary people' were acted out."[2] Thomas

Dyja captured the spirit in his book *The Third Coast*: "The stories were about individuals within a community that accepted all different kinds of individuals. Visitors to Chicago looked for the real *Studs' Place*, but unlike the original Bull and Finch Pub in Boston, it was too good to be true."[3]

Studs' Place was about the uncelebrated. It was the first TV show to include a pregnant woman, which necessitated network clearance. There was a segment on deafness. The waitress, Grace, always wore a union button. Though some of Studs' friends saw politics in the show, Garry Wills wrote: "There was nothing political about *Studs' Place* but the red-checked tablecloths, like the red-checked shirts and red socks and ties that Terkel always wore as a sign of his radical sympathies."[4] Whether or not *Studs' Place* was radical was immaterial within the U.S. political climate in the 1950s. While *Kukla, Fran, and Ollie* and *Garroway at Large* advanced to New York and were nationally syndicated by 1953, both *Studs' Place* and Studs became victims of Senator Joseph McCarthy's anti-Communist blacklist. The last episode of *Studs' Place* aired in January 1952.

Studs often told the story of the show's demise. It involved a visit from a New York NBC executive who explained to Studs that his show was in jeopardy because Studs had signed petitions for organizations like the Anti-Fascist Refugee Committee and the Committee for Civil Rights. In a discussion with Calvin Trillin, Studs contends that the NBC executive had proposed to him, "Why don't you say you were dumb, you were stupid, you were duped."[5] Of course Studs refused and *Studs' Place* was terminated. In the final episode the diner loses its lease.

Blacklist

The FBI began compiling files on Studs and Ida in the 1940s and didn't cease their surveillance on the couple until 1990. Listed for the years between 1945 and the cancellation of *Studs' Place* were the many rallies Studs attended. The various organizations that Studs supported were cited as Communist as were the people who he embraced—Henry Wallace and Paul Robeson for example. Studs' FBI file includes 269 pages but only 147 are available for viewing. In the file, it is revealed that in 1952, Owen Vincent testified before HUAC that Studs invited him to join the Communist Party (CP) in the 1930s. One informant explained that the *Daily Worker*, the newspaper of Communist Party USA, was Studs' inspiration. However, various entries in his file begin by stating that it is unknown if the informant was reliable. Subsequently, the listings are too spurious to deserve individual or collective attention. There was never a HUAC subpoena for Studs, which was something of a disappointment. With humor, he told Trillin that he could not believe that Zero Mostel, Arthur Miller, and Lillian Hellman were on the list but not himself.[6]

This book relies heavily on conversations with many people on the political left, some of whom have great curiosity as to whether or not Studs was a card-carrying member of the Communist Party. Studs' son Dan and his friend Ed Sadlowski offer some alternative possibilities. First, Dan Terkell:

He didn't have much patience for actual transactions of a technical nature of any kind. So, it's possible that he could have unwittingly signed something that our friendly crusaders in D.C. were able to link to the Communist Party. But you know he wouldn't bother to read the document.[7]

Sadlowski proposes a different interpretation:

Terkel didn't belong, he wasn't a card-carrying member of too many anythings. If he did he probably would have had a chest or two of those cards, you know, because his nose was into everything. You wouldn't find him at anything that was snobbish to the left to such a degree that you were frowned upon if you stood in the shadows. You would find him listening and out front.[8]

Friendships with people who acknowledged their participation in the Communist Party, his support of left-wing political organizations including the Abraham Lincoln Brigade, at the very least, placed

Studs within the scope of the Popular Front. Putting Dan and Ed's views aside, Studs would not have been unique in being sympathetic to Communist Party ideology but abhorring the organization's rigidity and even the meetings.

Studs would have looked askance at Party edicts, but he was involved with people in the Party, and union members in the Congress of Industrial Organizations (CIO), especially steelworkers in Chicago. One can envision Studs within Mark Naison's definition of the Communist Party, which is actually more a definition of the Popular Front. After noting the diversity and breadth of the Party and the Popular Front, Naison asserts: "The Popular Front developed a unique U.S. chemistry, a vision of a nation repudiating ethnic prejudice and class privilege and employing the strength and resilience of its common people to prevent a fascist triumph."[9] Oral historian Ronald Grele was astute in his thinking on Studs' politics saying, "For Studs it was a matter of his own life in Chicago that informed his politics, not the theory."[10]

The aggregation of Studs campaigning for Henry Wallace for president in 1948, his serving as the master of ceremonies at political meetings, his petition signings, and his continued support of unions and workers led to his blacklisting in 1951. That meant lean times for the Terkels. The family had to rely on Ida's social work paycheck to get by. Studs wrote of the time with humor, but losing his television show due to his perceived politics clearly altered his path. Win Stracke was also blacklisted, resulting in the loss of his children's program and his firing from the choir at Fourth Presbyterian Church. He and Studs began referring to themselves as the "Chicago Two."

Studs' nephew, Sandy Terkell, remembers his father, Meyer, on the phone trying to encourage Studs at the time. Dan Terkell refers to Studs' McCarthy-era fate as both a curse and a blessing: "As perverse as this may sound, I think we actually owe a great debt to Joe McCarthy, because had the blacklist not existed, he wouldn't have become who he was."[11] Other people who knew Studs concur. Sydney Lewis, who worked closely with Studs for over twenty years and co-authored *Touch and Go* explains, "Blacklist time was his library time, reading time, and he used it well."[12]

Studs had various acting roles and public appearances during his blacklist years. For a short time, he even worked as a manager at the Senate Theatre. However, in the early 1950s, a local florist and American Legionnaire named Ed Clamage decided it was his mission to destroy the livelihoods of progressives like Studs. Clamage was the chairman of the Chicago American Legion Anti-Subversive Subcommittee of the Americanism Commission. He sent out copies of Vincent's HUAC testimony to Chicago media outlets and called civic organizations that had offered Studs speaking venues, pressuring them to cancel his engagements.[13] Studs recalls these were usually talks on jazz and folk music for women's groups.

Studs regarded Clamage as "the Joe McCarthy of Chicago." In *Talking to Myself*, Studs presents a letter he sent to his nemesis: "The ladies to whom you have written have, in response, decided to double my fee. Instead of paying me $100, they have given me $200. How can I show my appreciation? You have $10 due as an agent's fee. Should I send it to your favorite charity? Please advise."[14] Despite his spunk, both his blacklisting and Ed Clamage's zeal had a negative impact on Studs' livelihood. For example, his music column for the *Chicago Sun-Times* was abruptly canceled. Clamage persistently protested outside of Studs' public talks. Another tormentor launched attacks via various neighborhood and community newspapers.

In the early 1950s, FBI agents visited Studs and Ida on more than one occasion. Studs reports that it was always Ida who informed the agents that they were not welcome. During these times, even the seemingly always optimistic Studs Terkel felt unsure. Studs knew a lot of people whom he viewed as progressive that had capitulated to the HUAC Committee. When interviewed many years later, he said that if he had been called to testify, he thought that he would have never "named names." One of his Chicago friends and political comrades, Timuel Black, recalls Studs' bravery during this period: "I will generalize and say he was a self-sacrificial, courageous person and that was what was so notable about him."[15]

WFMT

Studs' life changed dramatically in late 1952. He was listening to Rita and Bernie Jacobs' radio station, WFMT, on Christmas Eve. A Woody Guthrie record was playing. He had never heard Woody on the radio. Studs dialed in to WFMT and Rita answered the phone. As Studs tells the story, he explained to her that he felt an affinity with the station and would like to work there. Rita knew who he was but she had to tell him that they didn't have any money, to which Studs replied: "I haven't any either, so we're even."[16] This was the beginning of a regular broadcast on Sundays that quickly became *The Studs Terkel Show*. The show would air daily for the next forty-five years. Among Studs' early colleagues at WFMT were Norm Pellegrini and Ray Nordstrand. Both men worked with Studs throughout his four decades at the station.

Initially broadcasting only on Sunday mornings, Studs continued his other part-time radio host job at an African American station, WAIT, which featured a jazz show. For a short time, he joined WAAF radio host Vince Garrity on a third radio program, *Sounds of the City*. The two men traipsed around Chicago interviewing various "characters" from eleven at night until one in the morning. Studs recalls that although there was little rapport between Garrity and himself, the people they met were fascinating.[17] Jamie Kalven comments:

> I think the expectation is that you can at any moment learn something really important from anybody. You might walk out the door and encounter somebody. You know, actually remarkably few people operate that way or make themselves available in that way. And that was truly who he was. I mean he truly did that. If he went to the corner to get a newspaper he was open to the possibility of something interesting happening, bumping into somebody, having a conversation.

The Studs Terkel Show went through various changes over time. Studs played all genres of music, but his interviews with Pete Seeger and jazz musician Bud Freeman in the studio inadvertently transformed the focus of the program. Reminiscing with Calvin Trillin, Studs notes, "A listener calls up one day, says, 'Why don't you do more of that?' I say, 'More of what?' 'More of talking that way. It sounds like I'm eavesdropping on a conversation I haven't heard before,' and that's what began."[18] Not only did the radio program diversify its format, but the listener's request eventually led to Studs' numerous oral histories. *The Studs Terkel Show* was not only quickly a success in Chicago, but was recognized as the leading cultural radio program in the country in an Ohio State University national survey. The show's success, as Sydney Lewis recalled, was directly due to Studs' magic. "He would find the perfect piece of music even, and it could just be a feeling. But his artistry was in his bones, you know? He just felt his way to things that worked together."[19]

In addition to his radio and television work, Studs continued to appear in theater productions and became a well-known figure around Chicago. He also constructed his first book, *Giants of Jazz*. Studs interviewed thirteen jazz greats—Joe Oliver, Louis Armstrong, Bessie Smith, Fats Waller, Duke Ellington, Benny Goodman, Count Basie, Billie Holiday, Woody Herman, Dizzie Gillespie, Charlie Parker, and John Coltrane. Studs, deeply connected to African American musicians in Chicago, was keenly aware of their generosity as they, in his words, "graciously offered me time, conversation, and information."[20]

As of 1954, he also became the host of Mahalia Jackson's CBS radio program. As they rehearsed for the third episode of the thirteen-week series, a CBS executive from New York appeared and handed Studs a piece of paper. It was a loyalty oath. As Studs and the executive talked, somewhat heatedly, Mahalia walked by and said, "Is that what I think it is baby? Are you gonna sign it?" Studs said, "Nah." And Mahalia responded, "Let's rehearse." The CBS man said that it was required and Mahalia replied, "No Studs, no Mahalia."[21] The show went on.

American Racism

Mahalia Jackson is another important figure in Studs' life, and is featured in his book *Race* as well as his other oral histories. Studs regards her as another teacher from whom he learned about racial discrimination and humiliation due to segregation. He recalls that one night after working on the show, Mahalia was exhausted, so he suggested they eat at the building's Wrigley's Restaurant. He remembers watching as Mahalia and her best friend Mildred recoiled at the suggestion.

Studs knew that Philip Wrigley, chewing-gum executive and owner of both the *Chicago Tribune* and the Cubs, was overtly racist. When Mahalia asked Studs if he had ever seen black people in the restaurant, he replied, "No, but they will now."[22] At Mahalia's insistence, they walked to a nearby hamburger joint for their dinner. Reflecting on this incident, Studs notes, "I am furious at myself. They have suffered these humiliations, not I."[23]

Although the early 1950s were challenging for Studs, both he and Ida rallied their spirits and commitment to social justice. They were included in the Bronzeville multiracial gatherings at African American sculptor and Communist Party member Marion Perkins's house. Among the guests were Gwendolyn Brooks, Margaret Burroughs, Si Gordon, and one of Studs' 1930s benefactors, Ed Gourfain. Studs and Ida were very much involved in the civil rights movement. Just as he answered calls to support labor and class equity, he made appearances at and emceed Chicago meetings for racial equality. Studs aired many broadcasts that focused on American racism. Even at this time in the 1950s, he hosted Paul Robeson, an act of bravery as Robeson was still considered persona non grata by both the FBI and the local Red Squad.

Social and Political Milieus

In the 1950s, the Terkels' inner social circle was composed of families who shared a history of involvement with the Chicago Repertory Theater. These families included Nathan and Matta Davis and their three children, and Win and Genevieve Stracke and their two daughters. Charlotte (Chucky) and Ray Koch were also part of Ida and Studs' social milieu, as was artist-activist Pearl Hirshfield.

Studs first met Pearl in the 1930s when she auditioned for the play *Morning Star* at the Jewish People's Institute on Chicago's West Side.

Studs was the play's casting director. Pearl recalls that her friendship with Ida and Studs truly began in the 1950s, when Dan and her daughters were at the same elementary school, and the parents mingled at PTA meetings. This also marks the beginning of the couples' political camaraderie.[24] Pearl and her husband, Hyman Hirshfield, a progressive doctor who worked with the Black Panthers in the 1960s and collaborated with Quentin Young for many decades in the quest for socialized medicine, hosted various benefits for social justice. Ida and Studs attended their first event at the Hirshfield home in 1952, a fundraiser for the defense of Ethel and Julius Rosenberg. For the next four decades, Studs was a consistent participant at these gatherings. "He supported everything I did. He was so generous with everything I was doing. In fact, he gave me a rubber stamp. We would stamp the letter with his name. And we got a lot of money, raised a lot of funds," recalls Pearl.[25]

Studs experienced a great setback in 1958 when his oldest brother, Meyer, died of a heart attack. He'd had two previous attacks in the 1950s, and, like his father, died before his sixtieth birthday. Sandy Terkell remembers Studs' discomfort with his brother's open casket and that he was too overwhelmed to stay in the room. In spite of this personal tragedy, Studs never appeared to waver in terms of his work or political energy. In 1959, he conducted close to one hundred interviews.[26] The list of interviewees would expand greatly in the next decade. In the 1950s Studs' interviews were mostly with authors, musicians, and actors. It was not until the 1960s that political activists began to appear on the program more frequently.

4

Politics, Disparity, and White Supremacy

THE POPULARITY OF *THE STUDS TERKEL SHOW* grew tremendously in the early 1960s, and the concomitant celebrity brought more travel for Studs and Ida. Close friend Nelson Algren started referring to Studs as "Transatlantic Terkel." In 1960, Studs and Ida journeyed to the United Kingdom and France. Algren, who was then staying with his long-term, long-distance lover Simone de Beauvoir, was the couple's host in Paris. While in the French city, Studs interviewed de Beauvoir as well as Marcel Marceau. Both conversations aired on his show. He compared de Beauvoir to American feminist Margaret Fuller,[1] while she touched on her own travels and the life experiences that led to her feminist perspective.

The same year, Studs also went on the air with a grandmother, young leaders of the Student Nonviolent Coordinating Committee (SNCC), Maya Angelou, John Howard Griffin, Geraldine Page, Langston Hughes, Norman Mailer, and Pete Seeger. He aired radio specials for New Year's Day, Memorial Day, Veterans Day, and Labor Day, as well as features about Eleanor Roosevelt, Mark Twain, and Jane Addams.

During this time Studs was also performing theatrical roles. He was cast as the King in William Saroyan's play *The Cave Dwellers*, at the Goodman Theater. This is when he started frequenting Riccardo's, a neighborhood haunt he shared with friends Algren, Mike Royko, and Herman Kogan. One of Royko's biographers, F. Richard Ciccone, somewhat smugly referred to Studs, Nelson, and Mike as a "mutual admiration society."[2] According to Studs, besides being a place where

journalists met, Riccardo's effused "openness and ebullience."[3]
When Philip Wrigley, the building's owner, challenged proprietor Ric
Riccardo about admitting black people, Riccardo responded by hang-
ing a sign at the entrance that read "All Men of Good Will Welcome."

The Impertinent Question

Around this time, the "impertinent question" became a focus of Studs'
interviews. In *Talking to Myself,* he explains that he was at a London
party with scientist Jacob Bronowski when he was introduced to the
term. During a conversation about the Cuban Missile Crisis, Bronowski
turned to him, saying:

> We haven't asked the impertinent question. . . . Until you ask an
> impertinent question of nature, you do not get a pertinent answer.
> Great answers in nature are always hidden in the questions. . . .
> Now the artist asks the same kind of question; not about dead,
> but living nature; not about the outside, but the inside world; not
> about facts but about the self.[4]

Studs expanded the concept to include politics. He inserted impertinent questions into all of his conversations, both on radio and later in
his oral histories. In this way, his conversations sought a deeper truth.
Mike Royko said: "He might not know what year someone was born,
maybe not what decade even—but he knows where their heart is, he
knows where their soul is, and where to find the things in them they
care about."[5]

The Struggle to Save Hull House

In 1961, Studs and Ida became involved in what would be a two-and-a-
half-year struggle to save the Hull House settlement on Chicago's Near
West Side from urban renewal. Possibly the most renowned social
settlement in the United States, Hull House was founded by reformer
and social activist Jane Addams in 1889. Although the institution's
wide-ranging programs had served working people for over half a century, the battle to save it was a losing cause. In 1963, the complex of

buildings at 800 S. Halsted Street was displaced by the University of Illinois's expanding urban campus.

Chicago activist and Studs' friend since the 1930s, Florence Scala, remembers Studs interviewing neighborhood people and publicizing Hull House's fight against the city. Studs marched and attended meetings, and he also welcomed Scala, longtime Hull House leader Jessie Binford, and other residents to his program. Scala, who lived in the Hull House community her entire life, appeared on Studs' show numerous times. Studs' interviews with Scala touched on community, politics, capitalism, and power. When Studs asked her about the struggle to save Hull House, Scala didn't deny that it was an impossible task. She even pointed out that Binford had always had carte blanche with the city's mayors, but not this time.

Scala told him that Hull House had opened up the world for both her and her mother, revealing, as she put it, "There was something else to life besides sewing and pressing."[6] The greatest disappointment for Scala was when she realized that it was the young, liberal, pro-Hull House board members who were facilitating its destruction and the removal of its community. Most disheartening for her, in fact, was witnessing the demise of Hull House's community spirit. When Studs eulogized Scala in 2007, he said, "She was my heroine. She tried with intelligence and courage to save the soul of our city. She represented to me all that Chicago could have been."[7]

In Conversation with James Baldwin

The year 1961 also brought new diversity to the *Studs Terkel Show*, through specials on women writers, American Indians, Abraham Lincoln, and Christmas folksongs with Win Stracke. Interviewees during the year included Algren, James Baldwin, Ethel Merman, Zero Mostel, Ravi Shankar, Shel Silverstein, Lillian Smith, Gore Vidal, Norman Thomas, and Tennessee Williams.

During Studs' first interview with James Baldwin on July 15, they conversed deeply about the personal and collective consequences of white supremacy. A Bessie Smith tune opened the show. Baldwin told Studs that he sought to write like she sang. Baldwin describes his experience of listening to Bessie Smith records in Switzerland, writing his first novel and being surrounded by "white snow and white people."[8] Their long conversation explored the social, political, and psychological aspects of American racism.

First, Baldwin spoke about having to find his identity as a black man because "I had told myself so many lies, that I really had buried myself beneath a whole fantastic image of myself which wasn't mine, but white people's image of me."[9] Then, Baldwin moved beyond his own psychological pain and talked about the humiliation for black men living in the United States, the invisibility of African Americans, and the cost white people pay for their own racism. Studs listened as Baldwin talked of the price *he* paid for American racism. This broadcast marked a milestone in Studs' commitment to bringing awareness to the state of race relations in the United States. Studs continued to dedicate many of his WFMT shows to the fight against racism, to advancing civil rights, and to introducing his audience to great black artists.

The Prix Italia

Beginning in late 1961 and finishing four months later in early 1962, Studs and Jim Unrath produced his most celebrated special, "Born to Live: Hiroshima." Studs acknowledges Unrath in *Touch and Go*: "He calls me 'Boy Fellini' because I don't fully say things; it's all in my head. But Jimmy has a sense; he's the one who gets what I'm imagining better than anybody."[10] Lois Baum expands on Studs' process: "He never wrote a script. . . . He began with a sketch of maybe five points, and a list of the people in the documentary that he wanted to include in the order in which they should appear."[11] When entertainment writer Clifford Terry interviewed Unrath, he highlighted Studs' lack of technical expertise:

> When we were doing "Born to Live," all I wanted him to do was press the "record" button at the same time I was doing something else. We must have tried it forty-five times. I was getting angrier and angrier. All he had to do was push a button! I think that's one of the

reasons his interviews come off so well. His mechanical ineptitude relaxes people.[12]

Studs conceived of "Born to Live" as a "collage montage of voices"[13] meditating on life in the nuclear age. The program included interviews with a woman who survived the bombing in Hiroshima, a *hibakusha*; a tattooed street worker; suburban parents; and artists Pete Seeger, James Baldwin, John Ciardi, and Miriam Makeba. The voices of Albert Einstein, Sean O'Casey, and Bertrand Russell were also part of the show.

At the urging of WFMT co-founder Rita Jacobs, the program was submitted in the competition for the fourteenth annual Prix Italia Award in 1962. "Born to Live" won the prestigious "East-West" UNESCO special prize for radio documentaries or dramatic works. In addition to the award there was a $3,000 cash prize.

En route to Verona for the award ceremony, Ida and Studs spent time in France, Italy, and the United Kingdom. As part of their travels, Studs conducted interviews with progressive educator A. S. Neill and philosopher Bertrand Russell in Wales. Russell was ninety at the time and he impressed Studs with his clarity and what Studs refers to as his "life force." He had conversations in Paris with playwright Eugene Ionesco and actor-singer Yves Montand. In Rome, he had interviews with film directors Federico Fellini and Vittorio De Sica. During his visit to the set of Fellini's *8½*, he also conducted an interview with Marcello Mastroianni.[14]

Studs and Ida's journey culminated at the Prix Italia ceremony in October. Studs wrote with humor about the ceremony, but he clearly viewed the award as a great honor. Sadly, he lost the award scroll on the 151 bus when he returned to Chicago.[15] WFMT still plays "Born to Live" every New Year's morning.

The Studs Terkel Show

Political spirit intensified on *The Studs Terkel Show* in 1962. Activist and educator Rick Ayers suggests that Studs "laid low" for a decade after the blacklisting. Ayers in 1962 was a high school senior in sub-urban Chicago. He and his friends had come to the midnight show and Studs chatted with them afterward in the hall. Ayers felt that he wanted to know what these suburban kids represented. "The thing that Studs does, which is uncanny, is he is so into you. You're the most important thing in the world. It's like he's trying to understand the meaning of life, and he suspects you have the answer. And that makes you feel important."[16] "Born to Live" was followed by specials on French prisoners, Bertholt Brecht, and Charlie Chaplin. Political guests included Clancy Sigal, Saul Alinsky, James Baldwin, Ossie Davis, Ruby Dee, Paul Goodman, and Herbert Hill. Musicians Louis Armstrong, Miriam Makeba, Carlos Levi, and Eartha Kitt were also featured on the show.

South Africa

In 1963, Lufthansa Airlines asked Studs if he would join four other journalists on its inaugural flight from Frankfurt to Johannesburg. Although he pondered the ethics of his participation, he ultimately made the journey.[17]

Studs' anti-racist perspective was magnified during his sojourn in South Africa. Unlike the other journalists on the trip, Studs carried his tape recorder everywhere he went, documenting the experiences of black and white South Africans living in what Bishop Desmond Tutu refers to as South Africa's "Pigmentocracy." Despite 1963 being one of the most intense and contested historical junctures of the struggle against the apartheid state, Studs, in the short time he was there, managed to touch the hearts of the people and their lives within the country.

Lufthansa had organized various tours for the journalists during their junket. One was to Kruger National Park, famous for its luxury safari lodges. The group stayed at a camp called Pretoriuskop where Studs met the attendant assigned to his room. The man wore black servants' shorts, one of many symbols of the oppressive and demeaning nature of apartheid. He introduced himself as "John" and explained to Studs that he would take care of him at the lodge. He called Studs "Mastah," to which Studs responded, "I'm not your master."[18]

After this brief and uncomfortable exchange, Studs asked the attendant about his life. He learned about his family and his aspirations for his children to become doctors. The man told Studs that he worked seven days a week and traveled home, a good distance, every day, to be with his family. And he told Studs that his name was not John:

> "What is your name?" I ask. "John," he says, as though speaking to a retarded child. "I told you." "No, no," I say. "What is the name your father gave you?" He looks at me intently. Who is this guy, anyway? He smiles. "Magwiana." He whispers it. I take out a piece of paper. Slowly, he spells it out for me. Slowly, I write it down. I show it to him. He laughs. There is a touch of surprise to his laugh. "John is not my real name. The white people gave it to me because they can't say Magwiana Hlachayo." We both laugh.[19]

The following day Studs and the other American journalists went on an excursion to view zebras, wildebeests, elephants, and lions. Before they left, Studs observed a black man sweeping the floor. Two white men stood near him conversing about the childish nature of black South Africans. One of the men told Studs that it would be useless to talk to the "boy" as he did not understand English. Later in the day, Studs spoke with Magwiana about what he had seen. He responded, "I'm feeling bad on it. My heart is sore."[20]

Studs' dialogues with white South Africans during this trip revealed their humanity, but also their privilege and the conflicting reality that within apartheid all individuals are dehumanized. Among the many people Studs met, the message was always somewhat similar. Whites who were privileged assured Studs that they were cognizant of the shortcomings of apartheid, but they often added that the system made sense for South Africa. Artist Cecil Skotness, a resident of Johannesburg in 1963, explained to Studs that South Africa was "a happy society for whites." He added, however, "One mustn't think too deeply, of course."[21]

Studs visited South African writer and political activist Nadine Gordimer in her Johannesburg home on the first leg of the trip. She trusted him enough to suggest that he meet with struggle leader Chief Albert Luthuli when he traveled to Durban. Knowing the reality of apartheid well, Nadine provided careful instructions on arranging a meeting with Luthuli:

> When you reach an Indian marketplace in Durban, find a public telephone and call this number. Ask for B.W. Medawar. He is a close friend and colleague of the Chief. His phone is undoubtedly tapped by the SB–Special Branch. . . . Simply say you're a journalist from America and a friend of Nadine Gordimer. Say nothing else. He'll know what you want.[22]

Studs followed the instructions that led to an interview with this great South African leader, then President of the African National Congress (ANC). The apartheid government had banned Luthuli, which was the equivalent of house arrest in the United States, except that in South Africa this did not require formal criminal charges. He had won the Nobel Peace Prize in 1960. In 1962, he authorized Nelson Mandela to announce a move from peaceful resistance to armed struggle. It is important to note that armed struggle was defined as attacks on electrical pylons and government facilities—not attacks on people.

Chief Luthuli was forced to live in the small town of Stanger, about thirty miles outside of Durban. His conversation with Studs defined the apartheid state's reality from the ground, from the struggle. When the two men met, Studs shared his stories of getting acquainted with Magwiana Hlachayo as well as that of the white men in the lodge's lobby who spoke of blacks as children in the presence of the black worker. He recalls that Luthuli laughed. Studs likened this to the experiences of his friend, blues musician Bill Broonzy, and the blues line "laughin' on the outside, cryin' on the inside." Studs suggested that it might be more like "raging on the inside." Chief Luthuli responded, "One of the sore points is that we are not regarded as human beings. But if occasionally we are, it is as ignorant children."[23]

Luthuli spoke with Studs about Zulu history and culture as well as his own personal story, including his education at Adams College and his teaching. He shared his hope of a South African society where cultures come together to live but also his anger at government oppression. He referred to himself as a militant but then quickly spoke of his hope for democracy.

Although his stay in South Africa was brief, Studs explored the heart of the apartheid state through individual and collective South African stories. He learned the contradictions of individuals as well as the system. Recounting these conversations ten years later in *Talking to Myself*, Studs managed to display these complexities without ever denying the evils of apartheid. Upon his return to Chicago, his interviews with Gordimer, Luthuli, and Alan Paton aired on WFMT as did his conversations with black miners.

"This Train"

Politics and racism were linked in Chicago. Correspondingly, Ida and Studs' antiracism efforts included combatting Mayor Richard J. Daley. Partnering with friends like Leon Despres, a lawyer and anti-machine Chicago alderman, Studs fought Daley until the mayor's death in 1975, twenty years against a racist political machine that employed both white and black soldiers to divide the classes and races. Studs was highly critical of Mayor Daley regarding many issues, but foremost was the mayor's racism. He was especially irate in 1963, when in spite of the documented segregation and expansive black "ghettos" in the city, Daley proclaimed on July 4th that "there are no ghettos in Chicago."

On August 27, 1963, Studs and Ida boarded an overnight train from Chicago to Washington with approximately eight hundred other Chicagoans en route to the March on Washington, a civil rights march led by Martin Luther King, Jr. Making the trip on the "freedom train" was Ida's idea. Timuel Black and Don Rose, the organizers of the Chicago contingent in the 1963 March on Washington, recall Studs with his tape recorder both on the train and in the nation's capital. As always, Studs was a participant-observer. He presented the event in the WFMT documentary "This Train."

The journey had begun in the late afternoon on Tuesday the 27th and culminated at 9 a.m. the next morning. As Studs recalls, "I wandered up and down the train, and at nighttime if people were only half asleep, even just a little awake, I'd join them. That was an incredible trip, being on that train, being part of something big."[24] Black people and white people, old people and young people, religious people as well as atheists united in conversation, song, and expectation.

WFMT first aired "This Train" soon after Studs returned from Washington. On the radio broadcast, Studs interspersed the music of Mahalia Jackson, Big Bill Broonzy, the Mormon Tabernacle Choir, the Freedom Singers, as well as other musicians. He had conversations with Ruby Dee and Ossie Davis. He spent part of the journey chatting with actress and vocalist Etta Moten Barnett. With "We Shall Overcome" playing softly in the background, she told Studs, "I'm hoping the train is a metaphor for more opportunities for people."[25]

The same spirit prevailed for most of the people Studs interviewed before the train arrived in the nation's capital. Studs' program featured various people talking about their commitment to the civil rights struggle. Reverend Howard Schomer, the head of the United Church of Christ seminary at the University of Chicago, spoke with Studs just after the train disembarked from Chicago. There was joyful noise in the background as he asserted that the freedom train symbolized "more freedom for more people, a better life, a much better America."[26]

An older African American woman told Studs that she grew up in Indiana and that both her community and the schools she attended were integrated. She admitted that there was racial prejudice in her town, but she recalled that it was nothing like racism in Chicago. "Never say America is the land of free. America is the land of prejudice."[27] Studs then inquired about her thoughts on the young white people on the train. She replied, "I think they are wonderful. I think that if every white man and woman in America could get on this train and see the good fellowship he'd either have a stroke or he'd have a change of heart. But I have a soft heart for all young people, all youth. There's hope there in them."[28]

Various people talked about commitment to the civil rights struggle and Studs recorded the words of two other individuals before arriving in the nation's capital. First, there was a woman who came to the march because of the inspiration of her fourteen-year-old son who had participated in the Chicago Freedom March. "It's an exhilarating feeling to watch them and you begin to feel it because of them. It's great seeing negro and white children on the train singing and laughing together."[29] An older African American man, Clarence Spencer, born in Louisiana in 1893, exemplified the same hopeful spirit: "This trip is something like a dream to me. I said to my wife and kids this is something I want to be in. I don't want to see it on the television or hear it on radio. I want to be in it! So this train can't get to Washington fast enough for me. I just want to be there."[30] In his conversation with Studs, Spencer confided his memories of being threatened by the Ku Klux Klan and reflected on his father being a slave. Many of these stories of hope were mixed with accounts of daily encounters with racism. An African American woman spoke about Jim Crow travel. A young child nearby responded, "You don't have to stand. You can sit on chairs. You can sleep here, it's just like home."[31]

Upon the train's arrival in D.C., Studs recalls marching toward the Lincoln Memorial. He was at 14th and Constitution Avenue, at the Washington Monument, when he heard the announcement that African American leader W. E. B. DuBois[32] had died the night before in Ghana. One of Studs' interviewees cited the great African American leader. He was both serious and hopeful: "You know DuBois died last night and as I look out there he keeps coming in my mind. It's such an excitement I feel, almost nervousness. I can't describe it. It's like being part of something that you don't know quite where it's going but you know it's going somewhere. . . . Oh, it's time, it's past time for this."[33]

The crowd of over two hundred thousand people and Dr. King's "I Have a Dream" speech was awe-inspiring for Studs as well as those in attendance. Later, when Studs first interviewed Reverend King, he opened the show with "'I have a dream. I have a dream in which the valleys shall be exalted, in which God shall be revealed, and all the flesh shall see it.' The man said this at the foot of the Lincoln Memorial. It was a glorious August afternoon last year."[34] Studs spoke with an African American woman who lived in Washington before talking with white onlookers. Their dispositions were dissimilar. The woman had two sons who were both in the service, one in the United Kingdom and the other in Vietnam. She spoke about American racism and her experience of having to explain to her children when they were younger why they were not allowed to eat at certain restaurants in the nation's capital: "You know it's hard to explain to a child. It's hard to explain . . . and you see I have two boys in the Air Force and when they serve their country they should come back and have the same freedom as everyone else. So I'm going to march because we've been waiting a long time."[35]

None of the white onlookers who spoke with Studs were totally supportive of equality or the march. One man was amazed at how well the police and military kept order. Another man from the South said, "If they want to do it they ought to do it. If they think it will do any good. I don't blame them and it may do some good and it may do some harm. You never know."[36] He added that he could never support "race mixing." A woman passerby said, "I ain't got nothing against colored people" and a man added that "it's okay as long as 'they' don't get violent."[37] Another woman harshly remarked, "Well, I think it's ridiculous—absolutely asinine myself. A bunch of people coming here and keep people from doing their work. I think they're going absolutely too fast and if they're not careful they'll trip themselves before it's over."[38]

The last interview Studs conducted before returning to the train brought a message of hope and solidarity. He conversed with a man who knew him well enough to call him by name: "My feeling is one of overwhelming gratitude, surprise, joy, pride. It almost reduces me to tears. It's almost a religious experience, Studs. This is one of the watersheds of history. I think things in this country will never be the same."[39] There were interviews on the return trip to Chicago as well. Reverend Schomer asserted that he felt immense hope and profound solidarity. He then added that it was "wrong to call it a march, it was a picnic for all people."[40]

Besides airing "This Train" and some of his South African interviews, in 1963 Studs welcomed Mahalia Jackson, Ralph Ellison, Gwendolyn Brooks, Dick Gregory, and Stokely Carmichael to his show. Charles Cobb joined Carmichael and they discussed civil rights, specifically the Student Nonviolent Coordinating Committee. Jackson's words were particularly heartfelt as they joined the political and personal:

> When I'm on the stage and on television and working with white people, they just hug me and love me and say I'm so wonderful and I'm so great. And then, when I'm walking down the street like an ordinary citizen, they don't recognize me. And when I go into the department store in the South, I can't get a sandwich. I can't get a bottle of pop. I can't even get a cab. And I'm just the Mahalia Jackson that they got through saying how wonderful I am. What I don't understand is, what makes people act like that?[41]

As a result of his friendship with Mahalia, Studs was invited to interview Martin Luther King, Jr. He was visiting Mahalia at her house on a Sunday afternoon and she called Studs to come speak with him. Their conversation aired on WFMT on October 22, 1964.[42]

Studs was thrilled to be speaking with King. He talked with Studs about his nonviolent mentors—Mahatma Gandhi, Henry David Thoreau, and Old Testament prophet Amos. Studs opined that the Reverend's father must have had a great influence, and King answered that he was foundational to his own life and work:

> The one thing I always remember, and always will remember, about my father, is the fact that racial segregation was an evil system in his mind and one that he was determined not to adjust to, and that he did not allow his children to adjust to in the sense that he always taught us that we—even though we had to face the reality of this system, that that was a sense of somebodiness within us that always kept us moving toward the sense of dignity and self-respect that any human being should have.[43]

Throughout the conversation, one of King's handlers repeatedly reminded him that there was a dinner to attend. However, Mahalia wanted to make sure that Studs was satisfied with the interview. She asked him if he'd gotten what he needed. Studs simply turned off his recorder.

Anna Terkel

Simultaneous with their ongoing involvement in the civil rights movement and protests against U.S. invasions in Southeast Asia, Studs and Ida faced issues and challenges. Anna Terkel, at age eighty-seven, while living in a Chicago retirement home, passed away in 1964. Studs recounts Ida's experience of visiting Anna during her early days there:

> When she first went there one of the social workers said to my wife Ida, who'd also in her time been a professional social worker, "My, what a sweet old lady your mother-in-law is!" And then it can't have been more than a month afterwards, the next time Ida visited, that same social worker called her into her office for a talk and she said, "I don't know how your husband survived his upbringing. His mother's a monster!"[44]

By the time Studs approached his fifty-third birthday his father, mother, and brother Meyer were all deceased. Only he and Ben were left from his birth family.

5

Civil Rights and WFMT

BEFORE DEPARTING FOR THE SELMA-MONTGOMERY march in late March 1965, Studs presented a special broadcast called *Joy Street* that aired in five segments between March 8 and March 12. This project, another collaboration with Jim Unrath, focused on children and youth in Chicago. Studs interviewed a ten-year-old girl at the newly built Robert Taylor Homes, a public housing project in Bronzeville, on Chicago's South Side. When he asked her what she wanted to be when she grew up, she answered, "How do I know I'll grow up? My life wasn't promised to me."[1]

Studs often repeated this story. For him, it was an archetypal example of the human reality of poverty as well as the ability of the uncelebrated, in this case a child, to articulate fear and trepidation. Similar truths would be portrayed in Studs' many books in the four decades to come.

Selma-to-Montgomery March

In late March 1965, urged by Ida and also Virginia and Clifford Durr, Studs traveled to Montgomery, Alabama, for the culminating rally of the Selma-to-Montgomery March. During his stay in the city, Studs spent time at the Durrs' house. Studs had met them in the 1940s and like himself, they were both investigated by the House Un-American Activities Committee. Clifford was a lawyer who had worked for the Federal Communications Commission (FCC) during FDR's presidency. He relinquished his government position under the Truman administration when he refused to sign a loyalty oath. Studs' impression was that "they didn't court trouble; neither did they run away from it; naturally, they were always in trouble."[2] Both Virginia and Clifford made multiple appearances on *The Studs Terkel Show* and were portrayed in his oral histories. Studs dedicated his book, *Hope Dies Last*, to the Durrs and also wrote the preface to one of Virginia's books, *Outside the Magic Circle*.

The Selma-to-Montgomery civil rights march was led by Martin Luther King, Jr. On Sunday, March 21, about 3,000 marchers set out for Montgomery. They walked twelve miles a day and slept in fields. By the time they reached the Montgomery capitol building on Thursday, March 25, they were 25,000 strong. King addressed the thousands of people in the crowd: "There never was a moment in American history more honorable and more inspiring than the pilgrimage of clergymen and laymen of every race and faith pouring into Selma to face danger at the side of its embattled Negroes."[3]

Studs arrived in Alabama with a group of other political progressives from Chicago. Frank Fried remembers Studs asking him to bring some of the musicians he worked with to join the march. Timuel Black, who was also part of the Chicago contingent, recalls: "Studs was in the line when we were about to be attacked and the Catholic women stepped in front, and because it was being televised they were not going to beat those Catholic women. . . . Studs was in that line with the rest of us."[4] Civil rights leader C. T. Vivian was also in the line. Montgomery sheriffs beat him on the steps of the statehouse. Vivian talked about his Studs interviews: "He wasn't running from nobody. He wanted to create a total picture of whatever it was he was dealing with. So that you got the sides, because you got these personalities that he was dealing with, right?"[5]

With tape recorder in hand, Studs walked with the marchers. He spoke with civil rights protesters and white supremacists alike. He was able to touch the humanity, or sometimes the lack of humanity, of the people he met. There were performances on the evening of March 24. Studs cites a rousing talk by Dick Gregory.[6] He bemoans the absence of Mahalia Jackson, who was ill in Chicago. He recalls his introduction to civil rights heroine Viola Liuzzo, who was murdered by white supremacists just after the march.

Studs observes the spirit being very high—there were great expectations of the event. Yet, as a counterpoint, he recalls his conversation with two local barbers. In particular, he remembers one of the men saying:

> I won't say everyone, but the majority of the thinking people or the educated people, they feel that the colored man has been abused to an extent, but I feel that they think that this could be worked out locally and not on a national basis…. I've had people in my shop who sympathize with them and I've had people in my shop who tell me that they could kill Martin Luther King like a snake and never have any second thoughts.[7]

The barber continues asserting his respect for Martin Luther King Jr.'s intelligence but then adds that he also respects tradition. The second barber was quieter than his friend, but more intense about the tradition of segregation in Montgomery. He explains to Studs: "The interest here is to keep separated in schools, in churches, in homes, in restaurants, in places we go. It's a custom, it's a tradition, it's an old tradition."[8] After their conversation the men went to the hotel bar where Studs was staying to have a drink. Management and a local detective took issue with Studs talking with the barbers and they were harassed and then asked to leave the bar.

Later that night Studs reflected on the evening and on white supremacy in the United States. In conversation with his tape recorder, he said:

> I talk now in my hotel room and have the strangest feeling, a feeling I had in South Africa two years ago, a feeling that what I'm saying may be heard, that the room may be bugged, it's a horrible feeling. It's probably not true, undoubtedly not true, but the feeling nonetheless is there. There's a terrible fear, and the fear is the fear of the detective who flashed his badge at me. I was a Northern man with a tape recorder.[9]

Studs continued to interview people as Martin Luther King readied to speak to the crowd in Montgomery. He discovered contrasting reactions: an African American man expressed glee while a local white man worried that the event was giving the city a bad name. At the conclusion of the speeches, Studs observed what was for him probably the most troubling scene of his Alabama journey. At a small neighborhood grocery he overheard young white men using the "N-word" quite freely. When two young black teens entered the store they were ordered in no uncertain terms to leave, which they did. For Studs, it represented the rawness of bigotry and hatred.

The atmosphere was quite the opposite that same evening at the Durrs'. Guests attending the open house were a veritable who's who of political progressives. Among the guests Studs chatted with were Myles Horton, founder of the Highlander Folk School, and former local NAACP president E. D. Nixon, organizer of the 1956 Montgomery Bus Boycott. He interviewed both men for his WFMT show. Horton compared past marches to Selma-Montgomery: "We knew one another by name, by face—old friends, old struggles. Today there were so many thousands, I hardly knew anybody out there. They were from all over. It was great."[10] E. D. Nixon, who had worked for years as a Pullman porter, spoke about the relative violence of racism in the 1930s and then about soliciting Clifford Durr to obtain Rosa Parks' release from the Montgomery jail. He recalled asking Virginia Durr for help on numerous occasions. According to Studs, Nixon's strong presence was felt just as it had been as he fought for equality and justice in Alabama.

A conversation with the cab driver who drove Studs to the airport—his final interview of the trip—illustrates the unadulterated racism and white supremacy in 1965 Montgomery. It also speaks to Studs' ability to reveal the core of the people he interviewed. In the backseat of the cab, Studs opened the newspaper to a headline announcing the murder of Viola Liuzzo. The cab driver commented that it was a shame, but it was not long before he provided confirmation of the very worst that Studs had heard from some of the people he spoke with on the street:

Martin Luther King is the worst kind of nigger and that's the kind of nigger that causes trouble. All he does is stirring up these people and causes trouble among our niggers. He's just doin' it to make money and he's makin' money off the local niggers. . . . These niggers down here are uneducated. They don't know everything that's goin' on.[11]

Studs just closed his eyes in response. Before he disembarked at the terminal he was forced to listen to an "Ode to Governor Wallace."

WFMT

In 1965 Studs' brother Ben died of a heart attack at age sixty-two. His death brought Studs sadness but also generated fear and trepidation as it mirrored the fates of his father and his brother Meyer. Although the brothers did not see each other daily, they often got together for White Sox games at Comiskey Park.

After Ben's death, Studs bought an Exercycle in an effort to improve his health. Friends Tony Judge and Clancy Sigal both recall that Studs taped a map on the machine and tracked his journey across the world. Sigal would ask Studs, "Where are you now, Studs?"[12] He remembered Studs once answering, "I just reached Johannesburg."[13]

While Ben's death made him anxious, Studs didn't slow his pace. In 1965, his guests at WFMT included Woody Allen, Stokely Carmichael, Martin Luther King, Jr., Buckminster Fuller, Margaret Mead, and newspaper columnist Mike Royko, whom he interviewed fourteen times between 1965 and 1989. Cartoonist Jules Feiffer visited *The Studs Terkel Show* on numerous occasions in the 1960s. His reflections on being a guest are similar to many others that appeared on the program: "It was his enthusiasm for the talk and his enthusiasm for ideas, and his love of conversation, that made everything work."[14]

Studs' process was unique among radio hosts. Yet he was astounded that it was not the norm. He viewed himself as a craftsman. In a short time, he would utilize this skill gifting the world with multiple books—oral histories.

6

Division Street: America

THE GROWING INTENSITY OF THE VIETNAM WAR and antiwar protests impacted both Ida and Studs' political dispositions. For Studs, the civil rights movement, antiwar movement, his WFMT program, his upcoming books, and his worldview were all integrated. Victor Navasky assesses the relation between Studs' work and politics as follows: "He combined this political, this minority dissidents' political orientation with the ability to connect to and talk with—without patronizing or arguing—people across the political spectrum. And that's something that is very rare."[1]

While taking a three-month hiatus from WFMT in 1966, Studs completed hundreds of interviews for his first oral history book project—*Division Street: America*. He spoke with people across class divides in the suburbs and the city. *Division Street: America* was published in 1967. In the book's introduction, there is a concise paragraph that explains the project: "I was out to swallow the world. My world was my city. What with the scattering of the species, it had to be in the nature of guerrilla journalism."[2] *Division Street* takes on the major schisms in American culture in the 1960s—generation gaps, racism, classism, and the Vietnam War—and at the same time expresses the character of Chicago's urban contemporary life and its inhabitants.

"Feeling Tone"

Division Street is actually a street in Chicago and Hull House was part of the neighborhood. No surprise, then, that Studs begins the book with settlement house activist Florence Scala and concludes with her comrade, Jessie Binford. But the people whose stories are told in the book represent the breadth of Studs' view of the world, politically and culturally. He tells filmmaker Tom Weinberg in *Studs on a Soapbox* that they are articulate and representative of their friends and neighbors. His unspoken plea to the people he met was "Amaze me!" Jamie Kalven explains: "He was open to and eager and hungry to have his view of things unsettled or changed. He loved being wrong about people. And many of his stories, I think, hinge on that—right. He was expecting one thing and he found another."[3]

"Amaze me" is also linked to Studs' interview with Nancy Dickerson, who familiarizes Studs with the concept of "feeling tone." Nancy Dickerson is portrayed as Lucy Jefferson in both *Division Street: America* and *Race*. She was an African American woman who worked in a Chicago hospital, helped put her daughter through college, and lived to see her grandson become a neurosurgeon. A voracious reader, she was known at work as the woman who was never without a book, titles ranging from *The Status Seekers* to *The American Dilemma*. Studs also featured her in *Touch and Go*, and quoted the same words: "Let's face it. What counts is knowledge. And feeling. You see, there is such a thing as a feeling tone. One is friendly and one is hostile. And if you don't have this, baby, you've had it."[4]

The portraits of people in Studs' first book guide "feeling tone" into multiple directions. One of the book's characters, a cab driver who finds his lost manhood in the John Birch Society, deeply affected Studs. The depth of the man was in his contradictions, his confusion, and his life within the class disparity and racism of American society. He disparages Martin Luther King Jr., yet he supports Florence Scala's political activism. "She was the greatest personality I've ever known among women."[5]

Studs commented on this particular interview shortly after the book was published: "I feel sad. You see, he to me was perhaps the saddest figure in the whole book. This kid was full of so much hurt and so many fears. I felt the most sympathy for him, and he was a John Birch member."[6] But of course his sentiment is predictable, as Studs' conversations were personal, political, and more than anything else humane. Most importantly, one can clearly identify one's own dispositions in his books. There is always commitment to the individual and collective story—whether progressive, transformational, or not.

Conservative Oral Histories

Studs never hid from his own progressive political character, but disparate positions were presented in *Division Street* and his other books. No matter what the political leanings, he always sought people's truths. He acknowledges the relationship between himself and the people he talked with in a way that exemplifies trust within human interaction. "I want them to talk about what they want to talk about in the way they want to talk about it, or not talk about it in the way they want to stay silent about it. I'll keep them to theme—age or the Depression or work or whatever—but that's all."[7] Elaborating on this, he tells Tony Parker: "A number of conservative people are in my books; not as many as more progressive thinkers, but that's not the point of my books at all. I'm looking for those who can talk about how they see their lives and the world around them. Who can explain how and why they became one way or another."[8]

Examples of conservative interviewees appear in each of Studs' oral histories and his conversation with Jim Campaigne in *Division Street* provides emphasis. Campaigne was twenty-five years old when he spoke with Studs. He was an admirer of Milton Friedman, William F. Buckley, C. S. Lewis, and even Ayn Rand, although he did have some reservations about the philosopher of selfishness. He spoke with Studs about the college he had attended on the East Coast: "I'm a little down on it. It's been taken over by radicals, really. They don't educate. They're promoters. A diluted Marxism prevails.... I got myself hauled up before the board of directors, because I was telling the alumni the teachers were indoctrinating instead of education."[9]

Consider the different views on the Vietnam War expressed in *Division Street*. Forty-year-old homemaker Helen Peters talks about antiwar protesters and what she perceives as the negative image of Americans they project on the world: "I think these Vietnam protesters ought to be taken home and whipped with a strap. . . . They're doing our country an awful lot of harm. This gives us a black eye in the eyes of the world."[10] And John Rath is even more extreme: "They should—what did Goldwater say?—clean 'em out, didn't he say that? Well, I believe that they should."[11]

More Vietnam

Seventy-five-year-old widow Elizabeth Chapin holds a newspaper photograph of a terrified Vietnamese woman and her child as she speaks with Studs:

> That woman has the same right to live and the same right for her— shall we say freedom?—or at least her chances to live and not be cowed down protecting her naked child, while soldiers go by.... It's not the soldiers' fault.... I shudder when I think what might happen in Vietnam. I can't understand, and never will, what gives the few men the right to hold all our lives in the palm of their hand.[12]

After *Division Street* was published, Studs shared his own views on Vietnam with author Denis Brian: "I get angry at stupidities and ignorance and what I call brutality.... My Lai: not at Calley or Medina, you know. Just the goddam thing that led to My Lai and we still go on and suddenly I believe I'm part of this thing."[13]

Transformational Stories

Studs loved the transformational story. Two powerful examples are told in a section of *Division Street* titled "Fallaways." First, Studs speaks with forty-three-year-old suburban Chicagoan Dave Williamson. He and his wife, Julie, had left their successful jobs and upscale North Shore suburban life to move to an African American neighborhood on Chicago's West Side and do volunteer work at the Ecumenical Institute. Williamson reflects on how this change affected their perception, including their self-perception, and some of the social impacts of their transformation:

> Things that were so important before appear to be superficial now. Utterly meaningless. Economic gain, status gain. . . . When we try

to get the discussion toward what we think is meaningful there's resistance. When we bring up the subject of the Negro or Vietnam, they shun away. . . . They don't even want to become involved in a conversation.[14]

Directly following the Williamsons' story is a discussion with Hal Malden, a thirty-five-year-old southern white male and ex-Nazi who became an inner-city social worker in Chicago. Malden tells Studs that he joined the American Nazi Party in 1961 at a time when he was in a "very confused, disorderly place that was on the brink of falling apart."[15] Reading his analysis of the Nazi Party, one becomes immediately cognizant of his ambivalence:

> They have this enemy called "they." You ask one of them who "they" is. They'll say, "Well, the Jews." You say, "Who?" "Well, you know." If you say, "No, I don't know, tell me," they become very frustrated, they get agitated and they say, "Hell, you wouldn"t believe it if I told you." "They"—the Negro, the communist. . . . "They" is someone who is keeping them from their rightful place in society.[16]

Malden's politics are juxtaposed with his love of jazz and his work at an Old Town club. This leads to a romantic relationship with an African American woman whom he credits with motivating his transformation: "She showed me a world, another society that I didn't know anything about. And I showed her. She had never met a southern white. I think we taught each other about different kinds of people."[17]

Reviews

Studs' insecurities about *Division Street* were evident during the editing process and even after publication. Tom Engelhardt was a young editor at Pantheon at the time. Schiffrin had solicited him to review the manuscript late in the editing process. He recalls Studs' response when he reported that the book was "wonderful, great."[18] "'Did you really mean that Tom?' His voice was shaking. And this was the most startling, I mean, I've never forgotten it because to me, at that age, you know, it never crossed my mind that a famous author would have doubt. That he'd need that affirmation from somebody he didn't even know."[19] Both Studs and Ida paid close attention to the reviews of *Division Street* as they came out in Chicago and New York newspapers. The reviews were mostly positive.

Peter Lyons's review in the *New York Times* was titled "Chicago Voices." After stating that the oral histories were "remarkable," Lyons, who like Studs was investigated by Senator Joe McCarthy during the Red Scare, writes that the book "astonishes, dismays and exhilarates."[20] University of Chicago scholar and theologian Martin Marty—with whom Studs conversed on his show in 1965—examined *Division Street* enthusiastically in *Book Week*. Michael E. Schlitz, a reviewer for *Commonweal*, asserts: "It should be required reading for bishops and bureaucrats, the people who would find in its pages the very people they are supposed to be serving."[21] There was a mention in *The New Yorker*, and positive reviews in *The Nation* and in the academic journal *AV Communication Review*. In the latter, Patrick Hazard, a professor of American Studies, chastises fellow academics, urging them to learn from *Division Street*. Precisely, he admonishes the American Studies movement to "bring its highly cerebral, highly ineffectual energies back into the mainstream of American life by sitting at the feet of Studs Terkel."[22]

In *The Reporter*, Chicago native Andrew Greeley presented a dissonant voice. Initially, Greeley wrote that if his contemporaries who grew up around Division Street actually read "Terkel's painfully beautiful interviews . . . they might understand much about their city, much about themselves, and much about the world in which they have been forced to live."[23] Acknowledging the poetry of Studs' oral histories, Greeley then condemns Studs for his sentimental romanticism, which he describes as "characteristic of many of Chicago's liberal intellectuals."[24] He concludes that this predilection colors Studs' rendering of the characters in his book.

According to Greeley, the people Studs interviews in *Division Street* are categorized as either good or bad: the good are the hardworking, the poor, those involved in social justice pursuits, and the bad are those who hold the lion's share of the city's money and power. Greeley's review holds Studs up as an example par excellence of the city's "liberal intellectual." But mostly Greeley was critical of the book because he viewed much of it as a critique of the Chicago Democratic machine and Mayor Daley in particular. For this, he accuses Studs of being "either naïve or sentimental or quite possibly both."[25]

Soon after the book's successful launch, Studs and Schiffrin agreed to work together on a second project, an oral history of the Great Depression titled *Hard Times*. For this book, Studs traveled throughout the country to speak with people about their memories and reflections of the 1930s. *Hard Times* would be published in 1970.

Amazing Grace

Simultaneous with the launch of *Division Street* was the opening of the play that Studs had written in 1959, *Amazing Grace*. It premiered at the Mendelssohn Theatre at the University of Michigan, Ann Arbor. Referred to in the playbill as "a striking and original tragi-comedy," the play was set in a hotel similar to the place where Studs was raised. The stars of *Amazing Grace* were British actress Cathleen Nesbitt and well-known American film and television actor Victor Buono.

Nesbitt had appeared on Broadway as well as in various films, including *An Affair to Remember* with Cary Grant and Deborah Kerr. Buono had acted in twenty-three movies, a multitude of television shows, and in 1963 was nominated for both an Oscar and Golden Globe as Best Supporting Actor for his part in the 1962 film *What Ever Happened to Baby Jane?* Like Studs, he had been blacklisted during the McCarthy era.

Unlike the successful reception Studs enjoyed with *Division Street*, critics nearly universally panned *Amazing Grace*. Studs' young friend Rick Ayers wrote the play's only positive review in the *Michigan Daily*. Some years later, talking with filmmaker Tom Weinberg, Studs recalls that *Amazing Grace* was "a horrible play—we bombed in Ann Arbor." When asked why the play failed, Studs replied, "Because it was no good."[26]

Rick's brother Bill was also in Ann Arbor at the time and he laughed when he reported that he actually liked *Amazing Grace*. In *Fugitive Days*—Ayers's memoir of his leadership in the Weather Underground—he writes about Studs' visit to Ann Arbor for the opening of *Amazing Grace*:

> When Studs Terkel's play *Amazing Grace* opened in Ann Arbor we hosted a cast party where, along with the beer and the wine and the chips, dope was passing hand to hand. I offered a fat blazing joint to Studs who said he'd never tried it, but what the hell. A cigar smoker, Studs held the thing between his thumb and first finger, took a puff and then blew it out in a big cloud without inhaling. Hey, he said, holding the fat thing aloft and admiring it like a connoisseur. That's pretty good stuff. Sure—he smiled broadly—I felt something.[27]

For Bill Ayers, the experience was an example of Studs not being "a guy who was going to judge us. He was not a guy who was going to stand aside from us. He was a guy who was going to be part of what was going on, and he wasn't dogmatic in his beliefs and he wasn't sectarian. He was living in the world."[28]

7

Engaging Youth: The Democratic Convention and Continuing Progressive Politics

STUDS AND IDA BECAME EVEN MORE politically engaged in the late 1960s as protests against the Vietnam War accelerated. British journalist James Cameron—who first appeared on *The Studs Terkel Show* in 1966 to discuss his book *Point of Departure*—visited the show again in 1968 and talked with Studs about his book and television film *Here Is Your Enemy*. Cameron was the first Western correspondent granted access to Hanoi after President Richard Nixon launched his two-week-long "Christmas Bombings" campaign on Hanoi and Haiphong in December 1965.

Much in line with Studs' approach to his oral histories, Cameron's work offers a portal into the lives of the everyday Vietnamese people he met during the winter of 1965. Because Cameron was not critical of the North Vietnamese, however, he was treated as a Communist by the American press. Cameron lodged with Studs and Ida while both men reported on the 1968 Democratic National Convention (DNC). Cameron referred to the convention as "Demofiesta."[1]

1968 Democratic National Convention

In *Talking to Myself*, Studs describes the demonstrations and rallies during the DNC at length. Young acquaintances from Students for a Democratic Society (SDS) as well as the Youth International Party (Yippies) were leaders in the protests. Older comrades, including doctors Quentin Young and Hyman Hirshfield, organized first-aid tents for injured demonstrators.

The DNC and ensuing protests took place August 25–30, 1968. Studs' reportage covered three nights. The first night he observed the police clubbing demonstrators and young journalists. On the second night, Studs and Cameron participated in a short march and rally in Lincoln Park. In fact, a young preacher asked Studs to address the demonstrators: "At a microphone, one doesn't have to bear too much witness, 'I am glad to be here, where life is . . . rather than at the Amphitheatre where life ain't.'"[2] Shortly before 11:00 p.m., a good portion of the 2,000-person crowd dispersed in accordance with the city's curfew.

That night in Lincoln Park the police enforced the clampdown. Studs remembers assuring Cameron that the police would not attack because Mayor Daley had received bad press throughout the world for his handling of the previous night's events. But before he concluded his conversation with Cameron police charged the demonstrators, wielding tear gas bombs and clubs.

Studs recalls young demonstrators applying Vaseline to his and Cameron's faces just before the gas was sprayed in their direction. Cameron and Terkel were led by demonstrators to the Lincoln Hotel, where they mingled with Allen Ginsberg, William Burroughs, Terry Southern, and Jean Genet. Genet, who had to sneak into the United States through Montreal, was covering the event for *Esquire*, as were Burroughs and Southern. Ginsberg spoke and performed throughout the week. They were all there to participate in the Lyndon Johnson Un-Birthday Party, a mockery of the president's sixtieth birthday organized by the Yippies as part of their Festival of Life, what organizers were calling the week-long demonstrations against the convention.

The third night, Studs and Cameron again bore witness to Chicago police attacking demonstrators. Sitting beside Jules Feiffer and William Styron at the Conrad Hilton's bar, they viewed the Chicago police riot against American citizens. Cameron later commented to Studs that within a few days, scribbles of "Fuck Daley" replaced "Stop the War" and "Peace" graffiti in Chicago.

During an appearance on Studs' show after the event, Cameron proclaimed, "It occurred to me that had Chicago had an even semi-literate police force, it could have, with one well-directed grenade, eliminated the basic core of the writing New Left."[3] Studs later wrote: "Was it at this moment that the Weatherman were born? Hardly more than one year later came Days of Rage. . . . Officially, 1969 was the year of their birth. But weren't they conceived in 1968? And was Richard J. Daley their unnatural father?"[4]

Chicago native Haskell Wexler's *Medium Cool* was filmed amidst the DNC and antiwar protests in August 1968. Prior to the convention, Studs had served as a conduit between Wexler and Uptown neighborhood people.[5] Steven North, one of the producers of *Medium Cool*, viewed Studs as an "inspirational fairy" for his continued assistance and advisement throughout the shoot. Haskell listed Studs in the credits as "Our Man in Chicago." Concurrently, Studs was awed by Wexler's work—shooting a non-documentary film in the midst of intense antiwar protests. "He's a certain kind of revolutionary, in the good sense—revolutionary in technique. He'd done something no one quite did before."[6]

Youth Culture

In a reversal of roles, Studs was interviewed by Denis Brian for his book, *Murderers and Other Friendly People*. He again spoke about the 1968 Democratic convention and the subsequent Chicago Seven Trial—this time warning young people to observe Mayor Daley and Judge Hoffman. "I think that Richard J. Daley and Julius Hoffman are the two greatest teachers the young have had since Socrates, because they made them know themselves. What was greater teaching to a newspaperman than a club on the head by Daley's boys? And Hoffman's incredible behavior in the courtroom, you see."[7]

The late 1960s were somewhat of a conflicting time for Studs. While he unequivocally supported the antiwar movement, he was confounded by the generation of the Students for a Democratic Society and Student Nonviolent Coordinating Committee. Rick Ayers remembers Studs' words from their first meeting in the early 1960s: "I'm trying to understand, you know, I'm an older guy, I'm trying to understand your generation."[8] Studs' colleague at WFMT, George Drury, reports that the 1930s, not the '60s, were formative years for Studs. But like Ayers, he recalls Studs being both curious and sympathetic toward the decade's activists.

> He would be there and very simpatico with the line of progressive, socially aware, socially committed anything. And little things, like when Abbie Hoffman died, and he'd had Abbie Hoffman on his show. Studs came into the library, and he wanted to know where John Prine's "Sam Stone" was. The song. And I was like, well, you know Studs, Roger McGuinn has a song called "Partners in Crime" about the Chicago Seven. He wound up using them both.[9]

Tom Engelhardt held different memories and reflections. He edited some of Studs' books and noted that there were a good number of 1960s generation people in *Hope Dies Last*:

> I felt he was weakest on people from the sixties. My generation. I used to think about this because I felt that there was something that Studs didn't understand, didn't quite know what to make of the kids who came out of the good times, the golden age of the fifties. He was sympathetic. He liked them. But there was something in that sixties generation. Some deep thing that he just didn't get. He got perfectly good interviews out of them, but they weren't his best. That's my opinion. I was very aware of this as an editor. I was aware that these were the interviews you had to work hardest on, because they somehow lacked something. They were good, well-spirited, well-intentioned, but they just didn't have the emotional depth that Studs got from everybody else.[10]

In actuality, Stud was friends with many of that time's activists, including veterans of the Students for a Democratic Society, Weather Underground, and the Student Nonviolent Coordinating Committee. With reference to generations, it is helpful to recall one of the lines Studs often said, "They didn't sing the same songs."

Ida and Late-1960s Politics

Ida appeared to be more relaxed with the differences between herself and the sixties generation. She was clearly a political activist. In 1972 she was detained for blocking the entrance to the Senate chamber and demanding that Congress stop funding the Vietnam War. Her cell-mates were Francine du Plessix Gray and Judy Collins. Garry Wills wrote about the protest in his book *Outside Looking In*. Ida had told him about her experience when the prison guards brought the women "stew in a Styrofoam cup and coffee thick as syrup with cream and sugar."[11] When some of the women balked at the food, Ida spoke, "Poor people all drink their coffee that way, since they are starved for nutrition."[12]

Studs often described Ida as more of a political activist than himself.[13] One of her political acts in the late 1960s deserves emphasis. The leader of the Black Panther Party in Chicago was the dynamic and charismatic Fred Hampton. He had spoken critically about Mayor Daley as well as state's attorney, Edward Hanrahan. At three in the morning on December 4, 1969, police assigned to Hanrahan raided Hampton and his partner Deborah Johnson's house, and cold-bloodedly assassinated Fred Hampton while he slept. The Black Panthers feared an attack on their offices, and an organization of which Ida was a member, Women for Peace, arranged a twenty-four-hour vigil. Jo Friedman, the daughter of Studs and Ida's friends, Matta and Nate Davis, sat the four-in-the-morning shift with Ida.[14]

WFMT

The late 1960s and early 1970s witnessed a myriad of guests on *The Studs Terkel Show*, including Diane Arbus, Stokely Carmichael, Doris Lessing, Clifford Durr, Eugene Ionesco, Mahalia Jackson, Ralph Nader, Victor Navasky, Florence Scala, and Mel Brooks. There were also special programs featuring welfare mothers, the DNC, and a tribute to Robert Kennedy.

Because Studs was writing without relinquishing his radio responsibilities, life was even more hectic in the early 1970s. He hosted his daily shows on WFMT while at the same time interviewing hundreds of people for his forthcoming books. In the first half of the decade authors, musicians, actors, filmmakers, and the uncelebrated continued to frequent *The Studs Terkel Show*.[15] Besides the annual theme shows, new programs included eclectic topics.[16] Studs' co-workers at WFMT have multiple memories of his interviews and their collaborations with him at the station. Many colleagues, with a glint in their eyes, describe Studs asking for assistance finding music as his show was about to begin. Yet Lois Baum stresses that the music Studs chose made the show magical.[17]

Everyone who worked with Studs during his forty-five years at WFMT speaks of his practice of seeking feedback from his colleagues of their impressions of the guests, music, and issues that were featured in his shows. While they all agree that he did most of the talking, Andi Lamoreaux has a vivid recollection of Studs polling fellow workers: "I also remember him walking around, sticking microphones in people's faces. If you were going to memorialize an important event, he liked to find out what his colleagues thought about it, and he would just ask for memories or, what do you know about a person?"[18] Both Donald Tait, an announcer at WFMT, and George Drury recall Studs asking for suggestions—poems, music, recordings.[19]

Studs' interview with Noam Chomsky, who appeared on Studs' show to discuss his 1969 book *The New Mandarins*, was exemplary. Much of the conversation focused on Vietnam. The show begins, though, with Studs playing a recording of his earlier interview with A. J. Muste, whom he thought had moral views that paralleled Chomsky's. On Muste, Studs had previously said, "He wasn't saintly. He had a marvelous raffish quality. You know, A. J. Muste, the old pacifist. He was pretty close up there I'd say."[20] Studs asked questions about colonial history and together he and Chomsky conversed on the amorality and immorality of conquest—both past and present. Asking a question, Studs asserted that policymakers "were shocked when their motives were questioned."[21] To which Chomsky replied that colonizers did not see themselves as having malice. Instead, they were bringing civilization to the heathen.[22]

The Studs Terkel Show also saw an increase in listener letters—both favorable and critical. One writer took joy in telling Studs that he had begun to work with children after educator John Holt was on *The Studs Terkel Show*. An ex-Chicagoan, referring to *Division Street*, asked: "Are there no Jews living in Chicago?"[23]

After praising Studs for his show with Mel Brooks, a Chicago woman took issue with Studs' interviewing skills: "In your interviews, you often, even to the point of habitually, interrupt your interviewee to tell us listeners what he is talking about (as if we couldn't get the drift)—(if we were that dumb we wouldn't even be listening to you or WMFT)."[24]

Another listener had little appreciation for Studs' political disposition: "If President Nixon is 'a sleazy used car dealer mental midget,' then you are an asshole. If he is not, then you are still an asshole."[25]

Journalist Harrison Salisbury, who thirteen years later would be responsible for arranging Studs and Ida's journey to the Soviet Union, held a very different opinion. "The interview with you is one of the greatest experiences. Yesterday's afternoon was no exception. I have been in the business for a long time and I can only wish I could do half as well."[26]

Soft Racism and Humiliations

Stokely Carmichael was on Studs' show as were other black nationalists and anti-Vietnam War activists. Interviewing those in the struggle, he uncovered the humiliations of white supremacy that still existed for African Americans in the 1960s and 1970s. Carmichael's undergraduate classmate at Howard University, Elaine Jones, who spoke to Studs about her father's humiliation of a decade earlier, recalled a similar incident that happened when she enrolled in law school at the University of Virginia in 1967. She tells Studs, "I was in the ladies' room during my first week, and an older white lady came through. She saw me sitting on the sofa and she said, 'I know you're taking your rest break now, but when you finish, would you clean the refrigerator?'"[27]

White people never encounter the humiliations that Elaine Jones and all African Americans face in the United States. In spite of Haki

Madhubuti saying that Studs was comfortable with all cultures,[28] he did contemplate his own white privilege:

> As I stepped onto the bus one early morning, the driver, a young black man, said I was a dime short. I was positive I had deposited the proper fare. I did a slight burn, though concealed. To avoid an unpleasant exchange, I fished out another dime and dropped [it] into the box. My annoyance, trivial though the matter was, stayed with me for the rest of the trip. Oh, I understood the man. Of course. I know the history of his people's bondage. It was his turn—a show of power, if only in a small way. If that's how it is, that's how it is. Oh, well. As I was about to disembark, I saw a dime on the floor. My dime. I held it up to him. "You were right." He was too busy driving to respond. In alighting, I waved: "Take it easy." "You too," he replied. I've a hunch he'd been through something like this before. In this one man, I had seen the whole race. In his behavior (especially before my discovery of the dime), I saw all African-Americans.[29]

Studs describes a second example in a *Chicago Magazine* article eulogizing WFMT engineer Frank Tuller, whom Studs viewed as something of a Huck Finn character. Tuller died in 1975 at the age of forty-one, but there was a time in the late 1960s when he worked with Studs broadcasting a remote show on the West Side in an African American neighborhood. They loaded a truck with equipment and after arriving at their destination met a group of young black men standing at the corner. Studs thought that the men were glaring at Frank and himself. As they walked toward the church he heard Frank ask them to lend a hand. Tuller sensed that Studs was worried:

> "What's up, Studs?" "Uh—nothin'. Nothing at all." "Oh, I thought I heard you say something." "No, just forget it." Frank's eyes widened. As though something quite remarkable had occurred to him. He looked at me with just the hint of a funny smile. I looked away. "Hey, Studs, you didn't think—did ya?" "Nah, nah, nah.

You kiddin'?" . . . I heard a light laugh behind me. "Oh, man, for a minute you had me goin', Studs. For a minute I thought you were scared the guys were rippin' us off. Geez!"[30]

Activism and Celebrity

Ida and Studs supported labor and politics through both financial donations and his appearances. Ida was totally involved in peace activism and would become an important member of the Gray Panthers and the Chicago Peace Museum. Bernardine Dohrn recalled thinking, "I want to be like her when I'm old."[31] Ida often carried an anti-Vietnam War placard as she picketed with her Women for Peace comrades on State Street in downtown Chicago. In addition, both Studs and Ida continued to support Pearl Hirshfield's political fundraising. These efforts included benefits for the Angela Davis Defense Fund, the December 4th Committee, the Political Rights Defense Fund, and South African socialist I. B. Tabata.

Studs' local and national recognition was growing. In addition to the notoriety brought on with the publishing of *Division Street*, *The Studs Terkel Show* was broadcast in various cities throughout the country. Locally, he continued to lend his name to multiple causes and made gratis appearances at various events. Occasionally there was a nominal honorarium. For example, he received four hundred dollars when he spoke for the Adult Education Council of Greater Chicago. But rather than a check, there was only praise following his appearance at the Journalism High School Institute of Northwestern University. The director, Raymond Nelson, thanked Studs, saying, "Even though I know you were dead tired, you were marvelous. The rapport you developed with kids in less than two hours was exciting to watch. I hope you felt, as I did, some sense of accomplishment in being able to share some of your thoughts, feelings so directly with this age group."[32]

The solicitations, both reasonable and not, would continue to increase for the rest of Studs' life. In 1970 and 1971 alone, political requests and appearances included moderating a program called Justice at the Crossroads at the First Congregational Church of

Wilmette, speaking at New Trier High School on Vietnam, and the World Federalists meeting in Chicago. Local teacher Hank DeZutter remembers Studs always being available. One example was DeZutter's alderman refusing to issue a permit for a street fair because the Young Lords frequented the area. "We called Studs up and Studs went there and stayed three hours interviewing everyone. You know, it's one block in Chicago and yet he came."[33]

Requests for support arrived from various politicians who challenged the Daley machine. And then came invitations that tickled Studs' ego. He was invited to attend the opening of a play based on *Division Street* at the University of Michigan-Flint. Publishing invitations were intriguing but impractical. Richard Gray of the American Library Association solicited Studs to write an oral history of censorship in public libraries. Senator Paul Simon, who at the time was Illinois's Lieutenant Governor, asked Studs, for the second time, if he might write a biography of right-wing politico Gerald L. K. Smith.[34] Finally, filmmaker Haskell Wexler's father-in-law inquired if Studs would consider recording a Talking Books version of *Division Street*.

Travel continued during the early years of the 1970s as Studs interviewed people for *Working*. Often he commented on Vietnam, Nixon, and, of course, Watergate. In 1970, he told Denis Brian that California governor Ronald Reagan, President Nixon, and Vice President Agnew represented the "evil of banality.... You see the banality itself is the evil, because it's non-imaginative, it cuts off imagination."[35]

It is not surprising that Studs became upset when he was not included in Nixon's enemies list. Andi Lamoreaux remembers watching him at WFMT: "I had never in my life seen Studs so angry. He didn't make the list. He knew half the people who were on it, but he wasn't on there, and he was furious. He didn't talk about anything else for days."[36] The list included individuals and organizations from many spheres including Studs' friends Quentin Young and Bernard Weissbourd. Other Chicagoans on the list and people Studs had interviewed were Garry Wills, Dick Gregory, John Kenneth Galbraith, and Noam Chomsky, in addition to Hugh Hefner and even Joe Namath. During the Watergate hearings Spiro Agnew resigned the vice presidency, and in response, Studs and some of his WFMT colleagues wore buttons that said, "One down, one to go."

Studs Terkel's political perspective was crystal clear—corporations and governments oppress the people. However, he transcended political definition. He spoke about ideology and labels with Brian: "I almost think that political ideologies, as we know them today, are going to become archaic. There's something new in the world and it has to concern itself with life against death, as simple as that. And the passion for life."[37] The "passion for life" and the quest for social justice that Studs possessed were wedded to his belief in transformation. They were topics of the two oral histories that Studs published during the first half of the 1970s, *Hard Times* and *Working*.

8

Hard Times and *Working*: Books and Life

HARD TIMES, STUDS' SECOND ORAL HISTORY, was launched in 1971. The original working title of *Hard Times* was *Bear Thursday and All That*, referring to the stock market crash of 1929. Studs' interviews took him to cities and towns outside of Chicago. Ida accompanied Studs on the Iowa and South Dakota portion of his travels and sat in on many of Studs' interviews during the trip. In conversation with Tony Parker, she discusses Studs' interview method:

> Oh yes, I have noticed certain things about the way he interviews, things that get people talking to him, that he's probably not aware of. One is that he often takes on the actual rhythm, the speech cadence of the person he's talking with. Or sometimes he might unconsciously imitate a slight accent the other person doesn't realize they have. It's the feeling of empathy he has with them that enables him to do it, and I think it makes the other person feel closer and that he's easier to talk to.[1]

Studs stressed that *Hard Times* echoed the words of the uncelebrated. In the book's Introduction he writes:

> This is a memory book, rather than one of hard fact and precise statistic. In recalling an epoch, some thirty, forty years ago, my colleagues experienced pain, in some instances; exhilaration, in others. Often it was a fusing of both. A hesitancy, at first, was followed by a flow of memories: long-ago hurts and small triumphs.

Honors and humiliations. There was laughter too. . . . In their rememberings are their truths. The precise fact or the precise date is of small consequence. This is not a lawyer's brief nor an annotated sociological treatise. It is simply an attempt to get the story of the holocaust known as The Great Depression from an improvised battalion of survivors.[2]

Studs kept notes and descriptions of some of the people he interviewed in a diary. These were combined with other interview commentary in a document titled "Notes on the Big D." In condensed form, his notations became the foundation for the individual introductions in the book. Studs' writing in the notes is both graceful and powerful.

The first oral history presented in *Hard Times* is of Bughouse Square comrade Jim Sheridan. He was living in a hotel where many of the other residents had previously lived in mental institutions. Studs writes: "There was a sense of life there, far, far more than among those who might be considered 'the normal people.'"[3]

It's easy to identify Studs as someone with progressive political leanings through those he chooses to interview. For example, in addition to Sheridan and a number of Studs' friends, there were interviews with people who worked for both Henry Wallace and FDR confidant Rex Tugwell. They were clearly proud of their perspective and believed that they had helped to ease class disparity in America. However, as with his other books, Studs included counterpoint subjects. *Hard Times* contains conversations with motivational guru and Combined Insurance Company of America president W. Clement Stone, as well as HUAC endorser Senator Hamilton Fish.

Studs' people shared divergent views of the past and the present in the late 1960s. IWW activist Fred Harris was hopeful: "The thing that gives me the most cheer are the young people today. They don't have a dogma. They're far more flexible, far more open-minded, far more feeling. They have the feeling."[4] Community organizer Saul Alinsky was skeptical: "They don't believe anything happened in the past. It's a wonder these kids don't reinvent the wheel. I think the McCarthy period broke the continuity—the handing over the torch. There is a radical gap."[5] Virginia Durr was pointed in her worldview: "What frightens me is that these kids are like sheep being led to slaughter. They are romantic and they are young. I have a great deal more faith in movements that start from necessity—people trying to change things because of their own deprivation."[6]

Shame, community, and transformation were among the multiple themes addressed in *Hard Times*. One story in particular that captured humiliation in the Depression belonged to Ida. Studs relates her tale of one of her first experiences as a social worker:

> I'll never forget one of the first families I visited. The father was a railroad man who had lost his job. I was told by my supervisor that I really had to see the poverty. If the family needed clothing, I was to investigate how much clothing they had at hand. So I looked into this man's closet—[pauses, it becomes difficult]—he was a tall, gray-haired man, though not terribly old. He let me look in the closet—he was so insulted. [She weeps angrily.] He said, "Why are you doing this?" I remember his feeling of humiliation . . . this terrible humiliation. [She can't continue. After a pause, she resumes.] He said, "I really haven't anything to hide, but if you really must look into it . . ." I could see he was very proud. He was so deeply humiliated. And I was too.[7]

Although he gave her the pseudonym Eileen Barth, Ida was furious with Studs for presenting her social work clients in the book without asking permission.

Two strike stories touch Studs' heart in reference to community. In the first instance, Evelyn Finn, a St. Louis seamstress, discusses organizing fellow workers during the Depression:

> I said to the girls: Just sit, don't do nothin'. We sat and joked about a lot of things and had a lotta fun. The boss was goin' crazy. The union officials came down. They went crazy, too. It was a hilarious day. They called us a bunch of Communists.[8]

In the second example, Tampa writer Jose Yglesias recounts a 1931 strike at a cigar factory in his hometown of Ybor City in West Tampa, an area known historically as "Tampa's Latin Quarter" owing to its large Cuban, Puerto Rican, and Hispanic immigrant population:

> The strike of 1931 revolved around readers in the factory. The workers themselves used to pay twenty-five cents a week and would hire a man to read to them during work. . . . He would read from newspapers and magazines and a book would be read as a serial. The choice of the book was democratically decided. . . . Consequently, many cigar makers, who were illiterate, knew the novels of Zola and Dickens and Cervantes and Tolstoy. And the works of the anarchist Kropotkin. Among the newspapers read were *The Daily Worker* and the *Socialist Call*. The factory owners decided to put an end to this, though it didn't cost them a penny. Everyone went on strike when they arrived one morning and found the lecture platform torn down. The strike was lost. Every strike in my hometown was always lost.[9]

Hard Times, inevitably, could not have been a Studs Terkel book without incorporating stories of change. It was the first time that Studs wrote about his friend, Chicago activist Peggy Terry:

> As long as you can say I'm better than they are, then there's somebody below you can kick. But once you get over that, you see that you're not any better off than they are. In fact, you're worse off 'cause you're believin' a lie. And it was right there, in front of us. In the cotton field, chopping cotton, and right over in the next field, there's these black people—Alabama, Texas, Kentucky. Never once did it occur to me that we had anything in common. After I was up here for a while and I saw how poor white people were treated, poor white southerners, they were treated just as badly as black people are. I think maybe that crystallized the whole thing.[10]

Terry had been raised in the South during the Depression, and her activism became a model in Chicago for community organizers in the Sixties. Studs interviewed her numerous times, and told her story often as it represented his political dispositions. In fact, her life, like those of many of the other lives described in Studs' oral histories, offers possibilities and hope.

Reviews of Hard Times

Similar to *Division Street*, the book elicited many favorable reviews. Henry Resnick's article in *The Saturday Review* was titled "When America Was Singing, 'Buddy Can You Spare a Dime.'" The author of the song, "Brother, Can You Spare a Dime," E. Y. (Yip) Harburg, was included in Studs' book. In his review Resnick credits Studs with breaking ground on a new type of literature—the "tape-recorded book." Addressing the people Studs selected, Resnick stresses that *Hard Times* offers a "huge anthem of praise of the American spirit."[11]

Other reviews included similar sentiments. In contrast, Studs' friend Nelson Algren didn't view *Hard Times* as a testament to the goodness of American exceptionalism at all. In his review for *The Nation*, Algren states, "The author has provided us with a definitive report on the psychological recoil of a generation that suffered a failure of nerve."[12] This is vastly different than a "huge anthem of praise of the American spirit."[13]

The most in-depth review was written by oral historian Michael Frisch. Frisch's essay uses Studs' book to help "discover the role of oral history in modern society."[14] Along with Algren, Frisch takes issue with the thesis of Studs' book presenting a testament to American exceptionalism. He argues that this paints a one-dimensional picture. Even more important for Frisch, many of the book's reviewers, with the exception of Algren, had no sense of history or memory. Studs understood both: his oral histories in *Hard Times*, as well as his subsequent book, *Working*, illustrate the complexities of individuals and capitalism in the United States.

Working

Studs' third oral history was published in 1974. The almost 600-page *Working* contains more than 130 interviews and is like an encyclopedia of different kinds of work and diverse views of work. But it is, of course, consistent with Studs' left politics. At the outset of the book, Studs states:

> This book, being about work, is, by its very nature, about violence—to the spirit as well as to the body. It is about ulcers as well as accidents, about shouting matches as well as fistfights, about nervous breakdowns as well as kicking the dog around. It is, above all (or beneath all), about daily humiliations. To survive the day is triumph enough for the walking wounded among the great of us.[15]

Working does include stories from people who found their days meaningful, who enjoyed and took sustenance from their efforts. Overwhelmingly, Studs found work in America "fomenting the malignancy of our souls."[16] For the majority of Studs' interviewees, the prevailing sentiments are distress, humiliation, and boredom. A number of these people regard their work with a "hardly concealed discontent."[17] Studs continues:

> The blue-collar blues is no more bitterly sung than the white-collar moan. "I'm a machine," says the spot-welder. "I'm caged," says the bank teller, and echoes the hotel clerk. "I'm a mule," says the steelworker. "A monkey can do what I do," says the receptionist. "I'm less than a farm implement," says the migrant worker. "I'm an object," says the high-fashion model. Blue collar and white call upon the identical phrase: "I'm a robot."[18]

To combat the dehumanizing monotony of their labor, many workers relay memories, often mischievously, of surviving the day. There is the switchboard operator who sometimes amuses herself by answering the phone with a name other than the business she represents. The gas meter reader who would quietly appear in backyards as suburban women sunbathed.[19] More ominous were the stories of autoworkers who sometimes let cars roll by them on the assembly line.

Studs shares the story of John Coleman, who at the time was president of Haverford College. In 1973, Coleman took a sabbatical from his position and went on the road assuming menial jobs. His recollection of being fired as a dishwasher is a summation of the nature of work in the United States. Coleman says, "I'd never been fired and I'd never been unemployed. For three days I walked the streets. Though I had a bank account, though my children's tuition was paid, though I had a salary and a job waiting for me back in Haverford, I was demoralized. I had an inkling of how professionals my age feel when they lose their job and their confidence begins to sink."[20]

But Coleman, like Studs, did have a profession and one that he believed had meaning. Studs almost always found value in his work. He especially delighted in his efforts at WFMT and worked incredibly hard. He was rigorous, talented, and always prepared. In his Introduction to *Working*, Studs writes poignantly on the topic:

It was the daily experience of others, their private hurts, real and fancied, that I was probing. In lancing an especially obstinate boil, it is not the doctor who experiences the pain. I was no more than a wayfaring stranger, taking much and giving little. True, there were dinners, lunches, drinks, some breakfast, in posh as well as short-order places. There were earnest considerations, varying with what I felt was my companion's economic conditions. But they were at best token payments. I was the beneficiary of others' generosity. My tape recorder, as ubiquitous as the carpenter's tool chest or the doctor's black satchel, carried away valuables beyond price.... The privacy of strangers is indeed trespassed upon. Yet my experiences tell me that people with buried grievances and dreams unexpressed do want to let go. Let things out. Lance the boil, they say; there is too much pus. The hurts, though private, are, I trust, felt by others too.[21]

At least partially, Studs' sensitivity dates back to the Wells-Grand Hotel. Those experiences helped to connect Studs to the workers he interviewed for the book. Studs Terkel indentified the dread that so many people experienced, and still experience, in their work in the "yet to be United States of America."

Reviews of Working

Critical reviews of *Working* were generally positive. Gus Tyler, who at the time was the assistant president of the International Ladies' Garment Workers' Union, wrote in the *Industrial Labor Relations Review*: "Terkel allows wide latitude to his subjects. Hence, they wander into self-search, social commentary, homespun philosophy. They become people first and 'workers' second. Through their eyes— not Terkel's—the reader is allowed to peek at worlds he has never seen or even been aware of."[22]

Marshall Berman, a professor at City College of New York, wrote an extensive review of *Working* in the *New York Times*. Berman discussed the book within the context of the democratic vision of the Popular Front. He writes: "Terkel gets closer than ever to the Popular Front vision in this book, he also diverges from it more radically than ever— or else, maybe, carries the vision to new heights and depths. . . . He is confronting all the explosive psychic realities that the Front generation did not care—or could not bear—to see."[23] Berman views Studs as an evolving spokesperson for the utopian mission and associated his writings with very good company—Pare Lorentz, Dorothea Lange, Walker Evans, Woody Guthrie, Sherwood Anderson, James Agee, Erskine Caldwell, Edmund Wilson, and Paul Robeson.

Aftermath

Studs kept extensive lists of each of the reviews of his books and was particularly haunted by rumors mentioning that he was a compiler of tape recordings rather than a writer. Shortly after *Working* was published, he told Monsignor John Egan, "Well, Jack, what I think about the critics is like asking a lamppost what it thinks about dogs."[24] But Studs was a superb writer as evidenced by the introductions in the three oral histories he had written at that point. Award-winning African American poet Haki Madhubuti explained, "But for me his own work crossed genres because he was not only a great interviewer, he was a great writer."[25]

The publication of *Working* brought a stream of letters to Studs. In an interview with Calvin Trillin, he talks about a response to *Working* that he received from an Atlanta librarian. She explains that she orders books for the library and then writes:

> One of my volunteers is a spy for Jerry Falwell, Reverend Jerry Falwell. And he spies so that I don't buy dirty books or pornographic books with dirty ideas. One day he says, "Ms. Cooper? I see you've ordered a pornographic book." And she, "What's the name?" He says, "I believe it's called *Working Studs* by Terkel."[26]

In Chicago, there was continuing excitement about *Working*. A dozen young filmmakers, including Tom Weinberg, who produced films on Studs until just before he died in 2008, worked together to produce *It's a Living: A Documentary Inspired by the Book* Working *by Studs Terkel*. It was the first locally produced, independent, portable videotape program broadcast in 1975. It made its debut on Chicago television channel WTTW on May 9, 1975.

It's a Living featured Studs, three of the people who appeared in the book, and three other Chicagoans. Just as Studs emphasized those interviewed in his books, Weinberg and his colleagues highlighted Studs. Weinberg recalls how he and his fellow filmmakers felt on the Sunday afternoon when Studs, with Nelson Algren at his side, came to the Videopolis on Clark Street to preview the video:

> We were nervous about how he'd react. Nothing like it had ever been done on video before. We consciously and deliberately modeled this new style of Chicago video after the way Studs created oral/audio history. His nonjudgmental process, getting people to say real things, and editing them into a piece with integrity, was the inspiration for the way we did it. What people had to say

and how they did it always trumped fancy technical production techniques.

Studs loved the documentary. At the conclusion of the screening, the filmmakers shot a conversation between Studs and Algren as they did a spoof on Nelson's anticipated move to Paterson, New Jersey. Studs laughed through the entire filming as Algren referred to Paterson as a "boomtown welfare city." Studs told Algren that Chicago would miss him and then asked, "Will you miss Chicago?" Algren was serious as he looked into the camera: "No, I never miss Chicago and I don't think Chicago will miss me. I mean, I went up to the public library the other day. Let's see? I've written ten, eleven books and there wasn't one there. They are in Tokyo. They're in the public library in Tokyo and in Paris and in about ten, eleven cities. Not in Chicago."[27]

Lois Baum reminisces about Studs' friendship with Algren and Mike Royko, culminating with Algren's final night in Chicago:

Oh, he had arguments with Royko and Nelson Algren, a number of which I witnessed, and they would always shout and yell and sometimes Algren liked to stand up because he was taller than everyone. He'd stand up to get the attention of the table. It didn't matter where we were, how many of us, or if there were women at the table, they would just shout and yell at each other. It was very funny and sometimes of course embarrassing. The only time that didn't happen was Nelson's last evening in Chicago, before he permanently moved to Long Island, and everyone was very aware, including the three men, of how important this night was and what it meant for Nelson to be leaving his hometown and all the memories he had here. Among the three of them there was no shouting that night. There was no standing up and no arguing. They were very respectful of one another. It was probably the only time I ever saw them together that they behaved like gentlemen. I don't want to use that word *gentlemen* because that gives a different connotation, but they were gentlemen with each other on Nelson's last night in Chicago and extremely attentive to one another. They were all such good storytellers that it was hard sometimes for them to listen to someone else if they had a story on the tip of their tongue and they wanted to tell it. That night, however, they each recalled one hilarious escapade or argument or fight after another—a whole lifetime of stories because they'd all grown up in Chicago and being together on that occasion brought out the best in each of them. It was very special.[28]

Algren did indeed move to Paterson, and then later to Sag Harbor on Long Island, where he died in 1981. Speaking of his friendship with Studs, Nelson was very "Algrenesque": "For emotional help I wouldn't call anybody because nobody can help you emotionally and all you do if you call for that is to drag somebody else. Financially, if it were a small amount, I'd call Studs Terkel. Studs is very easy to borrow from."[29] As Lois Baum describes, Studs was deeply affected by Nelson's move. But Studs rarely exposed emotion, and thus radio, political, and writing life went on unhindered.

9

Memoir Meets Oral History

FOLLOWING THE SUCCESS OF *WORKING*, Studs published his memoir *Talking to Myself*, and a third oral history, *American Dreams: Lost and Found*. He turned sixty-five in 1977. In contrast to many of his age who were entering their retirement years, his work, activism, and travel widened and accelerated. As *The Studs Terkel Show* flourished between 1976 and 1980, he participated in two third-party presidential campaigns, partook in the theater production of *Working: The Musical*, spoke at conferences and various universities, and became more of a celebrity.

The Studs Terkel Show

In 1975 and 1976, besides James Cameron, Zero Mostel, and Muhammad Ali, Studs hosted an exciting mix of guests, including feminist author Susan Brownmiller, experimental composer John Cage, activist Dave Dellinger, Marxist historian Eric Hobsbawm, and anti-apartheid activists Hilda Bernstein and Dennis Brutus. Because Studs' traveling increased each year, he began to organize playlists of his favorite interviews for rebroadcast. Included from this time period were his interviews with Cameron, Judy Collins, Jacques Cousteau, and Ring Lardner, Jr. Will Leonard on baseball and a show titled "Children Look at Our World" were also rebroadcast on WFMT.

Studs' 1975 interview with Muhammad Ali represents the quintessential Studs Terkel interview. Culture, politics, class, and race are all addressed within the framework of genuine conversation. It is evident from the start that Studs had carefully read Ali's book, *The*

Greatest. Throughout the segment he honors Ali's words. They talk about racism as Ali explains to Studs why he threw his Olympic gold medal into the Ohio River after being refused service at a restaurant in his hometown. Studs asks Ali about the ramifications of refusing Army induction during the Vietnam War. When Studs asks about not taking the safe way out, Ali's response is "I took the safe way out—not going."[1] Studs also wanted to know what Ali thought when white people joyfully chanted his name, "Ali, Ali, Ali!"[2] He replies:

> I think the masses root for me because they're scuffling. They've been persecuted and they're thinking of the high taxes and whatever and they're for the underdogs. People are basically underdogs as a whole. And the things that I say for my people, black people, and for the freedom of all people. And I don't stop thinking of everyday man and I think this is what they recognize. Whether they be black or they be white, the masses of people are hardworking people. And the things I say and the places I go and the things I do when the odds have been so much against me—they see themselves. They don't see me and they don't see color. They see themselves fighting against untold odds and they're with me because I'm the underdog.[3]

As the conversation nears an end, Ali recites a poem. Studs concludes by comparing his guest with improvisational jazz musicians before playing Jimmy Rushing's especially inventive piece, "Going to Chicago."

In 1977, *The Studs Terkel Show* produced numerous special programs on diverse topics such as the Palestine Liberation Organization (PLO), his memoir *Talking to Myself*, and old age. Phillip Levine, Joan Didion, Woody Guthrie, Nelson Algren, Mike Royko, Leon Despres, and Win Stracke were among the many guests that year.

Studs' interview with poet Phillip Levine on March 13, 1977, was a standout for its political and conversational spirit. Studs describes Levine's writing as "poetry from the pavement."[4] The men discuss two specific verses that Levine had written on racism in Detroit as well as his poem "For the Poets of Chile," Levine's tribute to Victor Jara and other Chilean poets executed or disappeared by Pinochet. He and Studs reflect on his writings, and how his subjects are Brecht's "the anonymous" and Studs' "the uncelebrated." Finally, Studs encourages Levine to reflect on being a political poet:

> I think a political poet is one who doesn't necessarily tell people how to vote or how to think and what specific attitudes they should have, but he or she's a poet who deals with the political facts of our lives, that for example we live at the pleasure of people with enormous power and very little compassion. And I feel, as a poet, that one of my functions is constantly to remind people of this.[5]

The year 1978 witnessed the appearance of Toni Morrison, Jerzy Kosinski, Anna Moffo, William Sloane Coffin, Mortimer Adler, Ousame Sembene, Tad Szulc, and Calvin Trillin on Studs' show. His promotional stints included *The Dick Cavett Show* where fellow guests were Rod Steiger, Robert Klein, and Bernadette Peters. Trillin remembers Studs being superior to any other interviewer he conversed with on-air regarding his books:

> People get to Chicago weary and irritated and also thinking if they heard themselves repeat that lame line from the book one more time, they'd commit suicide. And then you go on Studs' show. Studs has not only read the book, he interviewed the book and underlined the book with big black marks everywhere, and he'd say, listen to this. And he'd read passages, and you start to think, that's not half-bad really.[6]

Throughout 1979 and 1980, programs about Hull House, gay rights, labor history, folk music, opera, Klezmer, jazz, dance, China, the Equal Rights Amendment, nuclear war, and Mahalia Jackson were aired on *The Studs Terkel Show*. Friends and frequent guests such as Nelson Algren, Mike Royko, Quentin Young, Rick Kogan, James Cameron, Quentin Crisp, Win Stracke, George Drury, and Burr

Tillstrom were interviewed. Barry Commoner, who was nominated by the Citizens Party as their 1980 presidential candidate, spoke with Studs about his campaign.

When Nadine Gordimer, who had been one of Studs' guides in South Africa, appeared on the show to discuss her book *A Badge of Honour*, Studs told her that her thinking on African independence reminded him of James Cameron's analysis of India. She asserts that Americans believed that black people could not handle freedom, but that it had been only twelve years since the first independence. "So it seems to me an absurdity to judge African countries on the strength of this little more than a decade."[7]

Fred Harris's Presidential Campaign

When John Nichols eulogized Studs in *The Nation*, he wrote, "Politics was never a game for Studs. It was the work of a lifetime. He wrote brilliant books about the lives of working people not merely because their stories were fascinating but because he wanted to get a conversation started about class in America."[8]

As a diehard third-party advocate, Studs supported former Oklahoma senator Fred Harris's presidential campaign in 1976. Harris had helped enact legislation for Native American rights and impoverished rural constituents while in the Senate. From 1969 to 1970—while retaining his seat in the Senate—he briefly served as the chair of the Democratic National Committee. Very disillusioned with the Party and by Oklahoma's steady move toward conservatism, Harris did not seek reelection for his Senate chair in 1972; instead, he ran for president.

Harris referred to his campaign as "New Populism." His platform was deeply influenced by reporter Jack Newfield's 1971 article "New Populist Manifesto." In 1975, Harris published a book titled *New Populism*. One of his 1976 campaign brochures outlined the New Populist mission that included grassroots democracy, decentralization, and local collective participation.

The platform was attractive for Studs. John R. MacArthur, political journalist and publisher of *Harper's* magazine, describes his first encounter with Studs, which happened to be at one of Harris's Chicago fundraisers:

> I confess that I also used to pigeonhole Studs as a "character" and "political radical"—that I didn't fully appreciate the subtlety of his intelligence or his writing. We first met at a 1976 fundraiser for Fred Harris's populist presidential campaign. . . . He ratcheted up the audience like no one I've ever seen; then, borrowing from some long-forgotten pitchman, played a kind of "Simon Says" trick: He told everyone to reach high up in the sky, then loooow down to the ground, and finally (after a significant pause for effect), deeeep into their pockets. It brought the house down—and the wallets out.[9]

Despite Harris's withdrawal from the presidential race due to inadequate funding, Studs maintained his third-party politics, and later went on to support both Barry Commoner and Dennis Kucinich's presidential bids.

Studs, however, never supported Richard J. Daley, Chicago's mayor for twenty-one years. On December 20, 1976, Daley suffered a fatal heart attack. Two days later, Studs penned an article for the *New York Times* in which he did not mince words: "Even to those of us that found so much of his work appalling, his death is astonishing. Such power, no more.... Yet the myth persists: Mayor Daley made Chicago work. The question is for whom?"[10]

Talking to Myself

As the United States' Bicentennial came to an end, Studs was immersed in writing *Talking to Myself*. He distinguished between interviewing the famous and the uncelebrated, stating that the former never astonished him. Talking about uncelebrated people he noted: "I am constantly astonished."[11] The memoir was a leap for Studs as his previous writing, in contrast, recounts other people's stories. While he includes selections from some of his previous interviews, *Talking to Myself* is in his own voice—a different craft. He had at least partially read too many of his reviews that accused him of constructing rather than writing. Studs noted that although *Talking to Myself* was a memoir, he was really writing about the world in which he was a reluctant participant and not just an observer.

Studs' life always involved listening and talking, observing and participating. Nora Ephron's review of the book in the *New York Times* captures Studs' spirit and that of *Talking to Myself*:

> This is not a personal book in the usual sense—there is nothing about Terkel's father, next to nothing about his mother, a bare smidgen about his brother, a couple of stories about his wife. What you see is what you get: Terkel's voice. Talking to himself . . . . In everything he does, in everything he tapes or transcribes, you can almost hear him saying, "Listen to this. *Just listen to this.*"[12]

Studs begins his memoir with a caveat, warning that certain personal memories will not be revealed. And believing that he respects the people that he interviews, the same rules apply when he writes about himself: "There is a private domain on which I'll not trespass."[13]

Working: The Musical

At the end of 1977, the musical adaptation of *Working* was running previews at the Goodman Theatre in Chicago. Opening night was scheduled for January 5, 1978. Stephen Schwartz, whose previous shows included *Godspell* and *Pippin*, had read halfway through Studs' book and decided to adapt it for the stage. He explains, "One thing that immediately appealed to me about *Working* was the fact that this was true, that you were going to be hearing from people in their own words."[14]

Schwartz flew to Chicago in 1974 to meet with Studs, who was tickled by the prospect of turning his best-selling book into a musical celebration of the unsung lives of ordinary people. He gave Schwartz the go-ahead.[15] Thinking back many years later, Schwartz explained what motivated him to approach Studs about the adaptation: "It was Studs' appreciation that everybody has a story. I still have retained that way of looking at people and looking at the world to this day.

Studs lived the attitude that appeared in his books, so being around him strengthened one's own internalization of that."[16]

Studs provided Schwartz with recordings and transcripts of the interviews he had conducted. He advised on the selection of music and offered opinions on character portrayal. One suggestion was to include the meter reader's story. He also urged Schwartz to include the story of Charlie Blossom, the twenty-four-year-old newspaper copy boy struggling to find his own identity. "He pointed the way to some characters that might not have occurred to me, certain interviews I might not have thought of," Schwartz said.[17] Some of the people who were depicted in *Working* attended the opening, as did Studs. Three-time Tony Award nominee Micki Grant wrote songs depicting two of the people in Studs' book, Maggie Holmes and Al Pommier. It was Grant who suggested to Schwartz that Holmes's voice needed to be part of the play. She remembered a smiling Terkel at the first performance. "It was great for Studs to see that it worked. I'm sure he probably had no idea as to how it was going to turn out. He just seemed to be very, very happy."[18]

Some of the people depicted in *Working* attended the Chicago opening, as did Studs. Reviews were lukewarm. The show was supposed to head to Washington for further work prior to the Broadway launch, but the producers decided to go to New York immediately in order to qualify for that year's Tony Awards. The move to New York, in Schwartz's opinion, came too swiftly. He did not think that the play was ready.

Ida and Studs flew to New York for the Sunday opening of *Working: The Musical*. They stayed at their usual hotel, the Royalton, but as was their practice they enjoyed drinks across the street at the Algonquin. The Schiffrins hosted a brunch at their apartment. It was a rainy Sunday night when *Working* opened at the 46th Street Theatre. Playing next door was Neil Simon's *Chapter Two*, and *Hello Dolly!* was staged across the street. Ida and Studs sat near the front with Andy Warhol and John Lindsay. Cathy Zmuda, Nelson Algren, and Win Stracke were among Studs' friends who attended the opening night performance.

Following the show there was a cast party at Gallagher's Steakhouse. Ida and Studs left the party just after midnight, before the New York reviews came out. As he was leaving someone asked him why he wasn't staying for the reviews, to which he replied, "Naw, fuck 'em."[19] As with his books, Studs was anxious about the reviews.

The show was panned with much more ferocity than it had been in Chicago. Although Studs appeared pleased at the opening night performance, he voiced criticisms in an interview with journalist Clifford Terry:

> You know, during the opening, I felt sort of detached. Because it wasn't my show. . . . There should be nuances and big things. It'd be a different play. I'm so mad. Because there's so much in it that's good. Just look at the audiences, standing up and applauding. If there's anything I've learned from all this it's that the New York critics are incredibly provincial. They don't know anything west of the Hudson.[20]

In spite of the fact that Craig Carnelia, Micki Grant, Mary Rogers, Susan Birkenhead, Stephen Schwartz, and James Taylor were all nominated for the Tony Award for Best Original Score, *Working: The Musical* closed after just twenty-four performances on Broadway.

Celebrity and Home in Chicago

Back in Chicago, Clifford Terry, who shadowed Studs in New York for a *Chicago Tribune Magazine* feature, continued to observe and talk with him for a few more days. In "The Wide World of Studs Terkel," published on July 2, 1978, Studs explains to Terry that listeners had suggested that he was "their college in a way."[21] He was quick to add a caveat, noting the contrast between his becoming a celebrity while writing about the underdog:

> Someone tells me I'm a celebrity. I say, "I am? So is Charles Manson." If Manson walked outside on Michigan Avenue, people, I'm afraid, would ask for his autograph. What does it mean, being a celebrity? Einstein was one, sure, but so is Zsa Zsa Gabor. What

you think of *yourself*—if what you're doing has a *meaning*—that's what matters.[22]

A few years earlier, Studs had actually written a narrative review of the *Celebrity Register* in *The Nation*. Citing C. Wright Mills, Studs maintained that publicity equaled celebrity. Viewing celebrity as somewhat absurd, including his own, he demonstrated his point in the review noting that Ralph Nader is listed next to Joe Namath. He also questioned the inclusion of Colonel Sanders.

Studs visited Vermont in 1978 at the invitation of Steve Robinson, the director of Vermont Public Radio. Robinson had received a grant from the National Endowment for the Humanities for a project inspired by Studs' oral histories. Students in Windsor, Vermont, were given tape recorders to interview elders in the town. Criteria in the grant included a "project humanist"[23]—that was Studs. Robinson recalled Studs eschewing the formal meeting. Instead, Studs talked with the kids. "We had a wonderful couple of hours with Studs, and he regaled them with stories."[24]

At home, Ida convinced Studs that the time had come for them to leave their apartment and purchase a home. Dan Terkel remembers when a large, old house—in what at the time was still somewhat of a precarious neighborhood—came onto the market. In an interview with *Mother Jones*, Studs describes the house at 850 West Castlewood Terrace and the neighborhood:

> This street is a have street. This is Uptown, which I like. It is a have-street enclave in a sea of have-nots. Beware of that. Here I am, the romantic again, without feeling the pangs of it. I like Uptown for the United Nations aspect of it. Uptown has more people from different societies and cultures than any area in the country probably. However, only about 100 yards away, there are the have-nots. Am I aware of that?[25]

The house actually belonged to a couple that Studs and Ida knew, Arlene and Harry Bouras. Harry Bouras, an award-winning artist, had a long-running show, *Art and Artists*, on WFMT. Ida and Studs moved into their new home in 1978. The house was built in 1906 and according to various friends the much larger house made little impact on ending the clutter.

Royko and Terkel

Shortly after the Terkels moved, Mike Royko wrote an article about Studs getting mugged near the new house. The most striking element of the story—told many times over by Studs, as well as his friends and colleagues—is that the mugger recognized Studs. And Studs, being the consummate oral historian, engaged him in conversation.

The tale always varied a bit. Sometimes the mugger entered the home. Occasionally the scene was the street. In every rendition, Studs asked the robber to return twenty dollars—sometimes for bus fare and at least once to buy Ida flowers. In some versions of the tale, Studs asked his assailant if he could interview him for his upcoming book.

Royko's son David worked for a couple of years at WFMT. He remembers parts of his father's relationship with Studs:

> It's funny, Dad, he loved Studs. But Studs could also drive him nuts. I remember one thing that used to bug him was when Studs would read his columns out loud on the FMT interviews. Dad had a very specific voice in his mind, especially somebody he's quoting with a specific kind of Chicago accent. And Studs always sounded like Studs when he was reading this stuff, and it would drive Dad nuts.[26]

Mostly, Studs Terkel and Mike Royko shared great respect for each other's work. Royko wrote columns that intensely supported Studs in the late 1980s when conflict, both personal and collective, became the reality at WFMT. Studs penned the introduction to the sixth edition of Royko's book *Sez Who? Sez Me*. He stressed the unique quality of Royko writing against the Establishment. "Usually they have concerned the 'ordinary citizen' or the wholly dispossessed, the one without a clout, pushed around by Authority. At such times, he appears possessed by a demon."[27]

The Citizens Party

Participation in the Citizens Party and Barry Commoner's political campaign were prominent activities for Studs during this period. The Citizens Party registered with the Federal Elections Commission at the end of 1979 as an effort to conjoin the diverse environmentalist and liberal groups into a unified political platform. Studs was a member of the party's Illinois committee, along with Quentin Young, Ed Sadlowski, and Sydney Lens. Labor union activist Dan LaBotz recalls this group's meetings as "talk-fests."[28]

The Citizens Party's Presidential Convention was launched in Cleveland with 275 delegates from 30 states. Studs gave the keynote address to a crowd of five hundred old radicals, environmentalists, feminists, and labor organizers. Addressing the crowd, Studs avowed that the party would "reclaim the American Dream from the predators who have stolen it."[29] The convention nominated Commoner and LaDonna Harris of Oklahoma for vice president. Commoner was best known for his research on the effects of radiation and his book on the environment, The Closing Circle. But part of his appeal to Terkel and other people on the left was presented in a different book, The Poverty of Power, in which Commoner went beyond the connection of science and politics and contended that environmental damage was directly connected to capitalism.

Studs introduced Commoner at various rallies in Chicago and also accompanied him to Los Angeles for an event at the Wilshire Ebell Theatre. In November 1980, Commoner and Harris received just over 200,000 votes—less than 1 percent—finishing behind another third-party candidate, John Anderson. The Citizens Party was short-lived, ending in 1984. By 1988, it had morphed into the Green Party.

American Dreams: Lost and Found

Studs traveled throughout the country to interview people about their real experiences with the mythical "American Dream" for American Dreams: Lost and Found. The critical mass of interviews for this oral history project would occur between 1977 and 1980. In 1978, he interviewed people in California, Oregon, Washington, Kentucky, Massachusetts, Mississippi, the Carolinas, West Virginia, Ohio, Iowa, and Minnesota.

Studs always acknowledged his "scouts," the people who aided him in identifying individuals to interview for his books. In the Northwest, for example, Sandy McCall, Elizabeth Furse, and John Platt assisted him. McCall was the nephew of Oregon governor Tom McCall, and two interviews that appeared in the book were with the governor and his mother, Dorothy Lawson McCall.

Studs journeyed to Oregon in 1975 to speak at Oregon State University in Corvallis. By this time, Sandy McCall had a Portland television program. Studs accompanied him for a story on striking loggers. At ten in the morning they visited a bar in Philomath that was filled with the men on strike. McCall began filming, then for some unknown reason asked Studs a question about George Wallace, to which, of course, Studs answered with a derogatory quip targeting the Alabama governor. Studs continued quoting Brecht and then added. "There are people in this town who are on strike now. They're right to be on strike, because in fact, as they're working, they cut down wood they're giving away to their employers by the federal government for nothing. And that wealth doesn't transfer down to them."[30]

McCall marveled at the response. "They started to clap. They grabbed him, took him over to the bar, back slapping, whole bit, line him up at the bar, he had to drink a couple of boilermakers, which didn't bother him at all. And he loved it. He loved it."[31]

The person whom Sandy McCall thought was perfect for Studs to interview, however, was his grandmother, Dorothy Lawson McCall. Sandy remembered that when he and Studs arrived at his grandmother's house she had already consumed a good amount of muscatel and her memories were rather vague. Then, according to McCall, "Studs became Studs":[32]

He got down on the floor and stuck the microphone right in her mouth, looked her right in the eye and said, "Miss McCall, what was it like when you were a little girl in Bar Harbor, Maine? Tell me the truth." And her eyes, it was just like a cash register came up. She went clear-eyed. She began to talk about her childhood in Bar Harbor. And she sobered up, and then she just came right back. I've never seen anybody get that, including any of her children. Studs got right down from her and he brought her back, and then she was just fresh as a daisy. He got these memories back from her; she told him some great stories. Not all of which appeared in the book. And he had really rung her bell. He had gotten memories out of her that she hadn't thought about in fifty years, sixty years.[33]

Sandy McCall introduced Elizabeth Furse and John Platt to Studs, which then connected him to Ramona Bennett who appears in *American Dreams*. Ramona was a Puyallup tribal activist and the chairwoman of the tribe. Furse recalls that meeting with Studs: "So I get this call from Ramona. 'Who the hell is this drunk you sent me?' But they got on like a house on fire, because he loved the interview, and Ramona was like that, she could be really straightforward."[34]

The other notable person Studs interviewed in Oregon was logger and environmentalist Bob Ziak. McCall had hosted Ziak on his own television show and he urged Studs to meet with him. Furse and Platt drove Studs from Portland to Knappa, near the Pacific Ocean coast, where he met with Ziak, who spent his life protecting bears and the environment. A large, almost archetypical-looking logger, he talked with Studs about conservation and the rapaciousness of the timber industry. Studs quoted Ziak in the Introduction of *American Dreams*:

The forest to me is an awesome and beautiful place. The young loggers were not here to see what was there before. If you've never known something, it's difficult to appreciate what's been lost. What happened to all that majestic timber? I believe that only by being in the presence of beauty and great things in the world about us can man eventually get the goddamn hatred of wanting to kill each other out of his system. The beauty is going.[35]

Citified Studs Terkel appreciated the beauty. According to John and Elizabeth, whether it was the loggers' café outside of Knappa where he and Ziak spoke, or the voluminous numbers of Canadian geese that Ziak fed at his home, or the red-tailed hawk that Ziak called the "doctor," Studs was "blown-away."[36]

American Dreams: Lost and Found was published in 1980. It was well received by most reviewers and was a National Book Awards finalist for nonfiction in 1981. The book's oral histories offer various definitions of the American Dream, or in some cases, the absence of one. Studs begins the book with Miss USA 1973, Amanda Jones,[37] and concludes with seventy-year-old Clarence Spencer, the son of a slave, whom Studs first met in 1963, on the "freedom train" trip from Chicago to D.C.

Amanda Jones did not meet the beauty pageant stereotype. She told Studs about a Chicago reporter who was astounded when she told him that she viewed herself as Ms., not "Miss." She shunned the organization's speechwriter, giving speeches instead that promoted environmentalism. She urged President Nixon to resign.

Jones spoke with Studs about the night the new Miss USA was crowned. That year's most popular film was *The Sting*. In the movie, Robert Redford and Paul Newman rubbed their noses when the con game was on. Jones describes her final walk on stage as Miss USA: "As they were playing that silly farewell speech and I walked down the aisle and stood by the throne, I looked right into the camera and rubbed my finger across my nose."[38]

New York City's progressive radio station WBAI featured Studs on its *Bread and Roses* program as he promoted *American Dreams*. In his interview with host Alex Paul, Studs emphasized specific interviews that powerfully related to "lost and found" American dreams. He explained that the subtitle for his book came from the hymn "Amazing Grace": "I was lost but now I'm found, was blind but now I see. Now, those last two words; 'cause in many cases people in this book have discovered something."[39] Studs cited the Amanda Jones interview and the ones he'd conducted in Oregon and Washington among his favorites.

The most moving portrait in the book for Studs was the story of C. P. Ellis, a poor white and a member of the Ku Klux Klan. He spoke with Studs about his youth, and about how the Klan were the only people who accepted him. He talked about needing to have an enemy—black people—and his slow but determined conversion from a disenfranchised angry racist to a union and civic leader fighting for social justice. On mastering his own prejudice, he declared: "I met a black person and talked with him, eyeball to eyeball, and met a Jewish person and talked to him, eyeball to eyeball. I found out they're people just like me. They cried, they cussed, they prayed, they had desires. Just like myself."[40]

Studs loved transformation stories like that of Ellis. Near the end of 1980, Dan Rather traveled to Chicago to produce a segment on Studs for CBS's *60 Minutes*. As Studs talked about *American Dreams*, Rather inquired about his optimism and Studs replied, "I wake up, I read the headline, I see the news, I say 'Oh gosh, we're not going to make it, the human race.' And then I talk to people, and I change my mind. People say power corrupts. I think powerlessness corrupts, and absolute powerlessness corrupts absolutely."[41] One of Studs' examples was C. P. Ellis, the man who at one point in his life taught Klan youth that Martin Luther King was a Communist. Yet, in his interview with Studs, Ellis said:

> I tell people there's a tremendous possibility in this country to stop wars, the battles, the struggles, the fights between people. People say: "That's an impossible dream. You sound like Martin Luther King." An ex-Klansman who sounds like Martin Luther King. (Laughs.) I don't think it's an impossible dream. It's happened in my life. It's happened in other people's lives in America.[42]

Studs explained to Rather that his hopefulness stemmed from the transformational stories he heard from so many of the people he encountered. The transformational stories of ordinary human lives, like that of C. P. Ellis, sustained his view of the world.

10

Chicago and Beyond: The First Half
of the 1980s

THE 1980S BEGAN WITH TRAVEL PROMOTING *American Dreams: Lost and Found* as well as interviews for two new oral histories, "*The Good War*" and *The Great Divide*. New York visits included the filming of a television talk show, *Nightcap,* which Studs co-hosted with Calvin Trillin. Internationally, in addition to the Soviet Union and the United Kingdom, Ida and Studs journeyed to China in May 1981. Travel, *The Studs Terkel Show,* controversy, politics, and fervent writing, were ever present through the first half of the new decade.

The Studs Terkel Show *and the Death of Nelson Algren*

WFMT featured seventeen shows on China. Studs held conflicting outlooks about the country; feeling positive that there would be more opportunity for poor people, but lamenting that progress was the new religion resulting in the displacement of people and the destruction of historic buildings. *The Studs Terkel Show* aired conversations with grade school children, former Chinese Red Guards, a cleaning woman, kitchen worker, train conductor, and a school principal.

On May 9, hours prior to his scheduled departure on his China trip, Studs received notice that Nelson Algren had suffered a fatal heart attack in his Sag Harbor home on Long Island. Studs immediately called Joe Pintauro, a writer and playwright who had engineered Algren's move to Sag Harbor and was the person Algren referred to as "the man who put an end to my losing streak."[1] Pintauro remembers Studs saying, "Just take care of him. He was a dear friend. Can you understand how helpless I feel?"[2]

As soon as he returned from China, Studs memorialized Algren in several radio tributes. He read from Algren's books and he editorialized the author to his audience: "His luck was not good; he was never praised by powerful literary brokers or endowed by great universities; yet he kept shuffling along, as do all true winners, to immortality."[3] Studs received numerous letters from WFMT listeners thanking him for honoring Algren and his work. Frank Walsh wrote acknowledging Studs for creating "a floating wake."[4]

Program themes for *The Studs Terkel Show* in 1981 addressed the Israeli-Palestinian conflict, abused women, political prisoners, Eugene V. Debs, El Salvador, magnet schools, the Skokie-Nazi conflict, Holocaust survivors, and social movements in Poland. In October 1981, Studs did a feature on *American Dreams: Lost and Found*. Among the many guests who visited *The Studs Terkel Show* that year were John Malkovich, David Attenborough, Jacques Cousteau, Toni Morrison, Gordon Parks, "Utah" Phillips, Orville Schell, Burr Tillstrom, Paul Wellstone, and Tennessee Williams.

In the following year, *The Studs Terkel Show* presented programs on nuclear disarmament, the Equal Rights Amendment, mill workers, nuns from Nicaragua, Maggie Kuhn and other Gray Panthers, Parents and Friends of Lesbians and Gays (PFLAG), Damon Runyan, and the peace movement in Northern Ireland. Among Studs' interviewees in 1982 were John Cage, Carlos Fuentes, Dizzy Gillespie, Nat Hentoff, Garrison Keillor, Tom Lehrer, Marcel Marceau, Mike Royko, Pete Seeger, Gloria Steinem, Edward Albee, Paul Theroux, and Calvin Trillin.

As Studs was working on the final edits of *"The Good War"* he welcomed a myriad of guests on his show: Rosalynn Carter, Stan Getz, Michael Harrington, Marcel Ophüls, Holly Near, Edward Said, Maurice Sendak, Denise Levertov, Gore Vidal, and Arthur Miller. Studs' old friends Pete Seeger, Burr Tillstrom, George Drury, Frank Wilkinson, and Garry Wills also made appearances. The year's programming highlighted the Haymarket Massacre, nuclear weapons, class and power, the Vietnam War, coal miners in the United Kingdom, Mark Twain, Virginia Woolf, D-Day, James Joyce, and political activists in Guatemala.

Around the time he performed on Studs' program, Pete Seeger also held a concert in Chicago. Studs served as the Master of Ceremonies. David Royko recalls a humorous anecdote involving his father, Studs, and Pete walking on Michigan Avenue after the concert, each carrying one of Seeger's instruments:

> At one point, a car with the windows open started driving slowly next to them, a middle-aged couple inside, staring. After a moment, the guy driving said out loud to his wife, "Oh my God, that's Royko!" And then a bit louder, "And, Studs!" And then almost hollering, "And, oh my God, Pete!!!" The guy, having been at that concert, was most likely an old-school liberal, and for an encore got to see a liberal Holy Trinity on Michigan Avenue.[5]

Investing in The Nation

Ida and Studs continued to lend their names and energies to various political issues and causes. On December 10, 1981, the *New York Times* reported that Studs, politicians Ronald V. Dellums of California, Robert W. Edgar of Pennsylvania, Patricia Schroeder of Colorado, Paul Simon of Illinois, and Tom Harkin of Iowa, actors Edward Asner and Jane Fonda, and singer and antiwar activist Joan Baez had all signed an open letter to President Ronald Reagan demanding that the United States discontinue its support of the Pol Pot regime in Cambodia.

Writing in *The Nation* since 1968, Studs increased his involvement in the early 1980s when he and Ida made a small investment in the magazine. Victor Navasky was the editor at the time, and he remembers that the magazine's publisher, Hamilton Fish, asked Studs to join the investors. In Fish's view, the work and worldview of Studs and *The Nation* were connected: "He was a crucial narrative spine of the sort of modern history of *The Nation*, and he was the chronicler. I mean, all of the stuff that he had done in *The Nation*, he had done in different ways in his books and on his radio shows, so there's a natural alliance."[6]

In 1981, Studs participated in the American Writers' Congress, an event sponsored by *The Nation*. The Congress was assembled, at least partially, because Navasky and other people at the magazine feared attacks on freedom of expression and publisher censorship following Ronald Reagan's election as president. Four thousand people attended the conference. Studs was on a list with other renowned writers and politicos. The event featured a live, onstage conversation between Studs and Calvin Trillin. This conversation provided the impetus for their television show, *Nightcap*.

Nightcap

Studs and Bud Trillin's show *Nightcap* first aired in 1982 on the Alpha Repertory Television Service (ARTS) cable television channel, a nascent version of the A&E cable network. *Nightcap* was acclaimed for its "highbrow programming." The program was filmed in New York City. It was shown on both the East and West Coasts, but ironically it was not broadcast in Chicago. One of the people who produced the show, Peter Meyer, remembered that Studs came to New York one day a month and four episodes were filmed each time.

The shows were somewhat thematic. Science-fiction writers Isaac Asimov, Gene Wolfe, and Harlan Ellison appeared together as did comedians Sid Caesar, Carl Reiner, and Mel Brooks. Another show featured animators Ralph Bakshi, Don Bluth, and Larry Elin. John Carradine, John Houseman, and Beatrice Johnson appeared with her a capella group Sweet Honey in the Rock. There were episodes on street performers, union workers, the blacklist, and jazzers.

After Studs died, Harlan Ellison recalled the day he appeared on the program. He rushed to the show thinking that he would be arrested as he had just physically assaulted his publisher at Grosset & Dunlap. Inside the studio he told the group of the event and remembered that he felt like Jean Valjean. "Studs Terkel that Great Man, looked at me and said: 'Kid, you got some real moxie there!' " [7]

The show's final program featured Caesar, Brooks, and Reiner discussing their contributions to the popular variety series *Your Show of Shows*, which aired on NBC from 1950 to 1954. *Nightcap* ran for about a year and a half. In an interview at the Academy of Television Arts and Sciences in 1999, Studs recalled, "I think people liked it. It had a spark to it. And then it was dropped because the guy who ran it made a whole lot of money on the little lady, the sex stuff, Dr. Ruth. So he dropped us like a hot potato."[8]

Classroom Controversy over Working

On February 2, 1982, Studs spoke at a rally in support of the Polish workers' movement sponsored by American Workers & Artists for Solidarity. Among the speakers joining Studs were Joseph Brodsky, E. L. Doctorow, Carlos Fuentes, Allen Ginsberg, Dick Gregory, Nat Hentoff, Ed Sadlowski, Pete Seeger, Daniel Singer, Susan Sontag, Gore Vidal, and Kurt Vonnegut.

Around the same time of this event, controversy broke out over Studs' book *Working*. Girard, Pennsylvania, was a blue-collar community on the outskirts of Erie. A veteran teacher named Kay Nichols had assigned selections from the book for her class, an English section for eight senior vocational education students. The dispute was supposedly focused on curse words in the book. The principal of Girard High School, Walter Blucas, viewed the event as "testing the authority of the teacher."[9] Many years later, Nichols stated:

> Well, everybody knew that that was a fraudulent position. There was resentment over basically having to work hard in class. They would've preferred a much less demanding environment. The actual protest, the inside information said they were in gym class before they came to my class, and that they cooked it up together and said if we do this, we won't have to do the work.[10]

Nichols had used Studs' book for eight years prior to 1982 with no problems. There were two students in this year's class, however, who were particularly vocal in their refusal to read the book because of the profanity—Robert Burns and James Richardson. Burns's mother, Linda, took up the charge and led a group of twenty parents who demanded that the school board ban the book.

The issue drew national attention, and media coverage of the controversy was extensive in Girard, Erie, and Pittsburgh. Kay Nichols became frightened about her security as a teacher and called Studs to explain the events at the school surrounding *Working*. She remembers Studs being very understanding and he suggested that she report back to him the following day.

After Nichols's subsequent call, Studs flew to Pennsylvania and met with different classes in the morning and the entire student body in the afternoon. He also had individual conversations with students and spoke at an open school board meeting in the evening. There was even greater media coverage of this event, including network television news reports and articles in papers throughout the country. Nichols noted that the community was not prepared for the controversy or for the attention it drew.

NBC covered Studs' visit with John Chancellor interviewing him on the national evening newscast. There was an extensive article in the *New York Times*. Studs recorded his memories of the event as well, and included them in his book *Touch and Go*. Nichols noted that Studs acted as an oral historian when he visited Girard:

He would wander out to the lunchroom and sit down at a table and talk to people. He had the freedom of the school. He certainly wasn't an unwelcome person. He charmed everybody. He disarms you when he speaks to you. He was like a grandpa. Just, you know, friendly, down to earth, no pretensions in language or attitude or manners. That's his persona.[11]

Documentation of some of Studs' conversations with students appears in both *The Great Divide* and *Touch and Go*. The dialogue was broad. Some students, using religion as their foundation, supported banning books with profanity. Others cited *Gone With the Wind* to challenge any ban on language or ideas. Most of the students appreciated Studs visiting their school. There was applause throughout his talk. It reached a crescendo when one of the boycotters said that he had changed his mind and told Studs that he owed him an apology.

Although Studs' words drew applause at the public meeting, the voices of dissent were louder. The loudest was that of Linda Burns: "We strongly object to profanity in the book and fear that students will receive a distorted view of the working world by reading it. We strongly oppose the work as required reading and would like to see it banned from the district."[12] Studs found Linda Burns empathetic. He felt that she was speaking from her pain and her heart. Yet he could not refrain from noting that his book was a chronicle of the townspeople's lives.

WFMT colleague Tony Judge had given Studs a ride to the airport when he departed on his trip to Girard. When he picked him up upon his return, Studs reported that he was very pleased by his reception in the community. His trip had been successful, as Kay Nichols was permitted to continue teaching *Working* in her classroom. Subsequently, Girard High School became one of the many schools to stage the musical adaptation of *Working*.

Studs and Ida in the USSR

In late July 1982 Studs and Ida, at the invitation of Harrison Salisbury, visited the Soviet Union for the Sixth Annual Soviet-American Writers Conference. Among the other invitees were Gwendolyn Brooks, Erica Jong, Arthur Schlesinger Jr., Robert Bly, Susan Sontag, Irving Stone, and their respective partners. The group toured from Kiev to Leningrad to Moscow, spending a few days in each city and exchanging views with Soviet authors.

Brooks recalled that the Americans and Russians sat at different tables at the various banquets. Except, of course, for Studs, who always sat with the Russian writers.[13] She also cited tension between the Soviet hosts and Erica Jong,[14] and Studs was disappointed because he found it impossible to meet with "ordinary people." For Studs, the second trip with Salisbury in 1990 was much more interesting. On each occasion he met with Yassen Zassoursky, the president of the faculty of journalism at Moscow State University, who recalled: "I think some of his books were published in Russian, they were very popular, but it's more important to know that he started a new trend in writing historical books, because he did a history of various professions of jobs, of people at their work."[15]

Studs included interviews from his journey in *"The Good War."* In addition, he welcomed Robert Bly on his show to discuss his experiences of the trip to the Soviet Union, and also broadcast his interview with Soviet physician, filmmaker, and editor Vitaly Korotich.

Korotich had guided Studs in Kiev and told the story of the Nazi invasion and the mass murder of Jews in the city. He spoke with Studs about the disbelief within the Jewish community of Kiev that the Nazis could prove so barbaric: "Some Jews who were killed didn't believe it, because they knew European culture. They knew Goethe's *Faust*, Heine's lyrics. They did not believe that in one nation it is possible to have Heine, Goethe, and Hitler. Beethoven and Himmler."[16]

Chicago's First African American Mayor

To usher in the New Year of 1983, Studs and Ida went to Don Rose's annual New Year's Eve party, an event they had attended for twenty years. Studs served on various boards—the Clergy and Concerned Laity in Chicago and the twentieth-anniversary committee of the Institute for Policy Studies in Washington. In autumn 1983, Studs was presented with the Eugene V. Debs Award for his public service. The award was conceived as a way of "honoring a person whose work has been in the spirit of Debs and who has contributed to the advancement of the causes of industrial unionism, social justice, or world peace."

Most importantly, Studs committed his support to Harold Washington in his bid to be elected Chicago's first African American mayor. Washington's campaign was dramatic. He strongly criticized Daley and his machine—as well as the nepotism that defined Chicago politics. In addition, he was vociferous in his critique of the city's systemic racism. Washington never hesitated to mention that black people in Chicago would finally be represented if he were elected. However, even when he was speaking to predominantly black audiences, he emphasized the fact that he would be mayor for all Chicagoans.

Studs spoke at rallies with great enthusiasm for Washington's candidacy. Don Rose recalls Studs' involvement in the campaign:

Studs was not the guy who came out to the office and made telephone calls or anything like that, but he used his public persona in a number of different ways—speaking at rallies, speaking at home meetings. He spoke in my backyard when I had a party to raise funds for the school boycott and other things. He always lent his time—air time if he could.[17]

Studs advocated strongly on behalf of Washington. One speech was included in Bill Stamets's documentary, *Chicago Politics: A Theatre of Power*:

> If by chance Harold doesn't win, runs a close second, some people are saying your vote was wasted. No. I would rather vote for something I want and not get it than vote for something I don't want and get it. And that's been the case in Chicago all these years. But I think, I think the intelligence of Chicagoans will result, and quite conceivably will be a victory for Harold. And to my white fellow Chicagoans, I say this transcends race. It involves vision. It involves self-respect, for yourself, for your intelligence, which I shall exercise on that day when I vote for Harold Washington.[18]

Washington won a close election over the incumbent, Jane Byrne, and Daley's son, Richard M. Daley. On April 28 he was sworn in as mayor at Navy Pier. While he restated his campaign phrase that he was mayor for all citizens of Chicago, he lost no zeal declaring: "Business as usual will not be accepted by the people of this city. Business as usual will not be accepted by this chief executive of this great city."[19]

The inauguration was accompanied by readings from Studs and Gwendolyn Brooks. The Chicago Children's Choir and the Morris Ellis Orchestra performed. Over twenty years after Harold Washington was elected, Studs still wished that he had not died so young. Speaking with Kurt Jacobsen from the journal *Logos*, Studs bemoans Daley's "plantation politics" and then adds: "But then came Harold Washington. Harold died too soon. He would have been fantastic. If he were alive today the country itself would have been affected for the better by him. There's no question in my mind. Harold was brilliant, funny, and heads above the others."[20]

Celebrity

With his ever-growing national reputation, the invitations to speak for organizations and on college campuses continued to increase. Studs Terkel's fee was strikingly different from that of his blacklist days. As was typical, however, he continued to appear gratis at the request of friends and sympathetic causes.

Studs made a number of appearances in 1984, including trips to the University of Alabama, Northeastern University, and the University of Judaism in Los Angeles. He also spoke in Jackson, Mississippi, at the annual meeting of the state's library association. His speaker's fee tended to be $5,000 plus expenses. One event that Studs attended without an honorarium was a student production of *Working*. He took the actors out after the performance.

Studs also acted in 1984. He had a cameo role in *The Dollmaker*, a made-for-TV movie starring Jane Fonda, who received an Emmy Award for her performance. Studs was on film for about two minutes in his role as a cabdriver. The irony being, of course, that in reality Studs never learned how to drive. After the film was screened, Jane Fonda signed a photograph of Studs in the movie that read, "What a thrill to be upstaged by you, Studs."

11

"The Good War"

BEGINNING IN 1981, STUDS' JOURNEYS included interviews for his book project on the Second World War. He traveled the country and, as in his earlier books, convinced people to share their stories, this time of participating in or avoiding the war.

California

Tony Judge acted as Studs' driver in California, where he conducted interviews for *"The Good War."* He describes Studs' interview with two African American pilots, Tuskegee Airmen:

> They didn't know who this Studs Terkel guy was. It was hardly the first time they did interviews because they were Tuskegee Airmen. And they were quite prepared, but they were obviously a little suspect because this was one more white guy, one more. And he completely disarmed them. It was really something to see. In the end they both looked at him and said, "Thanks for letting us tell you our story." They had told it dozens of times to others but to no one who had listened like Studs—that "feeling tone."[1]

"Feeling tone," is emphasized by Judge, who sees it as eternally present in Studs' conversations. "Studs thought the feeling tone was really at the essence, at the heart of conversation and the way that we think of each other. It meant everything to him."[2]

While in San Francisco interviewing Milton Wolff and Irving Goff, surviving members of the Abraham Lincoln Brigade—a volunteer unit that fought for the Popular Front during the Spanish Civil War in the late 1930s—Studs stayed at the inexpensive Beresford Hotel. He liked its "tattered elegance."[3]

Stewart McBride of the *Christian Science Monitor* conducted an interview with Studs at the Beresford. Studs told him that he had finished two-thirds of the interviews for *"The Good War,"* and talked to him about his reason for doing the book, the people involved, and the process. He explained that many of the interviews were about people at home in the United States rather than in the war zones. He also noted:

> You see, World War II was a real benchmark. During the Great American Depression, the nation's beautiful machinery slipped on a banana peel; the gears were stripped. World War II ended the Depression, and then came the bomb—and the Cold War. It was such a different world before World War II. Not only the U.S., but the whole world.[4]

Studs expounded on John Garcia, a Hawaiian whose fiancée was killed during the attack on Pearl Harbor. Except she was shot by "friendly fire":

> I'm thinking of starting the book with Garcia. He later got a job as a cop in Washington, but refused to use a gun. He'd walk empty-handed into a liquor store that three guys were robbing and say, "The cops are waiting outside, so you might as well surrender." It sounds crazy, but he got away with it.[5]

When McBride asked Studs about his process, he replied, "I've got hundreds of interviews, and so far it's a wild mural. I'm waltzing along now, but when I start editing the stuff will evolve in my mind."[6]

Kentucky

Mike Edgerly, who is currently news director at Minnesota Public Radio, was a young news reporter in Kentucky in 1983. When Studs arrived at the Lexington Airport, he was greeted by Edgerly who drove him to Harrodsburg to interview two Second World War veterans, Ken Hourigan and Jack Wilson. Edgerly noted:

> Wilson had saved lots of newspaper clippings, had lots of mementos from that period, and was really real talkative about his experience. Ken Hourigan, on the other hand, was one of those quiet vets who emerge from something really horrible and was not talkative. I think Studs actually liked Ken a little more, but Jack was so voluble and so helpful in telling a story that it seemed like a natural for the book.[7]

Studs crafted this chapter in the book by noting Wilson's words and juxtaposing excerpts from Hourigan within the story.

From Harrodsburg, Edgerly drove Studs to Louisville where he was to speak with members of the Kentucky Oral History Commission the following day. Edgerly's goal was to broadcast a radio story on Studs. With Studs' permission, he kept a tape recorder running in the car. His memories of their trip together were of Studs providing commentary on scenes that interested him as they drove. Edgerly reflected on his observations of Studs: "His gift was relating even to someone who had a completely different background from him and pulling the story out. You combine his love of conversation with his empathy for his subjects, and you know, it just seemed to work."[8]

Two years after chaperoning Studs on his Kentucky trip, Edgerly applied for a William F. Benton Journalism Fellowship at the University of Chicago. He asked Studs for a letter of recommendation. Among the documentation that Studs was sent regarding Edgerly's application was the twenty-five-minute radio program he had produced on Studs' visit. Not only did Studs write the recommendation for Edgerly, he called him shortly after finishing it to read it aloud:

> The phone rings at the news desk, I pick it up, and I announce, "Newsroom." It goes, "Can I talk to Mike Edgerly here?" And I said, "Well, you got him." And he goes, "Well this is Studs, hang on a second." So you know, it's fumbling with the phone and all that stuff.

He says, "Listen to this." And he reads, he just reads this, not very long, but a very pithy endorsement, very wonderful, warm endorsement about my application to the Benton Fellowship. And I thought, Holy shit. This is Studs Terkel. He said, "How's that sound to you?" I said, "God, it's incredible, what are you talking about?" And he says, "Okay, I'll see ya in Chicago!" And lo and behold, a few months later, I was in for interviews and I got the fellowship.[9]

Because he was a noteworthy Chicago writer, Studs was asked to speak at one of the Benton Fellowship seminar sessions. Edgerly was in attendance. Along with the other fellows, who represented CNN, BBC, and other big networks, he listened as Studs began the session by playing the first moments of the radio show Edgerly had produced on Studs.

For Edgerly, this experience with Studs was extraordinary—influencing him for the rest of his life. An occurrence similar to multitudes of others who had conversations with Studs: "His whole body language, everything is into you. You're the most important thing in the world."[10]

The Book

After completing the editing of *"The Good War,"* Studs began the book with the story of John Garcia, the Pearl Harbor Navy Yard apprentice who survived the attacks but lost his fiancée to an American bomb. He presented cogent portions of the narratives of the people portrayed in the book in the Introduction, juxtaposed with his thoughts and even analysis of the American spirit(s). He wrote of Hans Gobeler, who served as a mate on a German submarine, and American James Sanders, the junior flight officer who tried to sink it. Studs interviewed them together at the Museum of Science and Industry in Chicago. They were attending a reunion for the crews of both ships. They agreed that it was easy to dupe young people, and that in observing their dead enemies, the most striking thing was how young everyone looked. Sanders told a story of capturing a German prisoner: "Within a week . . . they were just talkin' like a couple of kids that grew up in the same neighborhood."[11]

Studs' edit began with placing the book's title in quotation marks. He spoke about it during his San Francisco appearance with Calvin Trillin. "Well, first of all, '*The Good War*,' you'll notice, is in quotes. That was my wife's insistence. Good and war, and even World War Two, no war she says, the adjective and the noun are incongruous and it'd be criminal of you to put down the book '*The Good War*' without it being in quotes."[12]

Even more prominent than in his prior oral histories, "*The Good War*" portrayed emotional, human insights that are seldom mentioned or even considered in historical studies of war. In addition to Americans, Studs interviewed people from Japan, Germany, France, the Soviet Union, and the United Kingdom. The Abraham Lincoln Brigade was represented and African American soldiers discussed white supremacy in the "Jim Crow" army. Characteristically, Studs unearthed the personal stories that are central to the collective spirit. He interviewed friends: Peggy Terry, Mike Royko, Win Stracke, Timuel Black, Virginia Durr, and Herman Kogan. Ida was again portrayed as Eileen Barth.

Camaraderie was a dominant theme in the book. One soldier explained to Studs, "It's that sense of not wanting to fail your buddies."[13] Studs' friend Win Stracke was emphatic concerning the responsibility borne of camaraderie. "We were in a tribal sort of situation, where we could help each other without fear. I realized it was the absence of phony standards that created the thing I loved about the Army."[14]

Other people with whom Studs spoke shared their stories of the prejudice and inhumanity of war. Milton Wolff and Irving Goff, members of the Abraham Lincoln Brigade whom Studs met with on his California trip, remember fighting against Franco and fascism in Spain in the late 1930s. For their commitment to democracy, they were labeled PAF—Premature Anti-Fascists—by the United States government. After the war, the FBI and the House Un-American Activities Committee subjected both men to intimidation. American poet John Ciardi, who as a student had signed an anti-Franco petition, was also labeled PAF. When he and Studs met, there was a discussion of the similarity between war and sport: "When you were on a mission and you saw a Japanese plane go down, you cheered. This was a football game. When one of your guys went down, you sighed. It was miserable."[15]

Virginia Durr's contribution was among the book's most forceful stories. The Durrs were living in the nation's capital at the time and were constantly providing refuge for people who needed a place to live. There was a Japanese-American couple who stayed with them at one point—the Yamasakis. After the bombs were dropped on Hiroshima and Nagasaki, they sadly informed Virginia:

> We hate to tell you this. You've given us a home and have been very nice to us, but we cannot stay here. I asked why. She said, "Twelve members of my family were evaporated in Nagasaki." He said, fifteen of his family. Made into atomic ash. They said, "We know that you are good people and you wouldn't have dropped the bomb, but we just can't stay with white Americans any more. We have to be with Japanese people."[16]

The most unique story on white supremacy in *"The Good War"* was that of Hans Massaquoi, the editor of *Ebony* magazine when Studs interviewed him for the book. Born in Germany in 1926 to a Liberian father and German mother, he was raised in Germany by his mother through the war. As one of very few German-born biracial children in Nazi Germany, he was shunned, albeit not persecuted by the Nazis:

> There was a drive to enroll young kids into the Hitler Youth movement. I wanted to join, of course. My mother took me aside and said, "Look, Hans, you may not understand, but they don't want you." I couldn't understand. All my friends had these black shorts and brown shirts and a swastika and a little dagger, which said Blood and Honor. I wanted it just like everybody else. I wanted to belong.[17]

These crises of identity borne of dual-status were not just a phenomenon in Nazi Germany, it was just as common in the United States. For example, Studs provides a story of being Japanese-American portrayed by Peter Ota. He remembered going to the prison with his mother and sister when his father was arrested after Pearl Harbor. "When my father walked through the door, my mother was so humiliated. She didn't say anything. She cried. . . . Shame in her culture was worse than death."[18] One of the survivors of Hiroshima, Hideko Tamura Friedman—a *hibakusha*[19]—spoke to Studs about looking for her mother after the bombing. She was eleven years old in 1945, and she cried as she told Studs that she never found her mother. Ursala Bender, who was an editor at Pantheon and worked with Studs, had a similar experience in Germany. The sirens had gone off, warning of Allied bombing, and her mother retreated with her to their basement for safety. She woke up to a burning smell and her mother was missing. Bender's story had a happier ending, as her mother was safe, working with other women who were distributing water to survivors.

There are so many potent stories in Studs' *"The Good War."* Erhard Dabringhaus, who was a German intelligence officer, reminded Studs that German soldiers had wives and children just as Americans did. Robert Rasmus viewed life as "B.W." and "A.W."—before the war and after the war. He said to Studs, "I remember letters I sent my buddies that came back: Missing in action. Killed in action. These were the eighteen-year-olds. It was only because I got the flu that I wasn't among them."[20] There were also allusions to Americans killing Americans. E. B. (Sledgehammer) Sledge, a biology professor whose book, *With the Old Breed*, was featured in Steven Spielberg's film *The Pacific,* had memories of both his own humanity and inhumanity after telling Studs, "There was nothing macho about the war at all. We were a bunch of scared kids who had to do a job."[21]

Arguably, the most powerful oral history was that of Betty Basye Hutchinson who served as a nurse as well as a friend of the severely wounded. She spoke of vomiting her first day on the job but then advocating for the wounded when they were shunned upon their return to the wealthy, privileged community of Pasadena. Hutchinson truly believed that a "good war" did not exist. Another woman in California, Dellie Hahne, was even more certain. "The good war? That infuriates me. Yeah, the idea of World War Two being called a good war is a horrible thing."[22] Both women's reflections relate to Ida's insistence on using quotation marks in the book's title.

Critical Reviews and the Pulitzer Prize

After *"The Good War"* was published, the critical reviews were overwhelmingly positive. Carol Brightman, writing in *The Nation*, noted, "*'The Good War'* is the fifth and finest entry in Studs Terkel's neorealist variation on Dos Passos' *USA*."[23] Her only criticism was that there was rarely mention of Nazi genocide. The *New York Times* review, written by longtime editor of *Life* Loudon Wainright, lauded Studs' book, saying, "It is hard to see how any reader now or then can fail to benefit from its 600 pages. . . . There is an amazingly visual quality to much of the detail. It amounts to a kind of mnemonic cinematography."[24]

"The Good War" became Studs' best-selling book in 1985. He was also the recipient of 1985's Pulitzer Prize for General Nonfiction. Studs did not dwell on winning this award. True to his character, he was somewhat self-deprecating. Maureen Dowd quoted him: "If you stick around long enough, anything can happen—look at Reagan. I didn't think I had a chance."[25]

Articles in the *Tribune*, *New York Times*, and *The Nation* praised the committee for honoring Studs' work, but there were some naysayers. Chief among them were the *Chicago Tribune*'s "Book World" editor, John Blades, and Joseph Epstein, a professor at Northwestern University in Chicago. Epstein would later write *Snobbery: The American Version* (2002), in which he uses Studs Terkel as an example of lefty snobbery. He is quoted in Blades' review as saying:

My sense is that his books are informed by his politics. . . . My guess is that he's selecting his material all the time in a way that suits his own bias. What he presents is Studs Terkel's version of the Common Man. He's one of what I call the Virtuecrats. He's always telling us how much he loves people, and everyone assumes he does. But the only evidence we have is that he keeps telling us he loves them.[26]

Royko wrote a response piece to this article in the *Tribune*. He titled it "Vintage Whines from Professors." You can almost hear him pounding the keys of his typewriter as he answers Epstein and like-minded critics:

> The names of the professors who denigrated Terkel's achievements need not be mentioned because no one would recognize them anyway. Of course the English teacher found Terkel's account of the war uninteresting—he would have preferred a novel about an English teacher with writer's block who goes to wartime France and meets this gorgeous . . . well you know. Of course history professors considered the book unscholarly, because no self-respecting historian talks with anyone living, and besides, historians consider anything that is not dull a sham.[27]

This time, Studs was not bothered much by the criticism. What touched his heart when he won the Pulitzer Prize were the innumerable letters of congratulation. Over a thousand listeners, fans, colleagues, and friends wrote to acknowledge Studs' honor. Most dear to Studs was a letter from Norman Corwin, which read: "Congratulations from here to both poles and around the Equator! All the past sins of the Pulitzer Award juries have been atoned and purged in a single stroke, as by a great judgmental Yom Kippur."[28]

As Studs celebrated the award, he was writing one book while on the road researching another. Much to his dismay, he was beginning to see changes in the climate and culture at his beloved WFMT.

12

Controversy at Work: But Life Goes On

STUDS' SPIRIT WAS ENERGIZED AFTER WINNING the Pulitzer. Subsequently, he worked to complete *Studs Terkel's Chicago* and traveled to interview people for *The Great Divide*. There were many new visitors to his show, including Richard Avedon, William Friedkin, Joseph Lelyveld, Wynton Marsalis, Leonard Boudin, Dr. Benjamin Spock, and many other academics, literary luminaries, activists, and scientists. There were also a variety of topical programs, such as the TWA flight attendant strike, Nicaragua, women political activists in South Africa (Black Sash), the Green Party in Germany, Tuskegee Airmen, Attica Prison, independent bookstores, WPA Artists Project, and Chernobyl. Circumstances surrounding his show at WFMT, however, were to be forever altered beginning in the second half of the 1980s.

Troubles at WFMT

Life at the station began to degenerate in 1985. Actually, WFMT's transition had begun in 1968 when the original owner, Bernie Jacobs, sold the independent fine arts station to the large, corporate WGN Continental Broadcasting Company. A group of WFMT listeners formed an organization, Citizens Committee to Save WFMT. The group supported staff and its charge was to conserve the original mission of the station. A legal battle ensued, and within two years, WFMT was donated to the Chicago Educational Television Network (CETA).

Studs referred to CETA as "overseers" and its management as "plantation style." In 1985, an outsider, John Diedrichs, was installed as the interim vice chairman of the station. Longtime station president

Ray Nordstrand lost his leadership status and was forced to step down as publisher of *Chicago Magazine*. In addition, the station was mandated to increase advertising time from four to six minutes per hour. For some, this portended the beginning of the end of WFMT as a semi-autonomous fine arts station.

The WFMT staff congregated at Studs' house. He wrote a long letter to the board in which he praised both the historical culture of the station and his colleagues. He noted the many awards the station had won internationally. Stating that they were all stunned by the events he added, "What had been a delightful place to work had, overnight, been transformed into Bleak House."[1]

Open animosity existed between Studs and Diedrichs. They argued in the halls of the station but mostly in Diedrichs' office. Reporting in the *Chicago Tribune*, Eric Zorn wrote, "Tempers flared and the exchange ended with Diedrichs suggesting that if Terkel didn't like what was going on he could quit, and with Terkel responding loudly that he would never quit."[2] In spite of this, Studs maintained hope that Diedrichs' attitude would change if he could understand the culture of the station.

In 1986 amidst the conflict and Studs' work on *The Great Divide*, Ida faced a medical issue that might have frightened Studs more than her. She was admitted to the hospital and underwent heart valve replacement surgery. Studs' WFMT colleague Sydney Lewis, very much a part of their lives at the time, remarks, "Studs was utterly distracted. He managed to work, but his demeanor wasn't normal, you could tell his mind was elsewhere, unsettled. He'd leave as soon as his interviews or work for the day was done."[3]

Ida's operation was a success and she recuperated quickly, thus allowing Studs to travel again to collect interviews for *The Great Divide*. While he was on the road in 1987, CETA sold *Chicago Magazine*. CETA received $17 million for the transaction. The sale was important for Studs and his WFMT colleagues on multiple levels. First known simply as WFMT's *Program Guide*, then *Perspective on Ideas and the Arts*, it became *Chicago Magazine* in 1975. Studs' work appeared in the monthly with his life at WFMT paralleling that of the publication.

Equally important was the fact that the magazine provided significant funding for WFMT.

CETA's general manager, William McCarter, working in conjunction with the CETA board, was making decisions for WFMT. Diedrichs' prior experience as an executive was at the Sunbeam Corporation—he was not a broadcaster. Staff at the radio station abhorred McCarter and held no trust for Diedrichs. The tension was too much for CETA and after a short time they reappointed Nordstrand, which was also short-lived as McCarter then named longtime WFMT engineer Al Antlitz as general manager. He became McCarter's lackey.

Studs believed that the board viewed McCarter as the ultimate fundraiser and that they had "utter disdain for the station."[4] The situation reminded him of Florence Scala stressing the meanness of "the good people." For Studs, the next blow came early in 1988, when, after airing at ten in the morning for thirty-seven years, *The Studs Terkel Show* was moved to the late-afternoon drive time. Antlitz claimed the move was precipitated by low ratings, but the numbers did not support that assertion. A year later the program was moved again. This time it aired at seven in the evening. There would be one more time change in the near future. By 1990, Studs' life at WFMT was totally altered.

The same year, the "Friends of WFMT" filed a lawsuit against the parent company, Chicago Educational Television Association, claiming funds from the sale of *Chicago Magazine* were the property of WFMT. Their case was dismissed because the organization did not have legal jurisdiction. Studs' response was that WFMT was "robbed of millions." In retaliation, CETA filed its own suits, one against Friends of WFMT and one against WFMT's employees. Management also began ordering WFMT to use "canned commercials," a practice that was antithetical to the culture at the station. Friends of WFMT were charged with trademark infringement. They counterclaimed and there was a quick settlement, with members from the organization added to the CETA board.

In spite of the legal compromise, there was little trust at the station. A tipping point was reached on January 12 when eight staff members, including Tony Judge, George Drury, Kathy Cowan, and Sydney

Lewis, who all worked intimately with Studs, were summarily fired. As Michael Miner reported in the *Chicago Reader*, each person was individually summoned to WFMT senior vice president and general manager Alfred Antlitz's office. There they were greeted by Antlitz, in addition to David Levin, director of the WFMT Fine Arts Networks, and Jim Barker, the general sales manager. One by one they were dismissed. Miner wrote, "Antlitz's way of letting people go lacked finesse. He told them to clear out by five o'clock and then he posted a security guard at the front door."[5]

Although Antlitz referred to their dismissals as a budgetary decision, Judge was clear that it was "the barbarians eliminating the opposition."[6] One colleague who was not terminated, Kay Richards, bravely wrote the board declaring, "The only common denominator among the people who were fired was that they were active and vocal dissenters to some of the management's policies."[7]

Studs expressed his anger in a letter to the *Chicago Reader*. Stating his disdain for McCarter, he emphasized that he detested the actions of the "good people" of the CETA board.[8] CETA, of course, would have loved to fire Studs—but they couldn't. Mike Royko wrote an article that challenged why, like most corporate entities, CETA did not know how to fire Studs "neatly, cleanly and with finality." Royko expounded on the contempt management had toward his friend as they were "sneaking about, nipping at him from behind, sticking him with tiny daggers, trying to make his life so miserable that he'll quit."[9]

Not pretending to hide his anger or disappointment, Studs collaborated with Lois Baum and other colleagues who remained at the station in a fight for union representation. CETA challenged a positive vote in the courts, but amidst the turmoil and negative feelings, the American Federation of Television and Radio Artists (AFTRA) was certified to represent WFMT workers. Conflict surrounding Studs' work at the station continued until he left in 1997.

Studs Terkel's Chicago

In 1986, Mayor Washington and Studs spoke at a rally for the Illinois Nuclear Weapons Freeze Campaign. This event also served as the public launch for *Studs Terkel's Chicago*. Unlike his oral histories or memoirs, this book was brief—only 144 pages—and included photographs from well-known artists, some of whom worked for the Farm Security Administration in the 1930s.

Referring to Chicago as two-faced—both blessed and cursed— Studs juxtaposes Jane Addams and Al Capone, Clarence Darrow and Julius Hoffman, the city of man and the city of things. He captures the sagas of the city, in addition to including some of his own. Various stories and anecdotes about his childhood in the book were previously published in *Talking to Myself* and would appear again in *Touch and Go*, but here he also chronicles his many years of riding the bus on his daily commute to WFMT. Union leader Ed Sadlowski, friend and comrade to Studs, thinks that the bus is a metaphor for Studs' life. He believes there is much to learn from the bus adventures:

> Most of his feelings and the direction that he traveled come off that bus ride to and from work and home. I think one of the things they should be teaching is a guy riding on the bus. The relationships and understanding why he's on that bus. Why is it going there? Where is it coming from? The architectural aspects. The whole history of the racial questions. All of those things.[10]

Studs loved everything about the bus—working people, ethnicity, and ultimately, conversation. While his aptitude for listening is well documented, his voice might have been the loudest on those daily rides. The bus represented what democracy was supposed to be.

Studs Terkel's Chicago, unlike his previous books, did not receive numerous reviews. John Palmer interviewed him nationally for NBC. Local television journalist John Madigan criticized Studs harshly on WBBM, calling him "a constant whiner about this city" and "a veteran lefty who has made a career out of attacking the American system." His only compliments were acknowledging Terkel's self-admission that he was no "Chamber of Commerce sycophant" and that the book accurately reflected his love/hate relationship with Chicago.[11]

Political Life

Now both in their mid-seventies, Ida and Studs' many political, social, and cultural commitments continued to grow. They answered Pearl Hirshfield's calls, this time for a fundraiser when South African anti-apartheid activist Dennis Brutus was honored by the Chicago Committee to Defend the Bill of Rights. Studs emceed the event at the Midland Hotel, titled "The Fight for Equality." In 1985, he had received the same accolade. He also appeared with Cesar Chavez at a Chicago rally for the National Grape Boycott where he spoke about our debt to farm workers and chided the growers about both fair pay and the chemicals hurting farm workers' children. Don Rose relied on Studs in his political campaigns. Working with AFSCME leader Roberta Lynch, Rose asked Studs to narrate a video for a progressive ticket running for offices in the Illinois Federation of Labor. "So I brought Studs into the studio and I told him I've got a script here for you and he says, 'It sounds just like me.' And he goes before the cameras like five minutes after that and does a perfect take."[12]

Bughouse Square still maintained its familial attachment when Penelope Rosemont would ask Studs to speak at the Newberry Library Committee oratory reenactments. Studs had been involved in the previous celebrations that were held each July and he would talk about Lucy Parsons and the other soapbox speakers whom he loved. In addition, Penelope or her husband, Franklin, asked Studs to endorse or speak at Kerr Publishing fundraisers. He joined Noam Chomsky, Ed Sadlowski, Dennis Brutus, Leon Despres, Sidney Lens, Les Orear, Pete Seeger, and Vicki Carr on a solicitation letter and he emceed various events. Rosemont recalls one such occasion where she feared confusion and chaos. "Studs just said, 'Oh don't worry about it, I'll take care of everything.' And he did. He was just magnificent, the way he could deal with people spontaneously."[13]

The invitations emanated from international as well as national and local venues. Political activist Alice McGrath, whose story was later recounted by Studs in *Coming of Age*, relays one invitation from the Cultural Workers' Union of Nicaragua for Studs to visit Nicaragua.

"You need not wait for a delegation—you would be a delegation all by yourself."[14]

Although neither Ida nor Studs traveled to Nicaragua, they contributed toward health care supplies in the country. There was also a donation at the time to Myles Horton's Highlander Folk School. Studs spoke at a Los Angeles fundraiser honoring radical International Longshore and Warehouse Union (ILWU) leader Harry Bridges at the Southern California Library for Social Studies and Research in February 1986. The library was the repository for publications on the history of social movements, labor, radicalism, civil rights, and civil liberties.

Similar to his prior books, *"The Good War"* elicited theatrical adaptations. Mark Taper Forum produced a play in Los Angeles, and a second West Coast organization, Stop the Arms Race, sought permission to do readings from the book to raise funds for their work. The latter group was led by one of Studs' friends, progressive political activist Rabbi Leonard Bierman. Finally, Studs discussed Ronald Reagan and Margaret Thatcher in a radio documentary, *Under American Eyes*, referring to the former as "a mean-spirited prick" and asserting that Thatcher "legitimized the basest of human instincts."

From the time Studs began writing oral histories, there was overlap between the individuals featured in his books and those who visited *The Studs Terkel Show*. The touring company for the production of *The Grapes of Wrath* appeared on the program in 1988. Ida and Studs had attended the opening night at Steppenwolf Theatre. Related to the play, and at the bequest of John Steinbeck's wife, Studs wrote the Introduction for the 1989 Fiftieth Anniversary edition of the book. Praising Steinbeck and equating his writing to the architecture of Frank Lloyd Wright, Studs drew comparisons between *The Grapes of Wrath* and the late 1980s. Studs also described Steinbeck's bravery, which he related to the people he interviewed representing organizations that were fighting to support farmers in Minnesota and Iowa.

The Great Divide

Amidst the troubles at WFMT, *The Great Divide: Second Thoughts on the American Dream* was published in 1988. Although he was unaware of it at the time, it was to be Studs' last book with Pantheon. Many of the interviews were conducted in the greater Chicago region, but Studs traveled to thirteen other states for further discussions. The Introduction is more political than his earlier books and stresses the loss of optimism amidst class disparity and racism. But because he is Studs Terkel, the vignettes almost all allow room for at least a sliver of hope. As in his prior books, themes are linked to the oral histories. The various individuals who Studs met shared contradictory stories. Studs asks questions about Ronald Reagan, who is described as both the savior and the devil:

> A young blue-collar housewife is ridiculed by her companions, especially her husband, at the neighborhood tavern. "They think anybody who doesn't agree with Reagan is dumb. Anybody who gets involved is called stupid. They laugh at me all the time." She has coined a word: ignorance-proud.[15]

Interviewees speak about the impact of poverty, unemployment, and suicide. They are farmers, steelworkers, miners, and they could not support their families.

In the opening pages of the book, Studs explains that we've become "anti-historical," and that the United States suffers from "collective Alzheimer's disease." Yet, he emphasizes, "In my prowlings and stalkings during these past three years, I've come across individuals, surprising in number though diffident in demeanor (call them the gentle people, if you wish), who are challenging the doctrine of the official idea."[16]

Shortly after *The Great Divide* was published, André Schiffrin, Studs' publisher, commented: "Studs has become the interpreter of America to people in other countries. In Germany, in England, in France, in Finland, wherever."[17] The stories in the book portray the "hurts," which Studs first attributed to the work of filmmaker Dennis Mitchell. There is also great depth as pain, bigotry, activism, hope, and transformation appear throughout the text. Again, as in Studs' prior books, there are oral histories of people whose politics and dispositions are antithetical to Studs'own. So while Studs portrays antiwar activists such as Jean and Joe Gump, Gray Panther leader Maggie Kuhn, progressive professors, and civil rights advocates like Timuel Black, he also includes members of the Ku Klux Klan, Ayn Rand devotees, and even a professional strikebreaker. There are sections that compare an anti-abortion protester with an abortionist, liberal and conservative clergy, and religious sanctuary leaders with Christians who oppose that movement. The oral histories throughout the book, possibly more than in his previous writing, correspond directly to his reflections on the people he interviews.

Unlike his previous books, which for the most part enjoyed a uniformly positive reception, *The Great Divide* received mixed reviews. Richard Eder lauded the book in the *Los Angeles Times* as did Willie Morris in the *Chicago Tribune*. Writing in the *Oral History Review*, Jim Stull of the University of Iowa praised Studs for his understanding that history discovers meaning through the "dreams, wishes, aspirations, and longings"[18] of real people. "Terkel's work encourages readers, as does all good history, to examine and question their collective future as well as their remembered past."[19]

In contrast, Mel Elfin of the *New York Times* accuses Studs of being stuck in the Depression Era—and of being anachronistic in general—as well as being guilty of romanticizing his activist heroes. He concludes by chastising Studs for not listening. He writes: "It's hard to understand what people are really telling you when you're listening from inside a time warp."[20] It was Jacob Weisberg's critical review in *The New Republic* that appeared to most aggravate Studs and his friends. Mike Royko challenged Weisberg and, years later, Tony Judge commented on how the critic's words affected Studs. Perhaps, Studs should have viewed Weisberg's phrase, "Terkel loves Americans and loathes America," as a badge of honor.

The Show Goes On

In spite of the negative reviews for *The Great Divide* and the time changes forced on *The Studs Terkel Show*, Studs and his program continued to thrive. Some highlights during the time include shows on

African American teenage girls, Japanese Americans and reparations, Cuban music, Francine du Plessix Gray on Soviet women, gay rights, Sandinistas, Italian American writers, Lincoln Park Zoo, the environment, and AIDS.

In 1988, John Sayles made an appearance on the program to talk about his latest film, *Eight Men Out*.[21] The film portrayed the Black Sox scandal of 1919 with Studs playing a substantive role, a crusty sportswriter, Hugh Fullerton, who was covering the World Series between the Chicago White Sox and Cincinnati Reds. Studs' colleague throughout the film was Ring Lardner, portrayed by Sayles. In the film, they discover that the "fix" was in. Together they keep scorecards identifying possible moments where players were "throwing" games. Studs personified the role and had a significant number of lines in the film. Sayles recalls thinking, "This was a Studs Terkel kind of guy. I thought, well, he'd be perfect for this."[22] Sayles knew that Studs was a radio actor and performer and solicited him for the part. Studs quickly accepted. Not able to not pass up the role, he told Sayles, "Let's get that bastard Comiskey, I'll do it."[23] After the film opened, Mike Royko teased Studs about his perception of himself as an actor: "He thinks he's Spencer Tracy. That's his problem. Since he's been in the movies he thinks he's Spencer Tracy. He says, 'Do I look like Spencer Tracy?' I say, 'You look like Dick Tracy.'"[24]

In addition to domestic travel to promote *The Great Divide* as well as to conduct interviews for his next book, *Race: How Blacks and Whites Think and Feel about the American Obsession*, Ida and Studs once again traveled to the Soviet Union. It was just as Gorbachev was entering reforms that would soon lead to the disintegration of the nation.

The journey brought greater hope for Studs than his prior visit in the early 1980s. He was able to speak with more of the uncelebrated and some lasting relationships emerged from the visit. Soviet footballer, poet, and PEN International leader Alexander Tchachenko had visited Chicago, and he and Studs communicated through the post. They wrote about literature, PEN, and each other's work. Studs forwarded *"The Good War,"* which Tchachenko was unable to purchase in Russia, and he reciprocated by sending his book of poetry, *Oglon*, as well as the journal he founded, *New Youth*. He also was appreciative toward Studs for helping a Russian friend who had moved to Chicago. In one letter, Tchachenko writes: "I love you and your books and your personality."[25]

Shortly after the Soviet visit, WFMT broadcast a conversation between Studs and Russian journalist Vitaly Korotich. They had become friends in the early 1980s during Studs' first trip to the Soviet Union. Korotich appeared on Studs' program soon thereafter.

In 1990, Korotich was editor-in-chief of the popular Soviet magazine *Ogonyok*. Their long conversation, published in *The Nation*, was somewhat controversial as both men speak about government censorship and surveillance in their respective countries. Similar to Tchachenko, Korotich compliments Studs, referring to him as a symbol of "American vitality, American optimism."[26] Likewise, Studs bestows compliments on Korotich: "The thing that attracted me to you was your sense of humor. You realize these big shots—they're clowns in a way—are really frightened of people who are independent, such as yourself, because they also know that you have a tremendous popularity."[27] Both men criticize American generals and Soviet generals, and the CIA and KGB for being more comfortable with each other than with the uncelebrated people in their own countries.

Fighting for André

In 1990, Studs also protested the dismissal of his publisher, André Schiffrin, at Pantheon Books. André was managing director of Pantheon for almost three decades. His father had started the Pantheon imprint, which was bought by Random House in 1961. For almost thirty years, Random House's president, Bennett Cerf, maintained a quiet remove from the radical imprint that didn't make much money but made up for its fiscal shortcomings in prestige.

Pantheon was well-known for bringing the works of Franz Kafka, Jean-Paul Sartre, Albert Camus, and Michel Foucault to an English-language audience. Schiffrin also championed the works of left authors Eric Hobsbawm, Noam Chomsky, Art Spiegelman, and Studs Terkel.

When Schriffrin was dismissed, five of his senior editors resigned, stating: "Pantheon's established role as a publishing house for unconventional and otherwise little-known writers was being ruined in the name of profits."[28]

As the news became public there were outcries in the publishing and literary communities. Joining ten writers in an open letter to the *New York Times*—including Dore Ashton, Noam Chomsky, and Dorothy Thompson—Studs announced that he would no longer publish with Pantheon. He was also a signatory in a full-page letter of protest in the *New York Review of Books*. Finally, when Barbara Ehrenreich organized a march at Random House, Studs protested with 350 authors, editors, literary agents, and sympathizers.

Most importantly, Studs announced that he would wait for Schiffrin's reemergence to publish *Race*. He told Chicago journalist John Blades, "A guy named Fred Jordan, Schiffrin's successor as managing director, called me about continuing with Pantheon and I told him to go to hell. I go with André, wherever he goes. He was really the visionary. Without him, there wouldn't have been all these books."[29]

As he approached his eightieth birthday, there was a great deal of chaos in Studs' life. Yet, *Race* was written, and there remained much to be accomplished in his ninth decade.

13

80th Birthday and Other Milestones

THE YEAR 1991 WAS FILLED WITH SADNESS for Studs. First, he spoke at a memorial for his musician friend Bud Freeman at the Blackstone Hotel. Freeman was one of the first interviewees on *The Studs Terkel Show* and had been honored with Studs by the Chicago City Council. Then, Studs was again heartbroken when one of his closest friends, Win Stracke, died of a stroke that same year. At the memorial, Studs reminisced of their days as the "Chicago Two" and teased that in the past at any event concerning Win, most of the people in the audience were FBI.

Early the following year, there was a scare when doctors found that Ida had a cyst that needed to be removed. Her spirits were high, but Studs was worried. Beginning in January when Ida was diagnosed, there were numerous letters from her sister Minsa, who was living in France at the time. She would remind both Ida and Studs about the importance of diet, deep breathing, and exercise. Her intensity rose as Ida's operation on April 20 approached.

The procedure passed with no complications. Inevitably, at eighty years old Ida needed time for recovery. Minsa's letters conveyed great concern and were simultaneously flighty and didactic. She drew diagrams of exercises and was especially pleased when Ida informed her that part of her therapy was dance. Minsa suggested that Vivaldi was the perfect music for exercise and emphasized the importance of regular movement. "She also admonished Studs, 'Dear, dear Studs, take good care of your beautiful wife. Caress her to sleep at night. Wake her with kisses'."[1]

Recovered, Ida quickly returned to her daily routine, including her volunteer work at the Peace Museum. Together, she and Studs supported progressive causes and tried to make socially responsible investments. In fact, their broker, Ron Freund, had letterhead that read, "Do Good and Do Well." They also grew closer to their neighbors, Laura and Bob Watson, who had moved to Castlewood a couple of years after Ida and Studs. The Watsons' sons, Anders and Brendan, absorbed lessons from both of the Terkels. Bob explained how Studs influenced their younger son, Brendan, who later became a journalist. The boys experienced Ida's political resolve. For example, during the first Gulf War, a neighbor organized a "Support the Troops" campaign. Anders Watson volunteered to distribute yellow ribbons to the people on the block. His mother recalls him talking with Ida about what the ribbons symbolized and why she wouldn't exhibit one:

> I remember him coming home and talking about what an interesting conversation that was, because she didn't want to do it because she felt that showed support for war activity, and that it was very jingoistic, that we should feel sorrow for both sides that got involved in the war. That it wasn't just the U.S. side. She was very strongly antiwar and in favor of peace, and it was very eye-opening for him as a kid to have that conversation with her.[2]

Studs, as well as friends like Lois Baum and Sydney Lewis, often emphasized the effect of Ida's sincerity, political and otherwise, and the influence it had on the people around her, Studs included.

Turning Eighty at the Studs Terkel Bridge

Studs was the recipient of an honor early in the 1990s that reflects the absurdity as well as the humor in American politics. On April 29, 1992, the Chicago City Council received a letter from Mayor Richard M. Daley, the son of the deceased former mayor, whom Studs spoke and wrote about critically too many times to catalog, proclaiming that the Division Street Bridge be renamed the Louis "Studs" Terkel Bridge. Just after Ida's operation, on May 16, 1992, Studs' eightieth birthday, the name of the bridge was officially changed. The proc-lamation cited *Division Street: America*, but did not mention his two more recent books on the social and racial divides in the United States: *The Great Divide* or *Race*. At the ceremony, Studs proclaimed that he was proud because the bridge represented the working class. "So whenever I'll see that bridge going up I'll feel good. But if a single sailboat goes through with a high mast with crew, a yuppie couple, NEVER!"

There were various speakers at the celebration for Studs. Rick Kogan joked about the city naming the bridge for him. Noting that at the time only two other Chicagoans, columnist Irv Kupcinet and broadcaster Paul Harvey, had been so honored, he said, "Kup, Harvey and Studs . . . sounds like a law firm."[3] Leon Despres described the three Studs—Cunningham whom James Farrell knew; Studs Lonigan, whom he called a "stupid thug"; and Studs Terkel, "the good Studs."[4] Mike Royko brought Studs a gift, Nancy Reagan's memoirs. He also publicly shared with the world that Studs hated the Cubs:

This is the wrong day because this is the opening day at Wrigley Field. I'd just like to point out that over his long career here in Chicago Studs has made a career out of dazzling many liberal Cubs' fans with his wit and wisdom, and selling tons of books to liberal Cubs' fans. If you did a survey of Cubs' fans and fans from that other group you'd probably find that Studs is held by Cubs' fans to be far more the Chicago legend than he is with the other group. And yet, Studs has a dirty, nasty, little secret: He hates the Cubs. Why does he hate the Cubs? Well, I'll tell you what I know. He was born in New York. Another dirty, nasty secret. Now Studs wasn't born in Uptown you know and to this day he's a San Francisco Giants fan. But he won't admit that. He gives this reason. He managed to come up with a humanitarian motive— noble motive. He says he's had a grudge against the Cubs because in 1947 the Dodgers signed Jackie Robinson and it took the Cubs five years to find a black player. So he says the Cubs organization were a bunch of bigots. And I don't want to be nasty, but, I think it was 1952 when the Cubs hired black players. It wasn't until 1981 that WFMT hired a woman announcer.[5]

Royko was right about Studs and the Cubs. Yet, shortly thereafter, Studs presided at Wrigley Field on a very sad occasion.

Race: How Blacks and Whites Think and Feel about the American Obsession

In 1992, André Schiffrin and Diane Wachtell, a former Pantheon editor, founded The New Press as an independent, nonprofit publisher of books "in the public interest." As a testament of Studs' loyalty to Schiffrin—and true to New Press's mission to publish "books that promote and enrich public discussion and understanding of the issues vital to our democracy and to a more equitable world"—*Race* was the first book it published. Of his relationship with Studs, Schiffrin remarked, "The fact that people like Studs Terkel stayed with us at The New Press made all the difference, and we couldn't have survived without them."[6]

When André Schiffrin phoned Studs with the proposal to write *Division Street: America*, one could not have imagined that their partnership would include seventeen books published between 1967 and 2008. No one could have anticipated the thousands of interviews that were included in those books or the equal number that were relegated to the cutting-room floor. Studs often suggested that the themes of his books were Schiffrin's ideas. Not surprisingly, the publisher also sang Studs' praises. "Studs could get people to speak openly and frankly even when they had lied to themselves. He had extraordinary respect for the people with whom he spoke. He wasn't looking for a sound bite. He wasn't looking for a quick fix. He wanted to know, really know, how they felt even if they didn't know themselves."[7]

Despite André and Studs' long relationship, there were writers and even some friends who didn't understand why Studs left Random House. In contrast, Victor Navasky, a friend of both men, maintained that Studs' choice to publish with Schiffrin motivated other authors to choose New Press for their own books. Sydney Lewis, also close to both men, reflected: "So different, in temperament, in bearing, energy levels, in obvious ways nothing in common but everything in common in terms of their values—politics. I think André really loved him and Studs really loved André—deep respect for each other."[8]

While most of the interviews for *Race* took place in Chicago, Studs also met with people in New York, California, Washington, Virginia, North Carolina, and Georgia. The book addresses the very real systemic issues of bigotry. The rawness of America's endemic disease, white racism, brought out ideology and feelings that crossed the spectrum from black nationalism to white supremacy. True to his involvement in antiracism throughout his life, Studs did interviews on issues of race on his radio show. Unforgettable were his conversations with James Baldwin and Muhammad Ali or the stories from apartheid South Africa. There were also portraits of race in his other oral histories. But never had he addressed the denseness of "America's dilemma" in a single book. Pondering his work in 1996, Studs referred to *Division Street: America* as a prologue to *Race*. Many of the individuals with whom he had spoken, both black and white, had addressed the depth of racism in their personal lives as well as in American society as a whole. Studs highlighted the systemic, asserting that Ronald Reagan's hostility toward civil rights legislation had served as permission for the exacerbation of white racism. As in each of his other books, Studs is energized by what he sometimes referred to as "ordinary but extraordinary" people and their stories that often, but not always, include transformation.

For example, there is public school teacher Mamie Mobley, mother of Emmett Till, the fourteen-year-old African American boy from Chicago who, while visiting family in Mississippi in 1955, was brutally murdered for allegedly flirting with a white woman. In her interview, Mobley talks with Studs about how an ex-student, a member of the Blackstone Rangers—one of Chicago's most notorious gangs—supported her and other teachers when they were on strike against the Chicago public schools. Mobley had been somewhat afraid because of the gang's violent reputation, and because they were on record directing teachers to get back into the classroom. However, she reveals to

Studs that gang members would bring the striking teachers food and offered protection during their time on the picket line.

Once again, Studs presented the story of C. P. Ellis, the poor white Ku Klux Klan member from Durham, North Carolina, who later became a multiracial union organizer. It was Studs' favorite transformation story. Ellis is featured next to the civil rights leader he worked with for many years, Anne Atwater.

Interviewee Mark Larson (his pseudonym in *Race* is Peter Soderstrom), a white teacher in a mixed-race school, thinks himself a liberal while his students and their parents see him as a racist. Sometime after the book was published, he spoke with radio host Dick Gordon about his conversation with Studs. He talked extensively about the personal transformation it inspired:

> It was truly my start of my thinking . . . am I a racist? You know, it was just not part of my upbringing. It was not part of what I thought I was. And it was not because I had ill feelings toward anybody. It was more because I was seeing myself pre-judging the situation and pre-judging the student.[9]

His interview with Studs lasted almost four hours. Near the end of the interview, as Larson returned from a break, he overheard Studs say to Ida, "His honesty is throwing me. He's so honest."[10] But Larson attests it was Studs, and the questions he asked, that facilitated his own impertinent questions and forever transformed his teaching.

Hank De Zutter, a teacher at a primarily black urban school, expresses similar thoughts about his experience being interviewed by Studs: "He takes you through your own mind and all of a sudden you're tinkering with something you didn't know was there. . . . Studs had a way of helping you know yourself. It's a privilege to spend time with someone who is truly concerned for the core of humanity—enough to help you find it."[11]

Chicago teacher, civil rights activist, and longtime friend of Studs, Timuel Black, makes an appearance in *Race*. In their conversation, Black recalls Chicago in the 1920s and 1930s, focusing on the schism between lighter and darker black people in the decade after the First World War. He tells Studs that four decades later, a white principal questioned whether light-skinned black children were smarter than dark-skinned black children. "I deliberately picked out a dark kid's grades and compared them to the scores of a dumb white kid. He was furious."[12]

Studs' lawyer, Gilbert Gordon, was also interviewed for *Race*. In his conversation with Studs, he sums up America's obsession with racism: "It is the most obsessive feature of American life. Every American, whether white or black, carries with him the consciousness of race, always, always, always. It obsesses everybody, even those who think they are not obsessed by it."[13]

A number of Studs' interviewees express their experiences of white racism in terms of psychological pain. Joseph Lattimore, a black middle-aged insurance broker, provides another apt summation of the experience of racism, focusing on how it affects one's daily life. He says, "Being black in America is like being forced to wear ill-fitting shoes. Some people adjust to it. It's always uncomfortable on your feet, but you've got to wear it because it's the only shoe you've got."[14] A young black teenager describes the hurt she felt when her music teacher had black students sing "I'm Dreaming of a White Christmas," just for a laugh at their expense. She tells Studs: "I just felt like crying. I had no respect for him after that."[15] A white housewife, Mary Fran Sheehan, tells Studs: "I felt like being white middle-class had a stigma to it. Everything was our fault. Every time I turned on the TV, it would be constant trying to send me on a guilt trip because I had a decent life."[16]

Many interviewees emphasize that it is imperative for black people and white people to know each other personally. Leola Spann, an African American woman who worked against racially segregated real estate practices, or "blockbusting," argues, "I think the main thing—and this is sad to say in the nineties—is not knowing one another. That's the key. I think if we ever know each other, we could iron out all our problems."[17] Betty Rundle, the matriarch of a white family, refused to leave the neighborhood when the blockbusters arrived. She tells Studs, "The black neighbors that we have are nicer and more loving than the white neighbors we had. You go down the street, teenagers, anyone, you smile at them, act decent toward them, they give you back what you give them. It's an exchange between two equals."[18] Mike Wrobleski, a former police captain in Chicago who was repeatedly harassed by his fellow officers because he would not tolerate racism, concurs: "They have the same concerns we have about education, about a job, about worshipping. The black ghetto and the middle-class suburb are equally isolated."[19]

Upon its release, *Race* was an immediate bestseller. It received overwhelmingly positive reviews in newspapers and magazines throughout the country. A release party for the book was held at the Algonquin Hotel in New York City. Tom Engelhardt remembers the event's hatcheck girl asking the New Press publicist, "What's this about a party for stuffed turtles—stuffed turtles?" She had misheard the buzz around Studs Terkel as "stuffed turtles."[20]

Ken Burns's Baseball

In 1994, Studs finally acquiesced to the urging of family, friends, colleagues, and his physician, Quentin Young, and purchased hearing aids, which he sometimes referred to as "ear amplifiers." In Young's reflections on Studs visiting his office, he remembers that he and Studs viewed the appointments as mutually shared political events.

Later in the year, Studs appeared in several cameos on Ken Burns's PBS documentary, *Baseball.* Burns loved Studs and thought that he provided a perfect voice for the documentaries:

> You could always count on Studs, no matter what he was reading, to interpret it just perfectly. Studs had a kind of perpetual twinkle in his eye and a love of life that was so infectious, and I think for him, human beings are there to talk to and to listen to and that means that everything is a story. He listened, you know? Ron Powers, the writer and biographer of Mark Twain, said that Mark Twain was an enormous noticer. I would like to sort of borrow that and say that Studs Terkel was an enormous listener, and he understood how to sort of funnel and distill and get to the essence of who somebody was, and that's what makes his works so enduring.[21]

The eighteen-and-a-half-hour historical saga was divided into innings, with Studs appearing in the third, fourth, sixth, seventh, and ninth innings. Speaking on camera about the famous home run that Ruth ostensibly predicted while standing at the plate, Studs quipped, "If everyone was there who said they were there, Wrigley Field would seat a half a million."[22]

Burns's favorite scene involved Studs' appearance in the sequel, *The Tenth Inning*. In the scene, interviews with George Will and Studs regarding free agency were juxtaposed. For Burns, it was an essentially human scene. Studs, a supporter of organized labor throughout his life and an admirer of baseball union leader Marvin Miller, opposed free agency and argued it was anti-community. How would you know the home team players? Will claimed to be semi-Marxist on the issue, arguing that those who do the work should get the rewards. Burns marveled: "We are in an age where we pigeonhole everybody instantly. Oh, George Will, he must be a right-wing conservative. Oh, Studs Terkel, he's a pink lefty. Then you begin to see in which other ways that dialectic doesn't hold up."[23]

WFMT and the Chicago History Museum

In 1993, much to Studs' chagrin, *The Studs Terkel Show*'s time was again shifted, landing in a late-night slot. Yet there were guests and segments on all phases of music, theater, and literature, as well as the continual wide range of individuals just as in the past.[24] In spite of the great interviews he conducted between 1993 and his finale in 1997 and the wide range of original programming, Studs felt resigned in his final years at WFMT. He said, "I'm like a yo-yo: up and down. The uniqueness is gone."[25]

Life was stressful for Studs within the walls of WFMT. He was still committed to doing his show, but he was never comfortable, as he had lost his private office—WFMT was no longer his home. Even though Tony Judge had been terminated in 1990, he kept his options open with CETA and did some contract work for their premier station, WTTW. He also represented Studs, working with one of the parent station's executives, Dan Schmidt, to relocate Studs' office as well as his papers and interview recordings to the Chicago History Museum—then called the Chicago Historical Society. Retaining his program until 1997, Studs' salary was paid by CETA. Initially, he came into his new office two or three days a week, and in 1998 he was given the title Distinguished Scholar in Residence. In addition, his papers and tapes were transferred to the historical society where they would be professionally archived.

As 1997 came to a close, Studs' forty-five-year career at WFMT ended. He never spoke about the final show, which was prerecorded and aired on Studs' final spot at ten-thirty at night. Donald Tait, a longtime engineer at the station, remembers it well and provides some insight:

> It was a Friday night. It was my shift to work until midnight and that was the last of Studs' programs. And I ran the tape. I said, "Everybody, if Studs didn't say anything about this, I just want to say, this is the last Studs Terkel program." I said, "I have no way, none of us has any way of telling you what we have learned from this man, here, off the air. What he is. You've only heard part of it. He has meant more than anything to all of us. I'm sorry." I couldn't, I couldn't go on. So I got back to the regular announcing. Anyway, I put a record on and the phone rang. It was Studs. And he said, "Thank you Don. Thank you, thank you." I said, "Studs, thank you."[26]

After leaving WFMT, Studs focused on his work at the museum. He began a project called "Vox Humana: The Human Voice," that includes forty-five years of his taped interviews from both his radio show and his books. This amounts to more than 9,000 hours of interviews. The president of the Chicago Historical Society who nurtured Studs' relocation to the museum, Douglas Ginsberg, refers to the collection as "the collected memory of our time."

Coming of Age

Studs completed his next book, *Coming of Age: Growing Up in the Twentieth Century,* in 1994. His sixty-nine interviewees for the book were all between the ages of seventy and ninety-nine. When *Coming of*

Age was published he was eighty-three. Originally, Studs wanted the title of *Coming of Age* to be *Rockin' the Boat*. The idea was to tell the stories of elders who for the most part challenged power throughout their lives. The critical mass of those Studs interviewed, more than in any of his other books, reflected his own progressive politics.

While some celebrities were interviewed in *Coming of Age*, most of the people Studs highlighted were among his core interest group of the "uncelebrated." The words of seventy-five-year-old Joe Begley, Kentucky storekeeper and strip-mining opponent, summarize the spirit of *Coming of Age*: "There's no way that a man can slow down. I owe it to the people in this county, and more particularly to my family and the people I live with in this community. There's no end to the battle. . . . The last flicker of my life will be against something that I don't think ought to be."[27]

The majority of Studs' *Coming of Age* vignettes are tales of social action—individual and collective. The interviewees in the book do not bemoan their age, but they invariably worry about the future for the young. One section of the book, "Whistleblowers," features individuals who confronted authority. Included are a retired admiral, an ex-CIA operative, a KKK infiltrator, and the scientist who discovered Uranium 233. One particular vignette stands out, that of seventy-one-year-old librarian Rochelle Lee.

In 1967, in the midst of heightened racial tensions in Chicago, Lee responded to an advertisement for substitute teachers. She was assigned to a school directly across the street from a school that was the setting of a student uprising just a day earlier. She arrived to a scene of multiple police cars and throngs of cops. She approached the seventh-grade classroom she had been assigned to but the students lingered in the hall. Janitors were cleaning the room because a student had thrown a chair through the window. She recalls luring them into the room with the promise of story time:

I didn't know what to do, so I said, "I'm going to read you a story." There was a sudden hush. They were stunned. "A story?!"

[Laughs.] I had some gang kids there. For some reason, they listened as I read. They loved it. So we talked about it. Somehow they related the story to their lives. The next day I came back and read and read. We talked and talked. . . . Oh, I loved these kids. They were so warm. And absolutely mesmerized by the stories.[28]

Afterward, the school principal asked her to become the school's librarian and for twenty-one years, until she retired in 1988, Rochelle Lee "read and read" and "talked and talked" with students in Chicago public schools. For Studs, her story was the quintessential transformative tale.

When she retired, ex-students sponsored the Rochelle Lee Fund to Make Reading a Part of Children's Lives. Accolades poured in from students, colleagues, and people who knew her. Lee recalls that one of those students, now a teacher in California, contacted her asking her to send biographies of Martin Luther King. He wanted his own students to learn about King in the same way that he had with Lee. She recalls "At the end of the letter was a P.S.: 'Would you please send your picture along with the books?' I wondered why. He replied: 'They love the stories, but the one thing they don't believe is that I learned about Martin Luther King from a white woman.' We just don't know what effect we have on people's lives."[29]

Studs traveled the country to promote *Coming of Age*. In Berkeley, Pacifica station KFPA sponsored the event and Jessica Mitford was the host. In Los Angeles, one of his venues was the Ground Zero Coffee Shop at the University of Southern California. Studs lectured about *Coming of Age* but also talked about *Working*. Raging against multinationals and the loss of respect for workers, Studs concludes, "They gave their blood, sweat and tears to that company. So how can you expect to have a healthy work ethic, if people are treated in this manner?"[30] He made appearances at bookstores and universities and did radio and television interviews. The *Los Angeles Times* featured an excerpt from the book and reviews appeared in newspapers, magazines, and academic journals.

Ida and Studs—Actively Aging

Beginning in the early 1990s Ida and Studs were both beginning to feel their age more potently. They went to New York during the 1996 Clinton-Dole presidential race and attended a *Nation* event where Studs was featured with Bella Abzug, Tom Hayden, and Norman Mailer. After Abzug spoke positively about reelecting Clinton, Studs retorted, "Clinton has to be criticized."[31]

Back home, Ida suffered a few falls and at some point enrolled in a Tai Chi class at a senior wellness center. Studs would sometimes accompany her to the Monday morning class, not as a participant, but rather as an observer. He himself was not feeling as healthy and in 1996 agreed to undergo quintuple bypass surgery. He was eighty-six. Sydney Lewis brought Ida to visit Studs as he recovered. She recalls:

> He was in intensive care so there were four beds, three occupied, two people flat out. It's the morning after and he's sitting up wolfing some soup down, "Hey, would you like some soup, would you like some soup?" 'Cause he was always generous. He was looking at a blank monitor, "You know there's a ball game on, can we get that on that screen up there?"[32]

Two years later, in his book *The Spectator*, he laments having to relinquish one of his lifetime joys, cigars. Studs writes, "The task has been made somewhat easier by the yuppies, who have adopted the stogie as the hallmark of success; as a result these smokes have become obscenely expensive."[33]

Mike Royko's Death

In April 1997, sixty-four-year-old Mike Royko suffered an aneurysm in Florida. After two weeks of post-surgical recovery, he was flown back to Chicago in one of the *Tribune*'s private jets. His doctors expected a full recovery, and Studs arranged a conversation with Jimmy Breslin, who had written about his own recuperation after having the same type of surgery. Then on April 22 Royko was rushed to Evanston Hospital after suffering from a second aneurysm. He died seven days later at Northwestern University Hospital in the city.

Royko was both a lover and critic of the Chicago Cubs. His funeral was held at Wrigley Field. Standing behind third base, Studs hosted the proceedings. He said of his friend:

> Mike was Chicago. He did it all and who was ever better about writing about the real Chicago, the Chicago of two-flats and the workingman? He was an investigative reporter of the highest rank but also wrote with great humor. Some day in the future, when people are trying to understand the city and the meaning of political power, they will have to turn to Mike. He knew the turf better than anybody.[34]

As he mourned Mike Royko's passing, New Press published another Studs Terkel edition, *My American Century*, which included oral histories from eight of his previous books. An eleven-page Foreword was written by Robert Coles, a professor of psychiatry at Harvard.[35] After explaining that anthropologists seldom tell the stories of their own countries, Coles wrote that we were lucky to have Studs Terkel because he taught us "about our fellow Americans, how their various lives go."[36]

Awards, Celebrity, and Politics

In 1995, Studs received the Chicago History Society's "Making History Award" for Distinction in Journalism and Communications. In addition, the Oral History Association honored Studs at their annual meeting at an event called the "Studs Terkel Tribute." There was some controversy within the organization relating to questions academics had always asked about Studs' work: was it history or some other type of expression? Ronald Grele, in attendance at the meeting, recalls: "When anybody said 'oral history,' it was immediately recognizable because of Studs. There was always that conflict in the Oral History Association. There was a certain amount of scorn for his informality, for what he did and how he operated, and a certain amount of grudging respect because he made oral history so popular."[37]

In September 1997, Studs visited the White House and received the country's inaugural National Humanities Medal. According to President Bill Clinton, the award was created to honor individuals "who keep the American memory alive and infuse the future with new ideas." When the president presented the award, he remarked: "No one has done more to expand the American library of voices than Studs Terkel. He has quite literally defined the art of oral history, bringing the stories of ordinary people to life in his unique style, and letting the everyday experiences that deepen our history speak for themselves."[38]

Due to his hearing loss, Studs missed most of Clinton's introduction. But Studs could not hesitate from creating a possible counter-reality in a later conversation with Calvin Trillin. He recalled that the president commented that he was wearing his typical red attire. "I was about to be cute. I was about to say the color of my politics. Had I said that, can you think of the headline next day? 'Clinton Honors Commie.'"[39]

In November 1997, the National Book Foundation presented Studs with the Medal for Distinguished Contribution to American Letters. Following in the footsteps of his friend Gwendolyn Brooks, who was honored a few years earlier, Studs received a $10,000 honorarium. Board member Don Logan delivered Studs' introduction:

> Studs Terkel's contributions to American letters have changed forever the way we view our history and ourselves. No one has produced oral history that speaks to the human condition with the same insight as Studs Terkel. No one has dared explore with the same empathy the social, racial, economic, and generational issues that so often divide our nation. And no one has challenged us with the same fervor to consider who truly makes history and what their place should be in the life of America.[40]

When he was called to the podium, Studs reviewed the stories of some of the individuals featured in his books. He shared something that was often on his mind: "I thought there is more than a touch of irony to this pleasant occasion. I am, after a fashion, being honored for celebrating the lives of the non-celebrated."[41] This was a topic that Studs mentioned often during interviews in his later years.

In autumn 1998, he endorsed a conference sponsored by the Brecht Forum at Cooper Union in New York. Entitled "Communist Manifestivity," the program celebrated the 150th anniversary of the *Communist Manifesto*. Early in 1999 he participated in placard marches and gave political speeches at progressive events in Chicago. For example, he spoke at a vigil organized by the Chicago Coalition for the Homeless when homeless Chicagoans were forcefully removed from taking shelter on lower Wacker Drive. He told the crowd: "To evict people from a public space where they have been for years, where they disturbed nobody. What is happening to us as humans?"[42]

In 1999, Studs was presented with various awards, but the honor he appreciated most was his induction into the National Literary Hall of Fame for Writers of African Descent. Studs was the only white member. He received the award alongside twenty-nine other inductees, including Maya Angelou, Ishmael Reed, Sonia Sanchez, Alice Walker, and close friend Vernon Jarrett.

He was introduced by poet and activist Haki Madhubuti. Acknowledging that Studs was comfortable among people of all cultures, Madhubuti added, "Studs is not part of the black community's genealogical line but its psychological line."[43] Thinking about Studs fifteen years after the event, Haki said:

> He was an unusual man and I say that in the context of being involved in the struggle—black, white, red, yellow—for all my whole life. There are very few European Americans or white men that I've met that I've really learned to love like Studs. I can even name them on one hand almost. He was one of the few men you could trust. He was like a handshake.[44]

Studs was awed by the award for numerous reasons: to be the only white person so honored, to be honored by Gwendolyn Brooks, whom he considered a close friend. She was someone he truly respected and his induction corresponded to his lifelong struggle against white supremacy.

The Spectator

The New Press released Studs' book *The Spectator: Talk About Movies and Plays with the People Who Make Them* in 1999. In contrast to his previous work, Studs blended autobiographical memories of theater and film with the WFMT interviews that he conducted with actors, writers, singers, musicians, directors, choreographers, critics, and a puppeteer, his friend Burr Tillstrom. Although *The Spectator*'s release received very little critical attention—compared to his other works—for many, it is their favorite Studs Terkel book. In the book's Introduction, Garry Wills states that this was Studs' best book because he had "show business in his bones."[45]

Unlike Studs' earlier books, *The Spectator* includes the questions that he posed to his interviewees. Studs explains that the book's narrative thread is each artist's "pursuit of their craft, their trade."[46] Throughout the book, two common themes appear in the mass of interviews: (1) politics; and (2) the complexities of human lives.

Predictably, the various movie and theater people express something of a collectively progressive perspective; that is, their politics correspond with Studs'. True to his history of speaking with the "uncelebrated," Studs featured Gilbert Moses, director of the Free Southern Theater, an African American troupe that performed for farmworkers in the South. Also, Rick Cluchey, who directed a theater group while serving a life sentence at San Quentin for armed robbery. Upon his release from prison, he pursued acting and playwriting and became the protégé of Samuel Beckett.

The complexities of human life resonate in *The Spectator*. Studs' interview with Arthur Miller is particularly revealing. Miller and Studs met in Miami. The playwright thanked Studs, telling him that *Hard Times* was the inspiration for his play that was then running, *The American Clock*. Conversing about the play, Studs talked about individual lives becoming tortured because of poverty. Miller agreed, saying, "*The American Clock* is a culmination of that concentration I've always had on what society does to the inner life of man."[47] Studs told him about a young man he had met in Kentucky who said that his father was Willy Loman, to which Miller succinctly replied, "The question is whether anybody can avoid identifying himself with his failure or his prosperity."[48]

Although Studs addressed human complexities and frailties through the people whose stories he presented in the book, he seldom, at least publicly, did the same concerning his own life. Before 1999 ended, however, he would be forced to become self-reflective.

14

Grief, and Then Again Life

STUDS AND IDA TERKEL CELEBRATED their sixtieth wedding anniversary in 1999. Now eighty-seven, Studs appeared to have recovered well from his earlier heart surgery. His hearing, however, was deteriorating quickly. Ida was battling with vertigo, but still attended her Monday morning tai chi class as often as possible. When friends worried about her falling, she would laugh and tell them that she fell gracefully.

Late in the year, however, she was advised to have heart surgery. Even though she had undergone a previous heart valve replacement operation, and more surprisingly, even at her age—she was eighty-seven—the doctors did not consider the 1999 surgery a great risk. They were in error. Complications arose and Ida did not survive the operation. She died on December 23, 1999, at Rush-Presbyterian-St. Luke's Medical Center in Chicago.

In a eulogy published in the *Chicago Tribune*, Rick Kogan quoted Studs: "It's hard. It's very hard. She was seven days older than me, and I would always joke that I married an older woman. That's the thing: Who's gonna laugh at my jokes? At those jokes I've told a million times? That's the thing. . . . Who's gonna be there to laugh?"[1] If Studs had still been on the radio, he would no longer have had his sounding board. According to Sydney Lewis, every day after Studs' show, the first thing he did was call Ida and ask, "How'd I do?" Lewis recalls, "She was the audience that mattered the most to him."[2]

Friends and colleagues grieved for Ida. They were also concerned about Studs. Years later, Quentin Young remembered that Ida "made it possible for him to function."[3] According to Young, "She made

Studs possible. If Ida wasn't there to organize things there wouldn't have been a Studs."[4] One week after her passing, relatives, friends, and fellow activists organized a memorial that celebrated Ida's life. WFMT program director Lois Baum welcomed people and jazz singer Polly Podewell, the daughter of Beverly Younger—who portrayed the waitress on *Studs' Place*—sang tributes to Ida. Podewell had worked with Benny Goodman and Woody Herman, but on this night she sang political folksongs at Studs' request. Podewell noted that her parents used to call her "St. Ida," for tolerating Studs.

Various guests came to the podium including Ida's sister Minsa, her son Dan, and of course Studs. Memories were shared of all the young guests Ida and Studs had welcomed into their home. Some had stayed a night and others were there for weeks. Mention was made of Ida's generosity and her extensive charitable work. There were other political anecdotes including Ida's mantra in her vigil for Fred Hampton—"All power to the people."

Dan Terkell talked about being in a stroller at political events and unsurprisingly, Studs told stories. Sydney Lewis, Garry Wills, and Gwendolyn Brooks elicited both tears and laughter. Lewis mentioned that when she asked Studs about speaking at the event, he said succinctly, "three minutes." She didn't comply with his directive, but her celebration of Ida elicited tears:

> I don't think Ida had a clue how much esteem she was held in. There are so many words that come to mind. Her grace, her dignity, her fierceness on behalf of people and their rights. She was just an incredible inspiration. You know Studs is so charismatic and frenetic and hyper-kinetic and Ida had just as much power but it was more magnetic power. Whereas Studs sort of tornados-in, Ida would just appear like a pool of beautiful water in a deep great forest that was waiting just for you. Any time I am dignified or graceful, or stand up for anybody, I'll be seeing Ida.[5]

Decades earlier, Wills and Ida were both arrested as they protested the Vietnam War. In the early 1990s, they were reunited in protest against the Gulf War. In his commemoration, Wills compared Ida to Jane Addams. He spoke movingly about her and Studs: "Studs Terkel is the conscience of Chicago, or the world. And where does that leave any room for Ida; leaves lots of room. She was the conscience of the conscience."[6]

Gwendolyn Brooks had last seen Ida earlier in the year, at Studs' induction into the National Literary Hall of Fame for Writers of African Descent. Her memories, though, were of Ida dancing with the Russian guides in the Soviet Union. Reading from her book, *In the Mecca*, Brooks concluded that Ida "is a lady among last ladies."[7]

Although Studs celebrated Ida joyfully with those at the memorial, it was evident that he was deeply pained. Friends and family were concerned about Studs, but in the midst of crisis he had begun his next book, *Will the Circle Be Unbroken? Reflections on Death, Rebirth, and Hunger for a Faith*. He would soon begin interviews for another oral history, *Hope Dies Last: Keeping the Faith in Troubled Times*. He also had people looking after him. His son Dan became more involved in his life and friends were ever-present. After Ida's death, his neighbors, Laura and Bob Watson, had Studs at their house weekly for Sunday dinners. "That was when we solved the world's problems," recalled Bob Watson.

There were also regular dinners out with friends like Quentin Young and Garry Wills. Roger Ebert, who was forever indebted to Studs for welcoming him when he first moved to Chicago, convinced Studs to join him and his wife, Chaz, at Dusty Cohl's Floating Film Festival just three weeks after Ida died. Cohl was the founder of the illustrious Toronto Film Festival and the Floating version attracted famous producers, directors, actors, and critics. Studs accepted the invitation, and took the opportunity to interview Chaz Ebert on her thoughts about death. The interview appeared in *Will the Circle Be Unbroken?*

"Without the laughter, there was work"

After Ida's death, "Without the laughter, there was work" became Studs' mantra. In spite of grieving, or maybe due to it, Studs was unprepared to alter his frenetic pace in the early months of 2000. For the next few years, Studs participated in political rallies and events, appeared on radio and television, including WFMT, had two public schisms, and published two more oral histories: *Will the Circle Be Unbroken?* and *Hope Dies Last.*

Politics

True to his lifelong support of unions and labor, Studs appeared in 2000 before the Chicago City Council with *Saturday Night Live* star Tim Kazurinsky, urging support for the striking members of SAG-AFTRA, currently engaged in a campaign against non-union commercials. Studs testified:

> Chicago has always been a great labor town. Here's where the industrial unions were organized. When Sandburg wrote the poem, "Chicago Hog Butcher of the World," he meant the packinghouse workers. He meant the steelworkers. And of course it means here the actors, writers, and singers who are so eloquent in the work they do.[8]

The strike lasted a bitter six months, during which SAG and AFTRA staged hundreds of protests and launched a boycott against Tide and Ivory Soap. In the aftermath, Elizabeth Hurley and Tiger Woods were fined $100,000 each for performing in non-union spots during the strike.

There were endless solicitations for Studs' comments on the Gore-Bush election, in which Ralph Nader was running as a third-party candidate. Although third party was Studs' preference, he became somewhat cagey as the year progressed on how people should vote. At WBEZ, he opined on-air that people in certain states might want to vote for Gore rather than Nader. Yet, in early October, Studs introduced Nader to ten thousand people at the University of Illinois-Chicago. Eddie Vedder played music and Studs shouted, "Gore or Bush, what's your choice? Influenza or Pneumonia, what's your choice?"[9] Just prior to the election, he wrote an article in the *Chicago Tribune* that compared the 1948 presidential election with the 2000 election, arguing that Nader might emulate Henry Wallace and help Gore beat Bush.

The Nation *Cruise*

Studs agreed to participate in *The Nation*'s annual cruise at the end of the year. Katrina vanden Heuvel remembers that Studs, whom she viewed as the great storyteller, "was funny on the cruise because he had a hearing aid that he wouldn't wear often, so he'd be shouting at you, which was sweet because he was so sweet."[10] During the weeklong event, Studs participated in a panel discussion with longtime *Nation* editor Victor Navasky, legal scholar Patricia Williams, historians Eric Alterman and Larry Goodwyn, and columnist Molly Ivins. The panel was called "The Ralph Nader Factor." Navasky was the panel's host and much to Studs' delight, he convinced him to begin with a sermon. Playing the ham, he thanked "Brother Victor" and told the crowd, "You are looking at a sinner":

> I have sinned shamelessly and grievously in support of that Satanic cult headed by Ralph Nader. In fact, I spoke before ten thousand young people in my pavilion, exultant young paying ten bucks a copy to get in, wouldn't pay a plug nickel to hit Gore or Bush, and then I was leading them down the garden path. I've sinned! Why do I feel so good when I sin?[11]

With the sermon completed, each of the panelists took their turn. Jim Hightower shared fond memories of being with Studs on the cruise, which was "always a place where you could visit with people you respected and admired, but seldom saw."[12] Patricia Williams also recalls her time spent with Studs:

> He kept asking questions. He would lean forward and put his hand to his ear and he would listen to you. He really wanted to hear what you were saying, and then he'd counter with some little story. But it was always, always in the sense that he wasn't just listening to you, but he heard you deeply. Then he had some trove of experience

that he related to some event that would enrich your whole view of your own story. It wasn't like he was exchanging a story. It was always in the context of exchange, of a real exchange. I remember thinking that talking to Studs Terkel is like creating a narrative.[13]

Politics, culture, but mostly conversation are at the heart of Williams's memories of Studs.

There were visits with friends in New York and inevitably meetings at The New Press. The primary purpose of an April 2001 trip for Studs was participation in a celebration of the Abraham Lincoln Brigade. The program, "The Activist Tradition," took place at the Tribeca Performing Arts Center. In addition to speakers and words from surviving vets, there was a performance of Peter Glazer's folk cabaret *Pasiones—Songs of the Spanish Civil War*. Studs was in his element with most of the audience being seventy or older. The topic was ingrained in his heart—not only had he narrated the 1984 documentary *The Good Fight: The Abraham Lincoln Brigade in the Spanish Civil War*, he knew all the songs.

Schisms

Young journalist and activist Danny Postel hosted the British political writer Christopher Hitchens as well as other Verso writers whenever they came to Chicago. He recalled that Hitchens was always keen to see Studs. He first introduced Hitchens and Studs in 1999 when Ida was still alive. During one visit, Hitchens asked Studs if he would appear in *Hitch Hike*, a documentary portraying his travels through the United States to promote his book on President Clinton: *No One Left To Lie To: The Triangulations of William Jefferson Clinton*. The documentary, shot by filmmaker Palash Davé, was fifty-seven minutes long and screened on Channel 4 UK. It begins with Studs depicting Hitchens as a "young James Cameron." He elaborates: "To British viewers that should say a lot because Jimmy Cameron was the nonpareil of journalists. He was independent in every sense. He was always against the grain, you know, against the grain."[14] Studs appears in a number of scenes talking with Hitchens.

In late spring 2001, Hitchens again visited Studs during his book tour for *The Trial of Henry Kissinger*. Once again, Danny Postel transported Hitchens to the Terkel house. This was the last positive visit between Hitchens and Studs as animosity between them arose after 9/11. January 2003 brought the infamous rift with Hitchens, who supported the invasion of Iraq. Studs penned an open letter to Hitchens in *The Nation*, in which he states:

> My point is a simple one: vanity. It's probably the least of our seven deadly sins; all of us have a touch of it, more or less. In some cases, more than less. Saddam Hussein is not the subject of this note; nor the nature of our approach toward the mass murderer. Chris has his opinion; *The Nation*'s editors have theirs. It is the manner in which he has behaved toward those who differ with him: his *ad hominem* assaults on their intelligence and integrity. It is his vulgarity of language.... It grieves me that one as gifted as you has chosen to play second banana to the wanton boy [Bush] in a burlesque skit that's not very funny.[15]

Although Studs' brief letter was generally regarded as light-handed and innocuous, Hitchens was violently stung by Studs' words. He lashed out publicly, calling Studs' letter "foolish, semi-coherent, and ignoble." He described Studs as an "idiot," an "ass," a "fool," as "deaf," and "full of himself."

Hitchens had a conversation with Postel about Studs' letter. Postel told him: "Let's remember who Studs really is. He is the great oral historian and spirit of the people of our time. These debates that you're involved in about the nature of fascism and Islamic fundamentalism and what the United States should do about it is not Studs' terrain."[16] Soon after this schism, Studs told his neighbor Bob Watson that he regretted criticizing Hitchens.

Numerous media outlets sought out Studs to comment on 9/11. On WBEZ he condemned the attacks, but then added that it was important for people in the United States to engage in a conversation of "who we are in the world." For *Chicago Sun-Times* columnist Steve Neal, Studs' comments conveyed borderline treason. In the title of Neal's article, he compares Studs to Reverend Jerry Falwell. He refers to him as "a silly old man and the village idiot."[17] In addition, he condemns Studs' blurb for *Fugitive Days* which read, "A memoir that is, in effect, a deeply moving elegy to all those young dreamers who tried to live decently in an indecent world. Ayers provides a tribute to those better angels of ourselves."[18] Ayers recalls Studs' bewilderment at this: "Imagine being critiqued for writing a blurb—not even your own book."[19]

Studs was puzzled by the attack. When Neal moved to Chicago from Oregon, Studs had introduced him to people at the request of onetime Oregon governor Tom McCall, who Studs had interviewed for *American Dreams*. Studs recalled, "On all occasions he had greeted me with an ingratiating smile and a firm handshake. It occurs to me now that the one was a bit too ingratiating, and the other a bit too firm. I was somewhat slow to catch on, being 'silly' and 'idiotic.'"[20]

This was not the first time Neal had attacked Studs in the *Sun-Times*. Two years earlier, in an article about Saul Bellow, Neal had referred to Studs as a "noted tape-recordist, transcriber, and a man of stale polemics."[21] Studs had let the first round of gibes pass, but this time he felt compelled to respond. His letter was published in the *Sun-Times*. The unpublished conclusion read as follows: "WBEZ and I invited Steve to join me in discussing the matter. He has declined, of course. I am relieved to know that he remains faithful to the tenets of Uriah—shaft irresponsibility and when encountered, run."[22] If Studs was affected by Neal's mean-spirited criticism, he was too involved in his next book to allow it to linger.

Stories and Culture

With Studs' support, Rick Ayers worked on a book, *Studs Terkel's Working: A Teaching Guide*, that was published in January 2001. Rick's younger brother John interviewed Studs for the project. When Rick delivered the transcript for Studs to review, he sat down and immediately smiled as he read. However, he then took out a pen. In the Introduction of the book, Ayers writes: "He kept stopping, pointing out parts that should be changed, clarified, cleaned up."[23]

Ken Burns also included Studs in his series *Jazz*, which made its debut on PBS in 2001. Studs spoke about the lure of Chicago for Louis Armstrong and other musicians. Burns talks about his inclusion of Studs in the documentary: "I like the fact that he knew about the race records; he knew about the district in Chicago; he knew about race; he knew about Louis Armstrong, he knew about how important this new black music was, not only to his city but to the whole country."[24]

Still a man of multiple projects, Studs contemplated returning to do limited work at WFMT. In 2000, Steve Robinson became the General Manager of the station. Foremost on his to-do list was reaching out to Studs. There were various projects Studs would take part in over the next few years. In 2001, he became one of two announcers for a segment called *War Letters*. Robinson had initiated the program before his WFMT gig, while working at the Nebraska Public Radio Network. It consisted of reading letters soldiers had written throughout American history. After coming to Chicago, Robinson received a small grant from the Illinois Humanities Council to continue the program.

Studs' role was to introduce the letters. According to Robinson, he was both "flattered and eager" as the correspondences were essentially stories. When Studs read some of the letters, however, he was displeased. He found a number of them, about the Korean and Vietnam Wars in particular, to be racist. Steve recalls: "We weren't making any political judgments, we weren't condoning anything, and I'll never forget the voicemail Studs left for me. I mean, he was furious. 'Steve, what are you doing to me! I can't be associated, what is going on here! I mean, did you read those letters?'"[25] Talking through the issue, Robinson recalled that the solution was limiting Studs' job to the introductions for World War Two and earlier conflicts.

In early 2001, *60 Minutes* did a segment on Studs. Chicago journalist Carol Marin conducted the interview at Studs' house. She was enthralled by the paintings on the walls and a poster near the kitchen that read "War Is Not Healthy for Children and Other Living Things." Studs informed her that it was Ida's favorite. Even more poignant for Marin was noticing that Ida's perfume remained in a downstairs bathroom. A large part of the interview concentrated on Studs' forthcoming book, *Will The Circle Be Unbroken?* Reflecting, Studs told Marin, "I have faith, but it's a here and now. I do envy those who have faith, because they believe that it gives them solace."[26] He spoke about Ida and how her death provided him with the impetus to finish the book.

Besides the interview, they spent time visiting Studs' local haunts. Marin notes that during filming she became increasingly aware of the extent of Studs' loss of hearing: "Whether we were on a park bench or we were at the bar in the Ambassador West, I just became aware that he was reading my lips. Part of the reason he stuck to his script was, like a lot of people who can't hear, they fill the space with their own voice."[27] She also said that filming this segment with Studs was one of her favorite journalistic experiences.

Studs attended a performance of Bertolt Brecht's *Mother Courage* at Steppenwolf Theatre the night before the *60 Minutes* interview. The show's director, Eric Simonson, would soon begin an HBO documentary on Studs. He and Studs spoke that evening, and his experience with Studs' hearing loss was similar to Marin's: "At the opening-night party he cornered me and told me that he could not hear a word of what was being said on stage, but he knew the story exactly by the way that it was staged."[28]

In May 2001, in recognition of his longtime support of the LGBT community—specifically Alderwoman Pearl Hart's representation of gay and lesbian clients in the 1940s—Studs was inducted into the Chicago Gay and Lesbian Hall of Fame. Studs' mantra, "Without the laughter, there was work," led to travel to Harrisburg, Pennsylvania, in early May. For Studs, it was somewhat of an odd forum. He presented the second annual Speaker's Millennium Lecture before the Pennsylvania Legislature. The series was jointly sponsored by the state's House of Representatives and the Pennsylvania Humanities Council.

Studs' topic was "The Importance of Remembering History." He explained to the crowd that he was a "radical conservative—getting to the roots of things and conserving what makes us civil."[29] He lauded President Eisenhower for understanding the dangers of the military-industrial complex: "This was a General talking, not a peacenik."[30] He took multiple questions from the legislators and others in the audience. When asked about his many interviews, he said that the one with C. P. Ellis was the "most indelible!"[31]

Studs again visited New York and made some local speeches in 2002. In June, he interviewed Gloria Steinem in his home while a *Washington Post* writer, Cindy Loose, visited for a story she was writing, "You Go, Studs: Chicago Is Terkel's Kinda Town." When Loose asked him about *Hope Dies Last*, he explained that nothing could be more hopeful than starting a book at ninety. Although he was trying to protect his time to work on the *Hope* book as well as *And They All Sang*, there were further public appearances. He visited New York during the summer. He lectured at Northern Illinois University as part of a month-long program, "Redefining American Spaces: The City, the Land, and the Body." When the American Psychological Association held their national conference in Chicago in late August, Studs presented the keynote address.

The year 2003 yielded more prestigious accolades for Studs. The National Book Critics Circle presented him with the Ivan Sandrof Lifetime Achievement Award. An accolade that held great meaning for Studs was the Freedom of Speech Award, presented by the Franklin and Eleanor Roosevelt Institute. At the ceremony in Hyde Park, New York, with Pete Seeger in attendance, Studs' speech roused the crowd.

There was an interview with Harry Kreisler, the executive director of the Institute of International Studies at the University of California, Berkeley, where Studs recalled various stories including civil rights memories from Selma. Moving through topics in the hour-long conversation, Studs asserted, "The thing we miss today is argument. We miss debate. We miss the whole idea of people going back and forth. I loved hearing those arguments."[32]

In April 2003, University of South Carolina professor Craig Kridel proposed the idea of inviting Studs to speak at the national meeting of the American Educational Research Association. Bill Ayers presented the request to Studs. When Bill asked Studs to confirm, he answered with a line he would use often in the coming years: "I'm on a deadline for this book I'm working on." Ayers said, "What's the deadline?" Studs replied, "I'm ninety, I'm the deadline!"[33] At the event, Bill and his brother Rick asked Studs questions, but as often as not, he spoke from many of his scripts to the delight of the people in attendance. Studs referred to *Hope Dies Last* as a guide for young activists. In addition, he stressed the need for teachers to be good listeners. In a homage to Studs, Bill Ayers concluded the program by saying, "Every time I have a conversation with Studs I feel like going out, being more purposeful, fighting harder, laughing more, and getting on with the business of changing the world."[34]

Studs signed books and spoke with various people, and then Rick Ayers was responsible for seeing him home. Studs wanted to take a bus, the principal means of transportation he had used throughout his life. Rick dropped him off at a bus stop in downtown Chicago. Ayers recounts his anxiety about not accompanying the ninety-one-year-old Studs home: "I watched him get on, engage the driver, the driver seemed to know him. I considered getting on. It was nerve-racking. But I let him go. That was such a Studs moment."[35]

The Lookinglass Theatre's Adaptation of Race

At the end of 2001, Studs consulted with David Schwimmer and Joy Gregory about their interest in doing an adaptation of *Race* for Chicago's Lookinglass Theatre. "We loved the kind of unflinching honesty in the book," recalls Gregory.[36] She was affected deeply by the "voices in the book that admitted to ambivalence on both sides of the issue, but particularly the white people."[37] Schwimmer and Gregory were also captivated by Studs' ability to invite people to discover truths they never realized they possessed.

Once Studs agreed to allow them to produce the play, they involved him in various aspects of the production. Schwimmer explained that Studs' respect and approval of the play was extremely important. "I really wanted to get it right. I wanted more than anything for him to be proud of what we were doing."[38] Part of their process included workshops with actors in order to understand the book as well as to further explore issues of race relations in the United States. Studs attended these workshops whenever possible. At one point he was asked to conduct an interview with a cast member at a workshop so the group could witness his interviewing style in action.

For David and Joy, the day was transformational. Schwimmer recalls: "There's a kind of trust. A genuine interest and curiosity and love and respect of people that you can just sense, in a very, very palpable way, visceral way. He talks about this thing, the feeling tone. He's got this. You can just feel that you can trust him."[39] Gregory adds: "I had done a play with Paulette [the woman Studs interviewed], I had spent hours in a van with her driving around the city doing this children's theater piece in schools. I had spent some quality time with her, and now I was learning all of this stuff about her political background and her values about raising her kids. So we were learning all this great stuff, and it was happening like jazz."[40]

Both David and Joy were thankful for the opportunity to have Studs as a collaborator. They realized that he had great insights and made it clear that they wanted him to express his ideas, but it was their show. Schwimmer explained to Studs that they needed his blessing that it was going to be okay if ultimately they made the last call on production details. Studs insisted, however, that the play needed to conclude with the song "We are Climbing Jacob's Ladder." In the spirit of collectivism, the troupe held one preview using Studs' ending. At that point, it was clear to Schwimmer and Gregory that the play needed to conclude with a curtain call where each of the characters presented a two-minute personal biography. They had agreed to disagree.

Lookingglass opened its new theater at the Water Tower with the premiere of *Race* on June 5, 2002. The location was apropos for Studs as the Near North Side had been his neighborhood as a youth. Studs attended the opening where he took a bow. He was present in the audience at multiple performances. After one of the shows he guided a question-and-answer session. When the play began its run, Studs had already turned ninety. In the months leading up to his May 16th birthday, he kept busy conducting interviews for *Hope Dies Last*. Many more people now visited Studs at his home for interviews than was the case for his earlier books.

Ninetieth Birthday

Just prior to his birthday, Studs wrote an article in *The Nation*, "Kucinich Is the One." Repeating what he had written in *American Dreams: Lost and Found*, Studs argued that Kucinich represented the possibilities of a grassroots-elected president. He claimed that Kucinich was the Democrats' only hope of obtaining the blue-collar Reagan vote. He even crafted an imagined Bush-Kucinich debate: "Imagine him in a televised, coast-to-coast debate with Dubya. Blood wouldn't flow, but it would be a knockout in the first round, and we'd have an honest-to-God working-class President for the first time in our history."[41]

Ten days after the article appeared, Studs celebrated his ninetieth birthday. The party began on Thursday, his actual birthday, and continued the entire weekend. Friends from throughout the United States as well as the United Kingdom came to Chicago to celebrate with him. The Chicago Historical Society hosted a public celebration. Garrison Keillor, Rick Kogan, David Schwimmer, Garry Wills, and Roger and Chaz Ebert were among the many attendees. Chaz Ebert gave a moving tribute to Studs. Schwimmer's speech contained the comment "*Studs' Place* was sort of *Cheers* as written by Clifford Odets," which was often repeated by Studs in the following years.

As part of his birthday extravaganza, Studs was asked to throw out the opening pitch of the Friday night game between the White Sox and the Anaheim Angels. Studs had watched enough baseball to know that often the celebrity honorary first pitch did not come close to home plate. He trained for a few weeks with his neighbor Laura Watson. They worked together to extend the distance of his pitches. Studs walked to the mound at Comiskey Park wearing a wool hat and a long red scarf. At the game, he felt bad for Laura, as his throw had taken a bounce to reach the plate. White Sox pitcher Jon Garland seemed to have a similar problem that day, as the Sox lost to the Angels 8-to-4.

15

Will the Circle Be Unbroken? and *Hope Dies Last*

BETWEEN 2001 AND 2003 STUDS PUBLISHED both *Will the Circle Be Unbroken?* and *Hope Dies Last.* The primary editor for the books was Tom Engelhardt. He had worked on some of Studs' earlier writing, and was one of the editors who left Pantheon with André Schiffrin. Engelhardt expressed the irony in the death book preceding the hope book, saying, "That's very Studs-ish."[1] He reflects on editing with Studs:

> We rarely worked in person. It was in those days pre-email, so it was letters, phone calls, and of course he was on the page, which is all that matters. . . . What he knew was you don't create oral history by simply putting it as it was told to you. Because if you just put those down and see an oral history like that it doesn't actually re-create the emotional experience of that person, nor does it even create the experience of listening. It was a process of actually shaping, getting the manuscript into a shape that gave the dramatic feel of these people. I would take what he sent me. I'd react to it. I'd often suggest cuts, reorganizations. And he would begin to have an ordering, and we would fiddle with it, absolutely. It wasn't just that he went out and interviewed a bunch of people and then put down shorter versions of what they said. I mean this was a very shaped experience. It was a book.[2]

While the majority of interviews for both books were conducted in Chicago, Studs had conversations with individuals across the country.

Will the Circle Be Unbroken?

Gore Vidal had first suggested that Studs write a book on death in the early 1970s. At the time Studs had no interest in the topic, but in 2001, he wrote, "It is a sweet irony that my first book of the twenty-first century (possibly my last) is about death. Yet these testimonies are also about life and its pricelessness, offering visions, inchoate though they be, of a better one down here—and, possibly up there."[3]

Will the Circle Be Unbroken? was a very personal book for Studs. When it was published, he was eighty-nine and mourning Ida. The book's dedication reads "Remembering Ida." Interviews had begun before Ida's death, but her passing surely affected Studs' construction of the book. In the Introduction, Studs writes autobiographically. He repeats three of his most well-rehearsed stories, constructs an ode to Quentin Young, and concludes with two pages lovingly applauding Ida.

Will the Circle Be Unbroken? included the stories of the uncelebrated as well as friends and topics that ranged from God, fear, war, after-life, heaven, hell, disabilities, AIDS, cancer, alcoholism, suicide to injustice, death experiences, terminal care, and conversation. The book features an interview with Ida's physician, Joseph Messer, the Chief of Cardiology at Rush-St. Luke's Presbyterian Hospital. Here, he speaks with Studs about the experience of Ida's passing from the physician's perspective:

> When it came to Ida, I had about ten different feelings. One was tremendous grief about her death, because I had enormous respect and affection for her. One was a sense of remorse: Had we made the wrong decisions in terms of recommending this particular course of therapy? What had gone wrong? One was: How am I going to confront you? I had learned that I was the one who was going to be telling you she had passed away. How am I going to break the news to you and your son? What words am I going to use? What's going to be your reaction? How are we going to interact in that terribly difficult period in your life and in my life? How can I help you after I've done that?[4]

Dr. Messer was an undertaker's son from South Dakota who learned about sensitivity and death by listening to his father speak with people who had just lost their loved ones. Of course, he showed the same compassion for Studs.

The book also features Studs' interview with neurosurgeon Marvin Jackson, the grandson of Lucy Jefferson, the woman who coined the phrase "feeling tone." In his conversation with Studs, Jackson explains that he was devastated by his grandmother's death. He wandered through his last two years of medical school at Stanford University. He reminisces about his grandmother, a nurse's aide who was never without a book:

> I look at the nurse's aides who work in the hospital, and I remember a long time ago when my grandmother was one of these people. I speak to them. I know their names. I see my grandmother, and I see the struggles that these particular women—most of whom are black, single, with children, trying to raise their families—are trying to provide. I see the path that they're on, because I'm at the other end of the path: I know where they're trying to go.[5]

Another interviewee, high school teacher Quinn Brisben, grieved for students who had died. He declared, "You're alive as long as your friends remember you."[6] He commented that Studs would be remembered through the individuals in his books. *This American Life* host Ira Glass said that he had thought about death every day since childhood. Kurt Vonnegut, who had just written *God Bless You, Dr. Kevorkian*, responded to death with a blasé "So it goes."[7] Studs' friend, political activist Peggy Terry, commented that she did not believe in heaven or hell because hell already existed on earth.

Studs' "death" book was released just after the September 11 attacks. Simultaneous to publication, both the *Atlantic Monthly* and the Center on Wrongful Convictions printed excerpts from *Will the Circle Be Unbroken?* The latter was Studs' interview with Delbert Tibbs, who spent two years on death row for a murder he did not commit. The book won the *Chicago Tribune*'s Heartland Prize for nonfiction.

Speaking with Bob Edwards on NPR's *Morning Edition* about *Will the Circle Be Unbroken?*, Studs explained the challenge of doing a book on death—the experience that none of us has had. "There are no experts, no bookmakers to make bets on it."[8] He commented on human vulnerability, mentioning Emmett Till's mother, Mamie Mobley, whose story is in the book, as well as the September 11 attacks on the World Trade Center and the Pentagon.

Barry Miles visited with Studs for a *Mother Jones* article on the book. He questioned Studs about the people he chose to interview and his inability to hear. Stud told him, "I earn my living as a listener. The trouble is I can barely hear anything anymore."[9] Then Miles asked, "There's a curious omission in this book. Everybody offers their views of an afterlife except you."[10] Studs pointed to an urn with Ida's ashes and explained that when he died their remains would be mixed together and spread at Bughouse Square. He said, "I think that when we go, we go . . . . This life is here on earth."[11] He continued, "I'll kick off when I kick off. Maybe at the typewriter, maybe chasing the bus. I'm not courting it—but it's courting me. In the meantime, I'll continue doing what I'm doing."[12]

The same month that the book was published, Studs appeared at the Printers Row Book Fair on a panel, "Chicago Stories," with Rick Kogan and a second journalist, Elizabeth Taylor. The following day Kogan's interview with Studs was published in *Chicagoland Magazine*. In it, Studs firmly proclaimed that his book was not about death, but rather life. Explaining that he did not fear death, he reflected on Ida: "There are roller-coaster days, but she's here. Is that immortality? Of course, if you touch one person's life and you die, you are alive as long as that person's alive. What you do with your life, who you touch, that's what it's all about."[13] Kogan expressed sadness when he realized that Studs no longer knew the people at his old hangouts. Studs replied, "I look to the obituaries and every goddamned day there's somebody who's gone. As a result of which it gets more and more lonesome. To not get lonely I have all these young friends, and by young I mean anybody under 75."[14]

Various newspapers published reviews of *Will the Circle Be Unbroken?* Whereas most writers appeared to focus on one aspect of the book, Herbert Mitgang's piece in *The Nation*, "A Microphone for Eternity," provides an exception. Claiming that Studs "captured large truths,"[15] Mitgang strikes back at some of Studs' recent critics:

> Terkel does much more than serve as a stenographer or a correspondent listening to talking heads. If it were that easy, there would be many authors doing what he does so gracefully. But he is always his own man in his books—first, in finding an important theme; second, in finding the right people to interview; finally, in panning for gold, in an interviewee's scattered ideas and words.[16]

Writing of Ida's death and Studs' bypass surgery, Mitgang concludes his review with the following observation: "His modest, self-prescribed Rx for life emerges in this and in his other oral histories: Keep going, expose hypocrisy, especially in government, and be an outspoken advocate of truth and progressive ideas."[17]

Hope Dies Last

The New Press published *Hope Dies Last: Keeping the Faith in Difficult Times* in 2003. Tom Engelhardt was once again Studs' editor. The "*Hope* book," as Engelhardt refers to it, held a special place for the editor. He says, "I love the book because I felt it was one of those books that taught me something as an editor. In good times, you can hope for anything. But in bad times, in order to hope, you have to act. That, I believe, is the essence of that book. And this I learned from Studs."[18]

Although Studs interviewed a diverse set of individuals in terms of class, race, and employment, Engelhardt states that hope was represented in the social and political activism of the people Studs portrayed. In the book, Studs broadly defines the term "activism:" "It can be in any form, freely expressing your grievance or your hope.... It's about action. You feel that things can happen, the possibility, the hope. You feel ordinary people can do extraordinary things."[19] At least thirty of the interviewees included in *Hope Dies Last* are activists, corresponding to Studs' lifelong devotion to grassroots politics. In addition, Studs interviewed several dozen people from all over the political spectrum:

teachers, military men including a whistleblower and the man who dropped the atom bomb, WPA Federal Theatre Project members, people from the Sanctuary Movement, exonerated former Illinois death-row inmate Leroy Orange, Democratic presidential candidate Dennis Kucinich, radical lawyer Staughton Lynd, and folksingers Arlo Guthrie and Pete Seeger.

Lynd discusses meeting and being dazzled by one of his students when he taught at Spelman College. The student was Alice Walker. Ken Paff, the founder of Teamsters for a Democratic Union (TDU), explains that when he traveled for TDU business he always stayed in other members' homes because "that's what builds a movement, when you start bonding with people."[20] Union leader Roberta Lynch explains that she remains skeptical about hope inciting action: "There are people who are what I would call hopeful people, maybe incurable optimists. You might be one of them."[21] Yet to this day Lynch continues to struggle for the rights of working people. Tom Geoghegan, at the time a junior law partner to Studs' good friend Leon Despres, declares, "He is ninety-four, yet still on the job. His secret is his constant sense of hope."[22]

Hope Dies Last was reviewed more frequently than Studs' other recent books. Margaret Atwood lauded Studs' work in her *New York Review of Books* article, "He Springs Eternal." She quotes John Kenneth Galbraith, saying, "Studs Terkel is more than a writer, he's a national treasure."[23] Thinking that Studs must have planned to end his writing with the "death" book, *Will the Circle Be Unbroken?*, she notes that the "hope" book reveals that hope is always anew.

Studs sat for various interviews after the book's debut. Ray Suarez quizzed him on the *PBS News Hour*. When asked by Suarez about the "connective thread" of the book, Studs responded: "The connective thread is simply that they are brave people who are active, who are citizens in an open society called the United States of America. In short, they are activists. . . . They want to have meaning in the world. And as a result of their hope, the rest of us are imbued with a little hope."[24]

He also made his first appearance on *Democracy Now* with Amy Goodman. Studs told Goodman many of his historical memories, including stories about the Durrs and Mahalia Jackson, and once again made a pitch for Dennis Kucinich's presidential campaign. He also took aim at Bush's war and the Patriot Act. With humor, when Goodman asked him to reveal his thoughts about his age and hope and death, he created a scenario of what would happen if he died during the interview. While Studs was joking, he did mention that it was probably time for him to "check out."

In an interview with *Religion & Ethics Weekly*, Studs provides analysis of the book that links the personal and political. Acknowledging the many reviewers who claimed that his last two books were abstract—whereas his previous work had been rooted in material matters like employment, race, and war—he said, "Hope is more abstract but, at the same time, this turns out to be the most personal of all the books. This, in short, is a tribute to all those people whom I call 'the prophetic minority.' "[25] The interview concludes with Studs being queried about what he hoped for. He replied, "I hope for peace and sanity—it's the same thing. I want a language that speaks truth. I want people to talk to one another no matter what their difference of opinion might be."[26]

Studs considered *Hope Dies Last* a political book. Resembling the people featured in it, he continued his own political activism. In September, he spoke at a rally for striking Chicago hotel workers outside of the Congress Hotel. Union leader Henry Tamerin introduced Studs as the "greatest advocate for change in the history of Chicago." Speaking on Labor Day, Studs reviewed a worker's history of the city and assailed the owner of the hotel. He concluded by thanking the crowd for keeping him young. Studs was young at heart, but his conversations with some close friends began to focus more on aging and death—Quentin Young comes to mind. However, interviews, some travel, and writing continued.

In October, Studs participated in the inauguration of StoryCorps at Grand Central Terminal in New York, the site of the organization's first Storybooth, a place where people would be able to record and share their memories and conversations with loved ones. The organization—and its ongoing oral history project—was founded by radio producer David Isay with a mission "to provide people of all backgrounds and beliefs with the opportunity to record, share and preserve the stories of our lives." Like Studs, Isay and his colleagues believe in the importance of listening to the stories of the "uncelebrated." Reflecting on the project, Isay notes, "Everything about StoryCorps, the kind of backbone of the project, is straight out of Studs's playbook."[27] At the New York launch, Studs spoke about the people that make up America, the working class. He concluded by reminding everyone in attendance that their lives have meaning—both individually and collectively.

16

Completing the Circle

IN FEBRUARY 2004, STUDS PENNED A WIDELY read critique of "Dubya" Bush's State of the Union address for *In These Times*. In the article, "Ghost Writer," Studs suggested that W. C. Fields was George Bush's speechwriter. Unforgiving of President Bush, Studs was equally critical of the Democratic Leadership Council. He concludes by trying to sell Dennis Kucinich as the best presidential candidate.

Katrina vanden Heuvel recalls Studs at a campaign function that her mother, Jean Stein, organized for Kucinich. She says, "Studs came to introduce Dennis and the funny thing was that everyone at the party wanted to nominate Studs to run for president after he spoke."[1]

In 2004, Studs returned to the air on WFMT. Steve Robinson, whom Studs had become very fond of in the short time since he had begun operating the station, facilitated the reunion. Airing on Saturday evenings, the program included reruns from *The Studs Terkel Show* and was called *The Best of Studs*. Robinson reminisces, "I set it up to run on Saturday night at 6:00, and then Studs called me up. 'Steve, Steve! You can't run it at six. It goes up against Garrison [Keillor]. I can't compete with Garrison! You can't do it at six!' And of course we changed it."[2]

Pleased to have his program back on WFMT, Studs became involved in additional collaborations at the station. In the spring, he decided to endorse an HBO documentary on his life, *Studs Terkel: Listening to America*. A member of Steppenwolf Theater in Chicago, Eric Simonson, had approached Studs about doing the documentary in 2002. At the time, Simonson sensed Studs was hesitant. They then talked about Simonson possibly doing a film about Studs' contemporary Norman Corwin. Studs was excited about that project and not only did Simonson make the film, *A Note of Triumph: The Golden Age of Norman Corwin*, it won an Academy Award for Short Subject Documentary. When Simonson approached Studs in 2004, he agreed to participate in the production of *Listening to America*. The documentary, which featured old footage and interviews recorded only months before his death, received an Emmy nomination for Outstanding Historical Programming, Long Form, in 2011.

On July 15, 2004, Studs fell at his Castlewood home. He broke his neck, requiring a two-month hospital stay. When he returned home in late September, it was in the company of a full-time caregiver. J.R. Millares was recommended by a social worker. He recalls coming to meet Studs at the hospital and hearing him tell one of his often-repeated stories: "I walked near his room. I overheard a loud voice talking to a nurse, 'Well, there it was, 1912. That's the year the *Titanic* went down, and I came up.' The nurse and the therapist giggled."[3]

Studs' son Dan was at the hospital when Millares arrived, and he explained the injuries as well as Studs' reticence about having a caregiver. Reflecting on his time with Studs, Millares says, "I was expecting a tough, challenging job and don't know exactly what transpired, but since day one, we were friends."[4] Millares, as was true for many others, was deeply moved by Studs' generosity toward him. Studs aided him with immigration issues. He was also wonderfully sensitive when Millares and his wife divorced.

It was no surprise, Sydney Lewis recalls, that in spite of Studs' health, he still wore her out. Referring to herself as a graduate of "The School of Studs," she claims, "Even recovering from a broken neck and two months in the hospital, he would still exhaust me. One day he talked for five hours."[5] At the same time, she recounts Studs' bigheartedness:

Dave Dellinger, the activist, came to the house. I don't know how many years ago, didn't have a lot of dough. Anyway, Studs interviewed him, and as he was leaving, I saw Studs go to shake his hand, and there was a check in his hand. I saw Dave go, you know, thank you. It was a small, graceful gift, and I thought it was such an elegant way to be generous. He made nothing of it, just quickly passed him some help.... His generosity was amazing.[6]

Millares often heard Studs lamenting the deaths of his friends. Much to his caregiver's dismay, at times Studs talked about "checking out." But there were also younger friends. Peace activist Kathy Kelly, whom Studs included in *Hope Dies Last*, was someone Studs respected and adored. She had been arrested numerous times, once just before Studs' fall when she protested the School of the Americas at Fort Benning. Studs had agreed to narrate a film, *A Time of Siege*, that Jackie Rivers-Rivet was making on Kelly. He accompanied the filmmaker to the train station when Kelly returned from prison. Rivers-Rivet gives an account of their ride together:

We're trying to get down to the train station and we come upon some kind of a thing, I don't know if it was the Taste of Chicago, but the traffic was just unbelievable. We were worried about missing Kathy's arrival, and this cop is standing there, and he's holding us back, but he leans in and he sees Studs and he says, "Studs! Oh my gosh is that you, Studs?" Studs rolls down the window and shakes his hand, says "Hello." The guy's like, "Oh my gosh, what a privilege. Just go right on through. Go right on through, Studs." So we went through all this traffic that's stopped, we're just bussing right by it, and Studs turns to me and says, "You know? Sometimes this goddamn semi-celebrityhood is good for something."[7]

Rivers-Rivet recalls Studs presenting Kathy Kelly with a rose as she disembarked the train. Kelly's reflections of Studs offer a composite of his politics and his craft. She says, "I think he had an unerring compassionate radical view. I'm happy for the ability that he had to find the nugget that would communicate the story to an audience and kind of create an opening."[8]

"The Human Voice"

Despite his constant activities and interactions with people, Studs' energy waned a great deal in 2005. He completed his work on *And They All Sang: Adventures of an Eclectic Disc Jockey*, originally titled *The Listener*, early in the year. The process was somewhat different than his other books because he included Jonathan Cott, who had previously interviewed him for *Rolling Stone*, as an editor on the project.

Studs participated in various interviews throughout August. Two in particular deserve emphasis. He had been part of the ribbon-cutting ceremony for Storycorps at Grand Central Station in 2003. In 2005, the organization sent one of their mobile units to Studs' home. It was the only time they made a visit to an individual. Storycorps viewed Studs as representing the heart and soul of their mission. The tale that he told upon their visit, "The Human Voice," eventually became an animated video that went viral. In it, Studs is on the airport train in Atlanta and is overwhelmed by the silence except for the computer-generated train announcements: "Where's the human voice?"[9] Amidst the silence he speaks to a toddler who then giggles: "Thank God for the human voice!"[10]

The second interview of note was with Carol Marin, who had interviewed Studs earlier in the decade when she worked at *60 Minutes*. Studs had great respect for her. In 1996 she had been the recipient of the Studs Terkel Humanities Service Award. Even though he was frail and ill at the time, he was determined to do the interview with Marin for *Chicago Tonight*. Marin was worried that because of Studs' health he would look poorly on the screen. But actually, when they began talking, Studs became animated. What made the interview special was that she encouraged Studs to go beyond his scripts. Studs talked almost as if he was not in a studio. When Marin asked him if he had any unfinished business, the response was "Well, maybe to make it up to some people that I hurt."[11] They talked about helping people understand that their lives had significance, about interviewing people whose views were divergent with one's own, and living too long. To the last issue, Studs offered, "In my case it might be so."[12]

Feeling weak as summer approached, Studs agreed to a second bypass operation in August. Before he was admitted for the operation, he did a series of radio interviews for *And They All Sang*, which was scheduled for publication in September. Steve Robinson made the arrangements, offering WFMT's studios. He recalls scheduling two days of intense interviews:

> He did this on a Thursday and a Friday, and there was something like eight interviews per day. Now, here's a ninety-two-year-old man doing these interviews, one after the other—I think there were sixteen altogether—and getting more energized as each interview went by. Well, Studs never opened the book. He talked about each chapter as if the book were right in front of him. He knew the content of every chapter. . . . And then he jokingly said to me he was gonna cancel the operation, he was feeling so good.[13]

The weekend before the surgery, Studs had dinner at the University Club with Chaz and Roger Ebert. The venue had been selected because it was quiet, giving Studs a better chance to hear the conversation. Writing about Studs in *Life Itself*, Ebert remembers Studs telling them that the odds were four-to-one for a successful operation. He said, "At age ninety-three, those are pretty good odds. I'm gonna have a whack at it. Otherwise, I'm *Dead Man Walking*. If I don't have the operation, how long do I have? Six months maybe. That's no way to live, waiting to die. I've had ninety-three years—tumultuous years. That's a pretty good run."[14] The surgery lasted six hours. Studs' cardiovascular surgeon, Marshall Goldin, told him that he was the oldest person known to undergo the operation.

And They All Sang

For the second straight year, at ninety-three, Studs faced a lengthy recovery. *And They All Sang* was published in September, and as with *The Spectator*, the book consisted of interviews that had been aired on WFMT. Instead of film and theater people, the content of *The Spectator*, the new book reviewed the breadth of the world of music:

folk, opera, classical, gospel, jazz, blues, and rock. Studs wrote in the Introduction about how music and art reached the masses. He quoted his friend, steelworker Ed Sadlowski, "Give a guy the opportunity to have time to read a book and he'll read it. Give him the opportunity to hear music and he'll listen."[15]

Many of the individuals who are portrayed in *And They All Sang* were longtime friends of Studs, including opera baritone Tito Gobbi, composer Leonard Bernstein, Big Bill Broonzy, Woody Guthrie, Pete Seeger, and of course, Mahalia Jackson. Marian Anderson, Andrés Segovia, Louis Armstrong, Bob Dylan, Janice Joplin, and Lotte Lehmann's stories also appear in the book. Throughout the text, the artists speak about their connections to the people that Studs often referred to as the "uncelebrated" and the humanity that could be found in all individuals. John Jacob Niles, who Studs referred to as "an American Original," was the first story. Niles recalled that his most famous song, "I Wonder as I Wander," originated from the singing of an impoverished girl in Murphy, North Carolina. When Studs suggested that Niles sang about outsiders, the fiddler's response was: "Absolutely, I never dealt with the respectable people."[16]

When Studs touched these artists' lives, the conversations transcended the stage and spoke to each person's own humanity. Studs knew Tito Gobbi very well. The opera singer had lived in Chicago for fourteen years, performing with the Lyric Opera. When they discussed the evil character Scarpia in Puccini's *Tosca*, Studs asked if there was any redemption. Gobbi pondered. "Yes, even though Scarpia is a monster, he's human."[17] Then, Gobbi explained a scene where the monster keeps a promise.

Leonard Bernstein and Studs talked politics and of their mutual respect for the author of *The Cradle Will Rock*, Marc Blitzstein. Studs interviewed Louis Armstrong, and also his second wife, Lil Armstrong. They both traced Armstrong's music to Ghana and spoke autobiographically. Marian Anderson, the first African American to perform with the New York Metropolitan Opera in 1955, told Studs of learning Negro spirituals as a child. She conveyed how nervous she would become before performances. Two examples were her first appearance at the Metropolitan Opera with her mother in attendance and performing before Arturo Toscanini. Classical guitarist Andrés Segovia also remembered his first encounter with the Italian maestro. While having dinner together in New York City, Toscanini requested that Segovia play for him because he did not value the guitar as an instrument. Segovia honored the request. He told Studs, "When I finished, the Maestro marched over, embraced me, and kissed my hand."[18]

The entirety of Studs' book was an ode to his love of music and its relationship to the human condition. Corresponding to the launch of *And They All Sang*, Studs contributed the segment on Woody Guthrie for inclusion in *World Literature Today*. Both the book and magazine pieces were adapted from Studs' introduction to *Ramblin' Man: The Life and Times of Woody Guthrie*.

Studs appeared on *Talk of the Nation* and *The Daily Show* to promote the book. After Jon Stewart warmly introduced Studs to his Comedy Central audience, Studs laughed, saying, "Keep talking, I like your style."[19] Stewart only had to ask Studs one question: "How do you get people to talk?"[20] Studs spoke for about five minutes—about curiosity, debate, and his parents' rooming house. "We were raised by argument. I can tell the President to bugger off—that is being American."[21]

And They All Sang was reviewed at home and abroad. Writing in the *Belfast Telegraph*, the author of *Search for the Blues*, Mary Beth Hamilton, called Studs' book an "homage to the life-changing power of music."[22] *Rolling Stone* columnist Anthony DeCurtis, in a review for the *Chicago Tribune*, emphasized that Studs' people believed that art had "humanizing power." "They reflect the author's conviction that if he treats his subjects with respect, listens carefully to what they have to say, takes their concerns seriously (though never humorlessly), they will repay him with honesty."[23]

Turning Ninety-Five

There was no doubt that Studs Terkel was feeling his age in 2006. Early in the year, André Schiffrin sensed that he was becoming somewhat disheartened, so he pitched the idea for a second memoir. The project evolved into *Touch and Go: A Memoir*.[24] Sydney Lewis assisted Studs on the book. She noted that Studs always had to have a project. But it was not only a question of being busy; he was clear on his views and he wanted to continue to express them publicly. Being blacklisted had meaning for him—he believed that he stood for something important and that was the need to participate, through debate and conversation.[25]

As Studs collaborated with Sydney on *Touch and Go* he refused to remain homebound. With the help of Dan and J.R. as well as various other people, he met with friends and made appearances at events in Chicago. In March, André was in Chicago to promote his new book, *A Political Education*. Rick Kogan was the master of ceremonies as André and Studs had a conversation at Stop Smiling Storefront. They talked politics—health care, the political party system, war and peace. Telling stories that would later appear in *Touch and Go*, Studs shifted to talking about André's book throughout the hour. He could not have been more attentive.

Studs' ninety-fifth birthday arrived on Wednesday, May 16. Tributes and best wishes were published in Chicago newspapers as well as the *Pittsburgh Post-Gazette* and the *Seattle Times*. Roger Ebert wrote a happy birthday essay on his blog. Chicago radio station WBEZ celebrated Studs by airing two clips of conversations between him and Garrison Keillor. Studs' laugh was infectious and the two men sang a duet of the song, "Rye Whiskey." In addition, Keillor's live variety show radio program, *A Prairie Home Companion*, honored Studs' birthday.

Studs' official birthday party was celebrated at the Chicago History Museum and hosted by *Chicago Tribune* reporter Rick Kogan, who reminded people, "Studs shined a light on the kinds of people that most people look right through: the waitress, the truck driver."[26] WFMT aired the birthday celebration. Between six in the morning and seven at night, the station's schedule was "All Things Studs." There was an interview with Andrew Pattner and the station played segments of Studs' favorite shows. The New Press hosted a website for people to write to Studs, and hired a skywriting airplane that spelled out in the Chicago sky: "Happy Ninety-Fifth Birthday, Studs Terkel."

Calvin Trillin wrote a tribute in *The Nation*. There were also two extensive interviews: one with Laura Washington for *In These Times* and the other with Amy Goodman, who had a conversation with Studs on the morning of his birthday on *Democracy Now!* Both Washington and Goodman asked Studs political questions and helped him reflect on his life.

When Washington entered Studs' Castlewood house, the first thing she saw was the final draft of the *Touch and Go* manuscript Studs had just received from New Press. They spoke about Studs' heart, Einstein, and the media. Studs also commented on Barack Obama, just as he did with Goodman. After Goodman introduced him, however, he explained that being ninety-five meant "feeling rotten." He used the opportunity to critique Robert Browning writing in "Rabbi Ben Ezra" that "the best is yet to be." He said Browning "lied like a rug."

Throughout the interview, Studs linked his personal history to progressive politics, citing Eugene V. Debs, David Dellinger, Henry Wallace, and Virginia Durr. As he had become wont to do, he emphasized the importance of making people know that they count. He told Amy, "Ordinary people are capable of doing extraordinary things, and that's what it's all about. They must count!"[27] Finally, at the end of their sprawling hour-long interview, Goodman asked, "When someone says Studs Terkel, what do you want them to think of?" Studs replied:

I want them to think of somebody who remembers them. To be remembered, whether it be me or anyone else. They want Studs Terkel, maybe as somebody—I'm romanticizing myself now— somebody who gave me hope. One of my books is *Hope Dies Last*. Without hope, forget it! It's hope and thought, and that can count . . . that's what it's about. That's what I hope I'm about.[28]

Terkel v. AT&T

Immediately following his birthday, Studs joined a number of Chicago luminaries—physician and health reform advocate Dr. Quentin Young, Illinois House Majority Leader Barbara Flynn Currie, Rabbi Gary

Gerson, Professor Diane Geraghty, and former Corporation Counsel for the City of Chicago James Montgomery—as plaintiffs in a federal lawsuit charging that telecommunications giant AT&T violated their privacy by secretly sharing the telephone records of millions of Americans with the National Security Agency (NSA). The American Civil Liberties Union's May 22, 2006, press release reads: "The group of renowned plaintiffs contends that AT&T violated their individual right to engage in telephone conversations without government monitoring under the Electronic Communications Privacy Act."[29]

Studs was quoted in the ACLU press release as saying, "Having been blacklisted from working in television during the McCarthy era, I know the harm of government using private corporations to intrude into the lives of innocent Americans. When government uses the telephone companies to create massive databases of all our phone calls it has gone too far."[30] ACLU legal director Harvey Grossman led a team of ACLU lawyers who represented the litigants. Other suits piled on, and in short order there were more than forty lawsuits filed against various telecommunications companies for spying on citizens and colluding with the government with regard to providing customers' calling records. The ACLU ultimately became lead co-counsel on a much larger case than the original ACLU of Illinois lawsuit, *Terkel v. AT&T*, which was dismissed by the U.S. District Court in 2006.

In addition to lending his name to the suit, the following year Studs wrote an article in the *New York Times* detailing the history of surveillance as he had observed and experienced it in his lifetime. The article appeared in the newspaper's Opinion Pages section on October 29, 2007. In it, he refers to his blacklisting in the McCarthy era and the material impact it had on his career at the time. He talks about Congress passing the Foreign Intelligence Surveillance Act in 1978, which subjected national security investigations—including wiretapping—to scrutiny by a special court. This was the law amended by Congress in October 2008 that granted what Studs refers to in this article as a "get out of jail free card" to the telecommunications companies that violated their subscribers' privacy.[31]

Awards and Activism

In July 2006, Studs published an article on Chicago, "A City Called Heaven," for *Smithsonian Magazine*. Much like his 1986 book on his city, Studs bemoans the city's contradictions. That same year, he was also notified that he had received the first annual Dayton Literary Peace Prize for Lifetime Achievement. The prize was established to honor "writers whose work uses the power of literature to foster peace, social justice, and global understanding." The ceremony for this event was held at the Schuster Center for the Arts in Dayton, Ohio, on November 5, 2006. It was Studs' last public lecture outside of Chicago.

As part of the weeklong celebration, faculty members from Wright State University read excerpts from "*The Good War*." Studs shared some of his many stories, but photographs from the event reveal his exhaustion and frailty. At the event, Studs explained that there are three stages of life: "Childhood, Adulthood, and You Never Looked Better."

With the help of his caregiver J. R. Millares and his son Dan, Studs appeared at a rally for his friend Dr. Quentin Young's primary cause, single-payer health care. Dan assisted him to the podium for his introduction of documentarian Michael Moore, who had just produced *Sicko*. Studs talked about labor, Moore's *Roger and Me*, and the United Auto Workers' 1967 sitdown strike. He presented Moore with the brick from the strike that Moore had given him many years earlier. Michael Moore felt great kinship with Studs, which he acknowledged by saying, "I can't tell you how much we appreciate all the years, everything you have done. Your place in this country, you are an American treasure, a national hero."[32]

Touch and Go

Studs' *Touch and Go: A Memoir* arrived in bookstores in November. The book was dedicated to Dan and the title page read, "Studs Terkel with Sydney Lewis." Studs participated in a series of radio interviews with stations throughout the country to promote the book. Steve Robinson delegated the task to two young colleagues at WFMT, Paloma Orozco and David Polk. Polk's roots, like Studs', were in Bialystok.

Polk was surprised when he received the list of stations Studs had approved for interviews. With the exception of WNYC's Leonard Lopate, the stations were almost all small community operations. Just a few of the NPR affiliates were included. The interviews lasted for two full workdays. Both Paloma and David were astonished by Studs' endurance. Polk recalls, "I don't know how he did it at his age, but it was tiring for us and there must have been six in a day." Studs asked David to join him in the studio. Polk was in some ways a surrogate interviewer. Like many of Studs' speeches and interviews as his hearing worsened, most of the interviews were scripted. "What most of these interviews looked like is that they would say hello, he would say hello, and then he would just start talking. And he could just talk; literally he could talk for the whole hour," is how Polk remembers the sessions. At the end of the second day of interviews, Studs gave both David and Paloma personally inscribed copies of *Touch and Go*.

Because the book was Studs' second memoir, there were stories and chronologies included in *Touch and Go* that had appeared in *Talking to Myself*. The new autobiography was, however, published three decades after the first. The concluding comment of André Schiffrin's editor's note was emphatic: "He is the same idealist, fighter, and chronicler of American life that he's always been."[33] Pages were spent addressing Studs' comments on Hannah Arendt referring to Nazi Germany as the "banality of evil." For Studs, in the United States it was the "evil of banality." The list of banalities that Studs provided included media, government, politics, and pop singers. But Studs Terkel had not abandoned hope. Among the people he praised were many who had appeared in his books—Peggy Terry, Florence Scala, Norman Corwin, Leon Despres, David Dellinger, and so many more individuals with whom he crossed paths.

Touch and Go was honored by the *Chicago Tribune* as the Best Book of 2007. E. L. Doctorow wrote the newspaper's review. Dan Barry gave the book a somewhat cynical review in the *New York Times*. One of the most thoughtful evaluations appeared in the academic journal *Oral History Review*. Jacqueline Lazu of DePaul University wrote that the book was "nothing short of incredible in its representation of the Oral

History of the Oral Historian."[34] She named Studs "the consummate oral historian."[35]

Still Working at 96

Travel ceased for Studs in 2008. Although his health was failing, he began working with Lewis on the volume that would become the posthumously published *P.S.: Further Thoughts from a Lifetime of Listening*. While the book read very well, Lewis recalled that working on it with Studs was not always a stress-free process:

> By that time, Studs was really pretty frail and his energy wasn't great. But he still wanted to do some of his own writing. At one point he was just tired and I was going over stuff. I tried to get him to do a little more. I said, "Okay, well if you're not going to do it then, I'm just going in the other room!" A little while later, I hear him go, "Hey kid. Come back here." And he had scrawled it out.[36]

Lewis coordinated the work, but as she noted, Studs was still an active participant. Simultaneously, it was becoming more and more difficult for him to leave his Castlewood home. There were occasions, however, where he was adamant. He spoke at an event commemorating Mike Royko. Upon seeing him in the flesh, Carol Marin, as well as other friends, expressed great worry. As Marin explains, when invited to present, Studs fully performed:

> J.R. brought Studs into the green room, and I thought, my God, he's gonna die onstage. He's gonna die onstage. And he needed a bathroom, and just looked frail. Each of us had some role, either to read something or to recollect something about Mike. When it came time for Studs, again, lights went on in the theater, boom. He was onstage. He was alive. He was succinct. He had a structure. He didn't go over in terms of time. He was funny, and then he stopped and got off stage and was frail again. I just remember marveling at that.[37]

In June, appearing for the last time at the Printers Row Book Fair, he mesmerized the audience for thirty minutes. His stream-of-consciousness address wove through history and ended with comments on Barack Obama and the current presidential race.

Before he was confined to home at summer's end, Studs fulfilled his desire to host a dinner out with friends. Carol Marin, Quentin Young, Don Mosley and other friends joined Studs at Tre Kronor, a Swedish bistro and one of his favorite places. Marin recalls the evening, again marveling at Studs' performativity, in spite of his frailty:

> As hard as it was to gather this little project together, it was sort of, I think, his testament that he still could go out and dine. He still could go out. So we arrived at Tre Kronor, and he's really slowed, but it's like the lights come on the stage, and zoom. He is Studs Terkel again. And he says, "You have to have the herring! It's fantastic!" Because the "tas" in *fantastic* was always where the accent was. Oh my God, he ate like a horse—lentil soup, which he always loved, herring, I forget what he ordered. He poured the wine. It was his event. It was proof positive that he could, you know, be the old Studs. But it took an awful lot of effort.[38]

As autumn progressed, Studs became even weaker. He invited friends, both local Chicagoans and people from afar, to visit. He referred more to "checking out."

Completing the Circle

When Studs fell again he asked his son Dan to contact hospice. He was at peace with the decision. Yet, despite all his frailties, he continued to write. *P.S.: Further Thoughts from a Lifetime of Listening* was completed through Sydney Lewis's prodding and their collaborative effort.

At the time, Studs received numerous requests from the media to comment on Obama and the election. He had reserved enthusiasm for the democratic presidential candidate. In 2001, when the future president was running for Senate, Studs was enthusiastic and referred to

Barack Obama as an "intellectual." By 2008, Studs' excitement about Obama was mostly due to the possibility of the country actually electing an African American president.

In October, good friends who had been ever-present or significant to his life and livelihood came to Castlewood to say their farewells. Studs was weak, but still talking politics, reading, and watching the World Series. In his memoir *Life Itself*, Roger Ebert recalls that even in his final days, Studs encouraged him in his own battle against cancer. He writes of "Studs reaching outside his failing body and giving encouragement, as he always did for me and countless others."[39] Sydney Lewis sent Ebert an email describing a later visit she had with Studs at Castlewood: "He said he's half interested in leaving, half in staying."[40] He came fully alive when she showed him a preview of *P.S.: Further Thoughts From a Lifetime of Listening*.

Studs Terkel was alive until he was not. He took his last breath on October 31, 2008. He was ninety-six years old.

Sydney remembers Dan telling her, "The night before he died, he was typing a new introduction to something. He was a little out of it, but he literally was writing until the very, very end."[41] On Studs' bedside table when he died was a copy of *P.S.: Further Thoughts from a Lifetime of Listening*. The book was scheduled for release in November.

Unfortunately, Studs passed away days before Chicagoans celebrated Obama's victory in Grant Park, the same park where Studs and James Cameron demonstrated among the 1968 Democratic Convention protesters. Upon learning of Studs' death, President-Elect Barack Obama declared Studs a "national treasure."

Following Studs' death, friends planted a tree in his honor in his beloved Bughouse Square. Six months later, Studs' ashes were mixed with Ida's and buried under the tree. His burial place was an outdoor extension of the rooming house that his parents operated. He had come home, with Ida, to the place where conversations and politics began for him.

Epilogue

OBITUARIES WERE UBIQUITOUS FOLLOWING Studs' death. Commemorations were held in both New York and Chicago. Almost all of the obits thanked Studs and lauded his life and work. At the tributes, of course, the praise was unanimous—a great deal of humor was included. The New York memorial was held in the Great Hall at Cooper Union. Laura Flanders hosted and exclaimed: "Studs set out to swallow the world but he gave it back to us."[1] Katrina vanden Heuvel quoted Garry Wills saying that Studs' "ism was underdogism."[2] André Schiffrin remarked, "He always surprised me from the beginning to the end."[3] "I don't know if there is a heaven or a hell. But just to be safe, I would bet that 'Tail Gunner Joe' and my father are not in the same place,"[4] jested Studs' son Dan Terkell. Sydney Lewis spoke as did Stetson Kennedy and Howard Zinn.

The Chicago memorial was held at the Chicago Cultural Center. Rick Kogan hosted and read his dad Herman's writing on Studs: "Asking questions of everyone and of himself. Evoking revealing answers, rarely lingering over woes that may have befallen him but ardent in his ire about injustices heaped on others."[5] Haskell Wexler sang a Pete Seeger song in Studs' honor. Chaz Ebert read comments for Roger and concluded by paraphrasing e. e. cummings: "If there are any heavens, Studs will all by himself have one."[6] Laudatory comments were shared from Quentin Young who also acknowledged Ida. Timuel Black joked about people thinking that Obama was not black enough, but then added, "There are probably a few who said Studs Terkel is not white enough."[7] Sydney Lewis and André Schiffin again spoke, as did Garry Wills.

He wore his honors lightly, as if not wanting anything to set him apart from the people he met every day on the bus, or the schoolchildren he used to visit, or his myriad friends from all walks of life. He lit up in the company of his fellow beings, and positively glowed when a friend came into view.[8]

Dan Terkell made the final tribute, but the comments that André offered are important because he, like Victor Navasky had done at the New York commemoration, addressed a critical *New York Times* article, "He Gave Voice to Many," that was published the day after Studs died. Written by cultural critic Edward Rothstein, the article was particularly cynical. Writing about *Working*, Rothstein argued that Studs only told stories about individuals who reflected his Marxist views: "It is, in fact, impossible to separate Mr. Terkel's political vision from the contours of his oral history. You grow more cautious as you keep reading. Mr. Terkel seems less to be discovering the point latent in his conversations than he is shaping the conversations to make a latent point."[9] Rothstein also contemptuously notes that Studs had praised Bill Ayers's book *Fugitive Days*.

In New York, Navasky had said: "Studs would have loved it. To be blacklisted when alive, and redbaited when dead, too good to be true."[10] However, the words Schiffrin delivered in Chicago were more serious: "So what Rothstein was trying to say was that the truths that Studs discovered were the very truths we did not want to admit about ourselves. And I think in that way, just as the McCarthy period had done, he paid an unknowing, unwitting tribute to what Studs had accomplished."[11]

Rothstein's article was fortuitous as it facilitated the opportunity to codify Studs' life of serious conversation and progressive politics. The *Times* cultural critic misunderstood the meaning and process of oral history and history in general, as well as progressive politics. Because of Rothstein's writing, though, oral historian Michael Frisch was prompted to respond. His 2010 article, "Studs Terkel, Historian," succinctly portrays Studs' life and work:

So Edward Rothstein was right. The title he intended as an ironic contradiction actually stands as the tribute Studs Terkel most deserves. Yes indeed, Terkel "gave voice to many, among them himself." This is what historians do, if they have great gifts, work hard and are lucky, and it's why they do it. Studs Terkel's enduring works of history preserve and present the voices of the many. And through the medium of oral history presentation, his own voice as a historian in dialogue with his sources could not be a more crucial, respectful, attentive, perceptive, informing presence.[12]

Frisch writes in detail explaining that being progressive or not being progressive does nothing to determine whether an individual is a historian. Rothstein's redbaiting is somewhat humorous because Studs never hid his political leanings. Going a step further, Frisch declares: "As a historian, he never forgot Marx's enduring challenge that the point of understanding and interpreting the world should be to seek to change it."[13]

Studs Terkel's life was one of serious conversation and thoughtful, progressive politics. On the former, he believed in the community and activism, in working people and hope. His serious conversation not only presented the voices of the "ordinary but extraordinary," but enabled us to know, individually and collectively, that "we" have meaning and that "we," and not "the faceless, often monstrous entities" that confront us, count. He amazed us!

Studs
1912—2008

as in metal,
confirmed loyalties and Farrell's Lonigan,
now, in the grandfather of your vision and giving
you have always understood the dominions of
words, money, privilege and organic liars.

you among the uncomfortable few,
an urban-tracker questioning influence and sovereignty,
questioning Texas spin, image and lineage,
used a worker's language to expose
the arrogance of the ultra-knowing wannabes
facing fear with your large heart
attached to the center of the people,
who are the colors of the planet
somewhat like southern quilts
the poor & poorer   landless   ownershipless
borderless tomato growers, green bean pickers,
indigenous fixers of anything with a motor,
hard workers of the muscular genre,
laborers,   after 10-hour days 6-day weeks
tolling for people who do not like them,
also known as the working classes,
still able to smile as they will the best for their children and others
always seeking solutions without resources or library cards,
as obscenely paid lobbyist and economic hit men
extend Washington's K street on to the capitals &
side roads of Mississippi, the Sudan, Utah & Iraq
bypassing the culture of comprehension, caring & birth
in concert with the nation's healthcare for the rich, connected &
self-serving politicians who spit clichés
more numerous than hyper-producing roaches,
while legislating the work of mercenaries into law.

you taught us to hunt cleanly and carefully
the opposite of televised preachers whose
lies are honeyed metaphors
wide-netting the uninitiated hungry
looking for a home, answers and the *truth.*

reading you is illumination & battle call
is flagless commitment to clean fire,
nutritious bread and comfort to the least of us.
it is not a paradox that children love you,
unlike bankers and agribusiness
you invest in co-ops, complex possibilities & dreams.

we grow observing the sun and language in your smile
the midnight musical moon that you ride,
the blues of your ideas & warnings
the manuscripts from the opening of your hands
cupping the trumpet of your recognized voice

you the red-shirted, boldly clear,
Robeson supporter & learned messenger   we
widely acknowledged that your children's children
populate the green fields, roads & spaces of the long marchers,
we are joyful that this is not an elegy or obituary.

your being among us is the rare, ripe, swinging musical
and we, the chorus, are still taking lessons, breaking only
to say thank you.

—HAKI R. MADHUBUTI
Poet, Founder, and Publisher of Third World Press,
October 31, 2008

Sources

Author's Conversations

Ann Atwatter
Christy Hefner
David Polk
Bill Ayers
Kenan Heise
Danny Postel
John Ayers
Jim Hightower
Jackie Rivers-Rivet
Rick Ayers
Pearl Hirshfield
Steve Robinson
Lois Baum
Judy Hoffman
Mark Rogovin
Ursula Bender
Deborah Holdstein
Don Rose
Audrie Berman
Dave Isay
Penelope Rosemont
Timuel Black
Tony Judge
David Royko
Ken Burns
Jamie Kalven
Edward Sadlowski
Michael Cole
Anya Schiffrin
Jonathan Cott

Charles Keil
Lena Schiffrin
Dan Schmidt
Kathy Kelly
Daniel Schulman
Richard Davis
Phil Koch
Stephen Schwartz
Robin Davis
Rick Kogan
David Schwimmer
Carol De Giere
Alex Kotlowitz
Clancy Sigal
Hank De Zutter
Dennis Kucinich
Art Shay
Bernardine Dohrn
Florence Kuttner
Eric Simonson
Bettina Drew
Peter Kuttner
Alan Stein
George Drury
Dan LaBotz
Tamara Tabb
Tom Dyja
Donna Blue Lachman
Donald Tait
Mike Edgerly

Mark Larson
Flint Taylor
Tom Engelhardt
Warren Leming
Dan Terkell
Jules Feiffer
Jesse Lemisch
Sandy Terkell
Hamilton Fish
Sydney Lewis
Calvin Trillin
Frank Fried
Penny Lipschutz
Katrina vanden Huevel
Jo Friedman
Roberta Lynch
C. T. Vivian
Michael Frisch
Haki Madhubuti
Laura Watson
Elizabeth Furse
Tony Macaluso
Robert Watson
Tom Geoghegen
Carol Marin
Tom Weinberg
Todd Gitlin
Sandy McCall
Bernice Weissbourd
Joy Gregory

Peter Meyer
Haskell Wexler
Ronald Grele
J. R. Millares
Patricia Williams
Jean Gump

Victor Navasky
Phil Wizenick
Jerry Harris
Prexy Nesbit
Wendy Wolf
Jeffrey Hass

Kay Nichols
Quentin Young
Tom Hayden
Andrew Patner
Lloyd Haywood
John Platt

Studs' Books

Giants of Jazz (New York: New Press, 2006).

Division Street: America (New York: Pantheon Books, 1965).

Hard Times (New York: Avon Books, 1979).

Working: People Talk About What They Do All Day and How They Feel About What They Do (New York: Avon Books, 1972).

Talking to Myself (New York: Pantheon Books, 1973).

American Dreams: Lost and Found (New York: Ballantine Books, 1981).

"The Good War" (New York: Pantheon Books, 1984).

Studs Terkel's Chicago (New York: New Press, 2012).

The Great Divide: Second Thoughts on the American Dream (New York: Avon Books, 1988).

Race: How Blacks and Whites Think and Feel About the American Obsession (New York: New Press, 1992).

Coming of Age: The Story of Our Century by Those Who've Lived It (New York: New Press, 1995).

My American Century (New York: New Press, 1997).

The Spectator (New York: New Press, 1999).

Will the Circle Be Unbroken? Reflections on Death, Rebirth, and Hunger for Faith (New York: Ballantine Books, 2001).

Hope Dies Last: Keeping the Faith in Difficult Times (New York: New Press, 2003).

And They All Sang (New York: New Press, 2005).

Touch and Go (New York: New Press, 2007).

P.S.: Further Thoughts from a Lifetime of Listening (New York: New Press, 2008).

Bibliography

BOOKS

Algren, Nelson. *Chicago: City on the Make* (Chicago: University of Chicago Press, 2011).

Atlas, James. *Bellow: A Biography* (New York: Modern Library, 2000).

Ayers, Rick. *Studs Terkel's Working: A Teaching Guide* (New York: New Press, 2001).

Baker, James. *Studs Terkel* (New York: Twayne Publishers, 1992).

Beck, Frank. *Hobohemia* (Chicago: Charles H. Kerr Publishing, 2000).

Bernstein, Arnie. *Hollywood on Lake Michigan* (Chicago: Lake Claremont Press, 1998).

Brent, Stuart. *The Seven Stairs* (New York: Simon and Schuster, 1962).

Brian, Denis. *Murderers and Other Friendly People* (New York: McGraw Hill, 1973).

Buhle, Paul, and Nicole Schulman. *Wobblies: A Graphic History of the Industrial Workers of the World* (London: Verso, 2005).

Ciccone, F. Richard. *Mike Royko: A Life in Print* (New York: Public Affairs, 2001).

Cutler, Irving. *Jews of Chicago: From Shtetl to Suburb* (Urbana: University of Illinois Press, 1996).

DeGiere, Carol. *Defying Gravity: The Creative Career of Stephen Schwartz from Godspell to Wicked* (New York: Applause, 2014).

Despres, Leon, with Kenan Heise. *Challenging the Daley Machine: A Chicago Alderman's Memoir* (Evanston, IL: Northwestern University Press, 2005).

Donahue, H. E. F., and Nelson Algren. *Conversations with Nelson Algren* (Chicago: University of Chicago Press, 1963).

Dyja, Thomas. *The Third Coast* (New York: Penguin Books, 2013).

Drew, Bettina. *Nelson Algren: A Life on the Wild Side* (Austin: University of Texas Press, 1989).

Ebert, Roger. *Life Itself* (New York: Grand Central Publishing, 2011).

Frisch, Michael. *A Shared Authority: Essays on the Craft and Meaning of Oral and Public History* (Albany: SUNY Press, 1990).

Godfried, Nathan. *WCFL: Chicago's Voice of Labor 1926–78* (Urbana: University of Illinois Press, 1997).

Green, Adam. *Selling the Race: Culture, Community, and Black Chicago, 1940–1955* (Chicago: University of Chicago Press, 2007).

Grele, Ronald. *Envelopes of Sound: The Art of Oral History* (New York: Praeger, 1991).

Hentoff, Nat. *Free Speech for Me—But Not for Thee: How the American Left and Right Relentlessly Censor Each Other* (New York: HarperCollins, 1972).

Kisseloff, Jeff. *The Box: An Oral History of Television 1920–1961* (New York: Penguin, 1995).

Klein, Joe. *Woody Guthrie: A Life* (New York: Dell Publishing, 1980).

Kogan, Rick. *A Chicago Tavern: A Goat, A Curse, and the American Dream* (Chicago: Lake Claremont Press, 2006).

Mangione, Jerry. *The Dream and the Deal: The Federal Writers Project 1935–1943* (Boston: Little, Brown, 1972).

Naison, Mark. "Remaking America: Communists and Liberals in the Popular Front." In *New Studies in the Politics and Culture of U.S. Communism*, ed. Frank Rosengarten and George Snedeker (New York: Monthly Review Press, 1993).

Navasky, Victor. *A Matter of Opinion* (New York: Farrar, Straus and Giroux, 2005).

Newell, Barbara Warne. *Chicago and the Labor Movement: Metropolitan Unionism in the 1930s* (Urbana: University of Illinois Press, 1961).

Nightingale, Carl. *Segregation: A Global History of Divided Cities* (Chicago: University of Chicago Press, 2012).

Parker, Tony. *Studs Terkel: A Life in Words* (New York: Henry Holt, 1996).

Odets, Clifford. *Waiting for Lefty and Other Plays* (New York: Grove Press, 1966).

Rabinowitz, Lauren. *For the Love of Pleasure: Women, Movies, and Culture in Turn-of-the-Century Chicago* (New Brunswick: Rutgers University Press, 1998).

Renehan, Edward. *Pete Seeger vs. the Un-Americans* (Wickford, RI: New Street Communications, 2014).

Rosemont, Franklin. *From Bughouse Square to the Beat Generation: Selected Ravings of Slim Brundage* (Chicago: Charles H. Kerr Company, 1997).

Rosemont, Franklin. *The Rise & Fall of the Dill Pickle Club: Chicago's Wild '20s!* (Chicago: Charles Kerr Company, 2013).

Rosenthal, Rob, and Sam Rosenthal. *Pete Seeger in His Own Words* (Boulder, CO: Paradigm Publishers, 2012).

Ross, Sam. *Someday Boy* (New York: Bantam Books, 1954).

Royko, Mike. *Sez Who? Sez Me* (New York: Warner Books, 1973).

Samors, Neal, and Michael Williams. *Chicago in the Fifties: Remembering Life in the Loop and the Neighborhoods* (Chicago: Chicago Neighborhoods, 2005).

Sandburg, Carl. *The Chicago Race Riots, 1919* (New York: Dover Publications, 2013).

Sinclair, Upton. *The Jungle* (New York: Dover Publications, 2001).

Storch, Randi. *Red Chicago* (Urbana: University of Illinois Press, 2009).

Street, Paul. *Racial Oppression in the Global Metropolis: A Living Black Chicago History* (Lanham: Rowman and Littlefield, 2007).

Taylor, David. *Soul of a People: The WPA Writers' Project Uncovers Depression America* (Hoboken: John Wiley & Sons, 2009).

Wills, Garry. *Outside Looking In: Adventures of an Observer* (New York: Penguin, 2010).

Young, Quentin. *Everybody In, Nobody Out: Memoirs of a Rebel Without a Pause* (Friday Harbor, WA: Copernicus Healthcare, 2013).

ARTICLES

Atwood, Margaret. "He Springs Eternal," *New York Review of Books*, http://www.nybooks.com/articles/archives/2003/nov/06/he-springs-eternal/.

Babwin, Don. "Studs Terkel's FBI File Unearthed, with a Few Surprises," http://www.huffingtonpost.com/2009/11/16/studs-terkel-fbi-file_n_360069.html.

Blades, John. "Prize Winner: Studs Terkel's Pulitzer a Popular Choice but Controversial to His Critics," *Chicago Tribune*, April 26, 1985, http://articles.chicagotribune.com/1985-04-26/features/8501250462_1_oral-histories-studs-terkel-critics.

———. "Notes Uprooted Legend: Studs Terkel Cries Foul at 'Bean Counters And Hit Men,'" *Chicago Tribune*, June 13, 1990, file:///Users/awieder/Desktop/studs/studsmarch/Tribune/Uprooted%20Legend%20-%20tribunedigital-chicagotribune.html.

Brightman, Carol. " 'The Good War:' An Oral History of World War II," *The Nation*, December 8, 1984.

Brooks, Gwendolyn. "Black Woman in Russia," in Elaine Lee, *Go Girl! The Black Woman's Book of Travel and Adventure* (Portland, OR: Eighth Mountain Press, 1997).

Davis, Robert. "The Election of Harold Washington the First Black Mayor of Chicago," *Chicago Tribune*, http://www.chicagotribune.com/news/nationworld/politics/chi-chicagodays-haroldwashington-story-story.html.

DeCurtis, Anthony. "Maestro of Chat," *Chicago Tribune*, October 2, 2005, http://articles.chicagotribune.com/keyword/studs-terkel/featured/4.

Dowd, Maureen. "Sunday in the Park among Winners of Pulitzers," *New York Times*, April 25, 1985, https://www.nytimes.com/books/98/07/19/specials/sondheim-pulitzer.html.

Eastman, Dan. "The MoJo Interview: Studs Terkel," *Mother Jones*, September/October 1995, http://www.motherjones.com/media/1995/09/mojo-interview-studs-terkel.

Elfin, Mel. "The Haves, the Have-Nots and the Have-Somewhats," *New York Times*, October 9, 1988, https://www.nytimes.com/books/99/09/26/specials/terkel-divide.html.

Ephron, Nora. "A Higgledy-Piggledy Life," https://www.nytimes.com/books/99/09/26/specials/terkel-myself.html.

Fitzimmons, Emma Graves. "Florence Scala: 1918–2007," *Chicago Tribune*, August 29, 2007, http://articles.chicagotribune.com/2007-0829/news/0708281426_1_hull-house-city-hall-studs-terkel.

Greeley, Andrew. "Wonderful Town," *The Reporter*, April 20, 1967, 53–54.

Hamilton, Mary Beth. *Belfast Telegraph*, http://www.belfasttelegraph.co.uk/life/books/and-they-all-sang-by-studs-terkel-28452993.html.

Hazard, Patrick. "Chicago's FM Whitman," *AV Communication Review* 15/4 (Winter 1967): 441–43.

Jacobson, Kurt. "A Conversation with Studs Terkel," *Logos*, http://www.logosjournal.com/terkel.pdf.

Kogan, Rick, "Conversations with Studs," *Chicago Tribune Magazine*, October 28, 2001, 10.

———. "Studs Terkel Dies," *Chicago Tribune*, October 31, 2008, http://www.chicagotribune.com/news/chi-studs-terkel-dead-story.html.

LaBotz, Dan. "Barry Commoner, A Great Presidential Candidate, 1917–2012," *New Solutions* 22/4 (February 2013): 419–21.

Lazu, Jacqueline. "*Touch and Go*, Review." *Oral History Review*, Winter/Spring 2009, http://muse.jhu.edu/journals/ohr/summary/v036/36.1.lazu.html.

Leonard, John. "Curtain Call with Terkel," *The Nation*, November 25, 1999, http://www.thenation.com/article.curtain-call-terkel/.

Lyons, Peter. "Chicago Voices," *New York Times*, February 5, 1967, http://www.nytimes.com/books/99/09/26/specials/terkel-division.html.

MacArthur, John R. *Harper's*, February 13, 2009, http://harpers.org/blog/2009/02/studs-terkel-radical-conservative/.

McBride, Stewart. "Studs Terkel," *Christian Science Monitor*, September 1, 1983, http://www.csmonitor.com/1983/0901/090144.html.

Miles, Barry. *Mother Jones*, Nov/Dec 2001.

Miner, Michael. "The Knife in Studs' Back/With New Teflon Coating," *Chicago Reader*, http://www.chicagoreader.com/chicago/the-knife-in-studss-backws-new-teflon-coating/Content?oid=906557.

———. "WFMT Takes a Turn," *Chicago Reader*, http://www.chicagoreader.com/chicago/wfmt-takes-a-turn/Content?oid=875087.

Mitgang, Herbert. "A Microphone for Eternity," *The Nation*, December 3, 2001, 32.

Neal, Steve. "Falwell, Terkel Fill the Air with Nonsense," *Chicago Sun Times*, September 21, 2001, 55, http://work.colum.edu/~amiller/nealat-tacksstuds.htm.

Naison, Mark. "Remaking America: Communists and Liberals in the Popular Front." In *New Studies in the Politics and Culture of U.S. Com-

munism, ed. Frank Rosengarten and George Snedeker (New York: Monthly Review Press, 1993).

Nichols, John. "Studs Terkel, You Will Be Missed," *The Nation*, October 31, 2008.

Pintauro, Joe. "Nelson Algren's Last Year: Algren in Exile," *Chicago Magazine*, February 1, 1988, http://www.chicagomag.com/Chicago-Magazine/February-1988/Nelson-Algrens-Last-Year-Algren-in-Exile/.

Rampell, Ed. "Q & A with Studs Terkel," *Jewish Journal*, March 2, 2006, http://www.jewishjournal.com/tag/studs+terkel.

Resnick, Henry. "America Was Singing, 'Brother Can You Spare a Dime'," *Saturday Review*, 27.

Royko, Mike. "Vintage Whines from Professors," *Chicago Tribune*, May 20, 1985, http://articles.chicagotribune.com/1985-05-20/news/8501310946_1_english-professor-oral-history-studs-terkel.

———. "A TV Masterpiece of Sneaking Around," *Chicago Tribune*, June 26, 1990, http://articles.chicagotribune.com/1990-06-26/news/9002210535_1_studs-place-studs-terkel-oral-histories.

Schlitz, Michael. "The Screen: Late Bloom," *Commonweal*, April 7, 1967, 101–4.

Stull, Jim. *Oral History Review* 17/2 (Autumn 1989): 186.

Terry, Clifford. "The Wide World of Studs Terkel," *Chicago Tribune*, July 2, 1978, http://archives.chicagotribune.com/1978/07/02/page/150/article/the-wide-world-of-studs-terkel.

Testard, Jacques, and Gwenael Pouliquen. "Interview with André Schiffrin," January 2011, http://www.thewhitereview.org/interviews/interview-with-andre-schiffrin/.

Tyler, Gus. *Industrial Labor Relations Review* 28/2 (January 1975).

Vulliaumy, Ed. "Studs Terkel," *The Guardian*, October 31, 2008, http://www.theguardian.com/world/2008/nov/01/studs-terkel-usa.

Wainwright, Loudon. "I Can Remember Every Hour," *New York Times*, October 7, 1984, https://www.nytimes.com/books/99/09/26/specials/terkel-goodwar.html.

Wieder, Alan. "South African Conversations: Studs Terkel on Racism and Apartheid," http://dissidentvoice.org/2014/02/south-african-conversations-studs-terkel-on-racism-and-apartheid/.

VIDEO RECORDINGS

The best source for video recordings about Studs is Media Burn, http://mediaburn.org/?s=studs+terkel.

Harry Kreisler, "Interview with Studs Terkel, University of California, Berkeley, 2003," Media Burn Independent Video Archive, http://mediaburn.org/video/keeping-the-faith-in-difficult-times-an-evening-with-studs-terkel/.

Tom Weinberg, "The Story of Studs Terkel and Nelson Algren," Media Burn Independent Video Archive, http://mediaburn.org/blog/the-story-of-studs-terkel-and-nelson-algren/.

Tom Weinberg, Media Burn Independent Video Archive, "Studs on a Soapbox," Media Burn Independent Video Archive, http://mediaburn.org/video/studs-on-a-soapbox-3/.

Carol Marin, "Interview with Studs Terkel," *Chicago Tonight*, 2006, http://chicagotonight.wttw.com/2014/05/08/celebrating-studs-terkel.

Eric Simonson, *Studs Terkel: Listening to America,* HBO Films, 2012.

Jon Stewart, "Interview with Studs Terkel," *The Daily Show*, Comedy Central, April 4, 2006, http://thedailyshow.cc.com/videos/yth8q7/studs-terkel.

Bill Stamets, "Chicago Politics: A Theatre of Power," https://www.youtube.com/watch?v=SUlNzbVwvJEIbid.er Eleven:had not died so young.atre of Power:ded in Bill Stamets't six decades--including Ibid.er Eleven:had not died so young.atre of Power:ded in Bill Stamets't six decades--including .

Ray Suarez, "Interview with Studs Terkel," *PBS News Hour*, December 1, 2003. http://www.pbs.org/newshour/bb/remember-july-dec08-terkel_10-31/.

"Studs Terkel Interview," *Religion & Ethics Weekly*, December 19, 2003, http://www.pbs.org/wnet/religionandethics/2003/12/19/december-19-2003-interview-studs-terkel/11022/.

AUDIO RECORDINGS

Many of Studs' WFMT radio interviews can be found at https://www.popuparchive.com/collections/938.

Bob Edwards, "Interview with Studs Terkel," National Public Radio, November 8, 2001, http://www.npr.org/templates/story/story.php?storyId=1132885.

Calvin Trillin, "Interview with Studs Terkel," San Francisco City Arts and Lecture Series, 2002.

Amy Goodman, "Interview with Studs Terkel," *Democracy Now!*, May 16, 2007, (http://www.democracynow.org/2007/5/16/studs_terkel_at_95_ordinary_people.

Sydney Lewis, "Working with Studs," http://transom.org/2010/working-with-studs/.

Notes

INTRODUCTION

1. Carolyn Kellogg, "Harlan Ellison, Isaac Asimov, Studs Terkel together in 1982 video," *Los Angeles Times,* May 6, 2013. Available at http://articles.latimes.com/2013/may/06/entertainment/la-et-jc-harlan-ellison-isaac-asimov-studs-terkel-together-video-20130503.

2. Author's interview with Jamie Kalven, 2014.

3. Frank Beck, *Hobohemia* (Chicago: Charles H. Kerr Publishing, 2000), 6.

4. Author's Interview with Bill Ayers, 2015.

5. Tony Parker, *Studs Terkel: A Life in Words,* 164.

6. Ed Vulliaumy, "Studs Terkel," *The Guardian,* October 31, 2008, http://www.theguardian.com /world/2008/nov/01/studs-terkel-usa.

7. Ibid.

8. Parker, *Studs Terkel: A Life in Words,* 166.

9. Ibid., 163.

10. Ibid.

11. Author's interview with Victor Navasky, 2014.

12. Ibid.

13. Ronald Grele, *Envelopes of Sound: The Art of Oral History* (New York: Praeger, 1991), xx.

14. Denis Brian, *Murderers and Other Friendly People* (New York: McGraw Hill, 1973), 288.

15. Studs Terkel, "Morning in the Streets," http://transom.org/2001/studs-terkel-in-conversation/.

16. Grele, *Envelopes of Sound,* 24.

17. Ibid., 32.

18. Studs Terkel to André Schiffrin, 1969.

19. Sydney Lewis, "Working with Studs," http://transom.org/2010/working-with-studs/.

20. Michael Lenehan, "Translating from Speech to Prose," *Chicago Reader,* October 31, 2008, http://www1.chicagoreader.com/features/stories/ourtown/081106/.

21. Grele, *Envelopes of Sound,* 72.

22. Author's interview with Jamie Kalven, 2014.

23. Ibid., 195.

1. FROM BIALYSTOK TO CHICAGO

1. Tom Weinberg, Media Burn Independent Video Archive, "Studs on a Soapbox," Media Burn Independent Video Archive, http://mediaburn.org/video/studs-on-a-soapbox-3/).

2. Bialystok was a predominantly Jewish city on the Russia-Poland border.

3. Studs told this story throughout his life with the quote changing a bit each time.

4. Shelley Berman would say that he didn't *listen* to radio, but rather *watched* radio.

5. Studs Terkel, *Touch and Go* (New York: New Press, 2007), 12.

6. Ibid.

7. Author's interview with Sandy Terkell, 2014.

8. Terkel, *Touch and Go*, 15.
9. Franklin Rosemont, "Introduction," Frank Beck, *Hobohemia* (Chicago: Charles H. Kerr Publishing, 2000) 8.
10. Author's interview with Lois Baum, 2014.
11. Ibid.
12. Eugene V. Debs, "Statement to the Court," September 18, 1918, https://www.marxists.org/archive/debs/works/1918/court.htm.
13. Terkel, *Touch and Go*, 30.
14. "Studs Terkel at 95," interview with Amy Goodman, May 16, 2007, http://www.democracynow.org/shows/2007/5/16.
15. See Tom Weinberg, Media Burn, 1990, http://mediaburn.org/video/studs-terkel-at-the-wells-grand-talking-about-thanksgiving-1933-and-prohibition-repeal/.
16. Studs Terkel, *Talking to Myself* (New York: Pantheon Books, 1973), 48.
17. Author's interview with Roberta Lynch, 2015.
18. Ed Rampell, "Q & A with Studs Terkel," *Jewish Journal*, March 2, 2006, http://www.jewishjournal.com/tag/studs+terkel.
19. Paul Buhle and Nicole Schulman, eds., *Wobblies: A Graphic History of the Industrial Workers of the World* (London: Verso, 2005), 3.
20. Thomas Dyja, *The Third Coast* (New York: Penguin Books, 2013), xxiv.
21. Terkel, *Touch and Go*, 139
22. Ibid., 57.
23. Studs Terkel, *Will the Circle Be Unbroken?* (New York: Ballantine Books, 2001), xxi.
24. Author's interview with Haki Madhubuti, 2014.
25. Julius Hoffman was the judge who presided at the trial of the Chicago Seven.
26. Denis Brian, *Murderers and Other Friendly People* (New York: McGraw Hill, 1973) , 295.
27. Studs Terkel in Conversation with Craig Kridel, Bill Ayers, and

Rick Ayers, American Educational Research Association Conference, Chicago, April 2003.
28. Studs has different stories regarding his passing the bar examination, which he did pass. It appears that the most accurate version is that he qualified the second time he took the exam.

2. WORK, THEATER, POLITICS, AND, MOST IMPORTANTLY, IDA

1. Terkel, *Talking to Myself* (New York: Pantheon Books, 1973), 256.
2. Babwin, Don, "Studs Terkel's FBI File Unearthed, with a Few Surprises," http://www.huffingtonpost.com/2009/11/16/studs-terkel-fbi-file _n_360069.html.
3. Henry Kreisler and Studs Terkel, UC Berkeley, February 2004, http://www.uctv.tv/shows/Keeping-the-Faith-in-Difficult-Times-with-Studs-Terkel-Conversations-with-History-8371.
4. Studs told this story many times and each version was a little different. Besides the Studs Lonigan reference, he also often said that there were already other actors named Louis.
5. Studs Terkel, Jeff Award celebration for Nathan Davis, 2012, https://www.youtube.com/watch?v=kIQ0noF6DsY.
6. James Baker, *Studs Terkel* (New York: Twayne Publishers, 1992), 16, 17.
7. See Sydney Lewis's interview with Studs, "The Dumbest Gangster," http://transom.org/2001/studs-terkel-in-conversation/; Kreisler and Terkel, UC Berkeley..
8. Terkel, *Studs Terkel's Chicago* (New York: The New Press, 2012), 32.
9. Studs Terkel, interview for the film *Soul of the People*, transcript, Washington, Spark Media, March 2004.
10. Ibid.
11. Ibid.
12. Tony Parker, *Studs Terkel: A Life in Words* (New York: Henry Holt and Company, 1996), 220.

13. Ibid.

14. Ibid., 219.

15. Scott Ackman and Christopher Schwarz, "Dubious Legacy," *Chicago Magazine,* August 2008, http://www. chicagomag.com/Chicago-Magazine/ August-2008/Dubious-Legacy/.

16. Author's interview with Haskell Wexler, 2015.

17. The song was anti-lynching and depicted hangings in the South.

18. Terkel, *Touch and Go* (New York: New Press, 2007), 115.

19. Ibid., 105.

20. Rob Rosenthal and Sam Rosenthal, *Pete Seeger in His Own Words* (Boulder, CO: Paradigm Publishers, 2012), xii.

21. Nathan Godfried, *WCFL: Chicago's Voice of Labor* (Urbana: University of Illinois Press, 1997), 232.

22. Kreisler and Terkel, UC Berkeley.

23. See http://www.normancorwin. com/the-poet-laureate-of-radio-an- interview-with-norman-corwin-dvd/.

24. Studs Terkel, "The Bard of Radio," http://transom.org/2001/studs -terkel-in-conversation/.

25. Virginia and Clifford Durr were southerners who dedicated their lives to the civil rights movement in the 1950s and 1960s.

26. Mary McLeod Bethune was a well- known African American educator and activist who dedicated her life to provide higher education for black women.

27. Terkel, *Touch and Go*, 142.

28. Author's interview with Don Rose, 2015.

29. Terkel, *Touch and Go*, 135.

30. Terkel, *Talking to Myself*, 297.

31. Ibid.

32. Ibid., 299.

3. TELEVISION, THE BLACKLIST, AND WFMT

1. Studs Terkel, *Touch and Go* (New York: New Press, 2007), 119.

2. Thomas Dyja, *The Third Coast*, 178.

3. Ibid.

4. Garry Wills, *Outside Looking In: Adventures of an Observer* (New York: Penguin, 2010), 135.

5. Calvin Trillin, "Interview with Studs Terkel," San Francisco City Arts and Lecture Series, 2002.

6. Ibid.

7. Author's interview with Dan Terkell, 2014.

8. Author's interview with Ed Sadlowski, 2014.

9. Mark Naison, "Remaking America: Communists and Liberals in the Popular Front," in Frank Rosengarten and George Snedeker, eds., *New Studies in the Politics and Culture of U.S. Communism* (New York: Monthly Review Press, 1993).

10. Author's interview with Ronald Grele, 2015.

11. Author's interview with Dan Terkell, 2014.

12. Author's interview with Sydney Lewis, 2014.

13. James Baker, *Studs Terkel* (New York: Twayne Publishers, 1992), 24.

14. Studs Terkel, *Talking to Myself* (New York: Pantheon Books, 1973), 42.

15. Author's interview with Timuel Black, 2014.

16. Studs Terkel, "The Cool Medium," http://transom.org/2001/studs -terkel-in-conversation/.

17. There was also another short-run late-night local television show, *The Briefcase*, which aired for less than a year. Studs jested that the audi- ence consisted of ten insomniacs. See http://mediaburn.org/video/ inter view-with-studs-terkel-about- chicago-tv-in-the-50s/.

18. Trillin interview with Terkel, 2002.

19. Author's interview with Sydney Lewis, 2014.

20. Studs Terkel, *Giants of Jazz* (New York: New Press, 2006).

21. Henry Kreisler and Studs Terkel at UC Berkeley, February 2004, http://www.uctv.tv/shows/

Keeping-the-Faith-in-Difficult-Times-with-Studs-Terkel-Convers ations-with-History-8371.

22. Terkel, *Talking to Myself*, 266.

23. Ibid.

24. Pearl Hirshfield reflected on Studs' discomfort at the school meetings: "Studs was so quiet and out of his element that I thought he wasn't focused. And the same thing happened when I had an art exhibit. He looked like he didn't know where he was at. It was very interesting because Ida was so vivacious." Hirshfield's description is insightful, as both colleagues and friends commented that it was very clear when Studs was not interested in a topic. He didn't like confrontation, but his body language was definitive. He once told the writer Denis Brian, "When I'm bored, I walk out, disappear."

25. Author's interview with Pearl Hirshfield, 2014.

26. The 1959 list includes conversations with Nelson Algren, Carol Channing, Lawrence Ferlinghetti, Tito Gobbi, Lorraine Hansberry, Hal Holbrook, Robert Hutchins, Julian Huxley, Alan Lomax, Dorothy Parker, Sidney Poitier, and Win Stracke.

4. POLITICS, DISPARITY, AND WHITE SUPREMACY

1. Margaret Fuller was a nineteenth-century transcendentalist, feminist, writer, and teacher. See John Matteson, *The Lives of Margaret Fuller: A Biography* (New York: W.W. Norton, 2012).

2. F. Richard Ciccone, *Mike Royko: A Life in Print* (New York: Public Affairs, 2001), 108.

3. Studs Terkel, *Touch and Go* (New York: New Press, 2007), 208.

4. Studs Terkel, *Talking to Myself* (New York: Pantheon Books, 1973), 234–35.

5. Tony Parker, *Studs Terkel: A Life in*

Words (New York: Henry Holt and Company, 1996), 40.

6. Emma Graves Fitzimmons, "Florence Scala: 1918–2007," *Chicago Tribune*, August 29, 2007, http://chicagotribune. chicagotribune.com/2007-0829/ news/0708281426_1_hull-house-city-hall-studs-terkel.

7. Ibid.

8. Studs Terkel with James Baldwin, WFMT, July 15, 1961, https://www. popuparchive.com/collections/938/ items/6901.

9. Ibid.

10. Terkel, *Touch and Go*, 160.

11. Author's interview with Lois Baum, 2014.

12. Clifford Terry, "The Wide World of Studs Terkel," *Chicago Tribune*, July 2, 1978, http:// archives.chicagotribune. com/1978/07/02/page/150/article/ the-wide-world-of-studs-terkel.

13. "About Born to Live with Jim Unrath," http://transom.org/2011/ jim-unrath-born-to-live/.

14. The interviews were broadcast on Studs' program.

15. Nora Ephron, "A Higgledy-Piggledy Life," *New York Times*, September 26, 1999, https://www.nytimes.com/ books/99/09/26/specials/terkel-myself.html.

16. Author's interview with Rick Ayers, 2014.

17. Much of this section is from my *Dissident Voice* article, "South African Conversations: Studs Terkel on Racism and Apartheid," http://dissidentvoice.org/2014/02/ south -african-conversations -studs-terkel-on-racism-and apartheid/.

18. Terkel, *Talking to Myself.*

19. Ibid., 109.

20. Ibid., 111.

21. Ibid., 114.

22. Ibid.

23. Studs Terkel with Albert Luthuli, WFMT, March 1963, https://www.

popuparchive.com/collections/938/items/8391.

24. Studs Terkel, "The Train," WFMT, August 1963, http://conversations.studsterkel.org/radio.php.
25. Ibid.
26. Ibid.
27. Ibid.
28. Ibid.
29. Ibid.
30. Ibid.
31. Ibid.
32. W. E. B. DuBois was a sociologist, Pan Africanist, and great African American leader. He was the editor of the NAACP journal *The Crisis*, and the author of *The Souls of Black Folk*. See Aldon Morris, *The Scholar Denied: W. E. B. DuBois and the Birth of Modern Sociology* (Oakland: University of California Press, 2015).
33. Terkel, "The Train."
34. Studs Terkel and Martin Luther King Jr. interview, WFMT, October 22, 1964, https://archive.org/details/dr-martin-luther-king-jr-talks-to-studs-terkel-a.CSVgaR.popuparchive.org.
35. Ibid.
36. Ibid.
37. Ibid.
38. Ibid.
39. Ibid.
40. Ibid.
41. Studs Terkel and Mahalia Jackson Interview, WFMT, May 17, 1963, https://www.popuparchive.com/collections/938/items/10725.
42. Terkel and King, October 22, 1964.
43. Ibid.
44. Parker, *Studs Terkel: A Life in Words*, 25, 26.

5. CIVIL RIGHTS AND WFMT

1. Studs Terkel, *Joy Street*, WFMT, March 8, 1965, http://pacificaradioarchives.org/subject-tags/joy-street-produced-studs-terkel.
2. Virginia and Clifford Durr, WFMT, June 1965.
3. Martin Luther King Jr.'s speech at the conclusion of the Selma-to-Montgomery March, http://mlkkpp01.stanford.edu/index.php/encyclopedia/documentsentry/doc_address_at_the_conclusion_of_selma_march/.
4. Author's interview with Timuel Black, 2014.
5. Author's interview with C. T. Vivian, 2015.
6. By this time, King often asked the comedian, writer, and activist Dick Gregory to appear at events. Subsequently, Gregory helped raise funds for various organizations including SNCC.
7. Interviews from Montgomery, Alabama (Part 1), WFMT, March 25, 1965, https://www.popuparchive.com/collections/938/items/22163.
8. Ibid.
9. Ibid.
10. Myles Horton, WFMT interview, March 25, 1965, https://www.popuparchive.com/collections/938/items/22163.
11. Interview with a Young White Cabbie, WFMT, March 25, 1965, https://www.popuparchive.com/collections/938/items/22370.
12. Author's interview with Clancy Sigal, 2015.
13. Ibid.
14. Author's interview with Jules Feiffer, 2015.

6. DIVISION STREET: AMERICA

1. Author's interview with Victor Navasky, 2014.
2. Studs Terkel, *Division Street: America* (New York: Pantheon Books, 1965), xx.
3. Author's interview with Jamie Kalven, 2014.
4. Studs Terkel, *Touch and Go*, 183.
5. Ibid., 55.
6. Denis Brian, *Murderers and Other Friendly People* (New York: McGraw Hill, 1973), 309.

7. Tony Parker, *Studs Terkel: A Life in Words* (New York: Henry Holt and Company, 1996), 166.
8. Ibid., 235.
9. Terkel, *Division Street: America*, 331.
10. Ibid., 164.
11. Ibid., 31.
12. Ibid., 29.
13. Denis Brian, *Murderers and Other Friendly People*, 309.
14. Terkel, *Division Street: America*, 321.
15. Ibid., 325.
16. Ibid., 327.
17. Ibid., 328.
18. Author's interview with Tom Engelhardt, 2014.
19. Ibid.
20. Peter Lyons, "Chicago Voices," *New York Times*, February 5, 1967, http://www.nytimes.com/books/99/09/26/specials/terkel-division.html.
21. Michael E. Schlitz, "The Screen: Late Bloom," *Commonweal*, April 7, 1967, 101–4.
22. Patrick D. Hazard, "Chicago's FM Whitman," *AV Communication Review* 15/4 (Winter 1967): 441–43.
23. Andrew M. Greeley, "Wonderful Town," *The Reporter*, April 20, 1967, 53–54.
24. Ibid., 54.
25. Ibid.
26. Tom Weinberg, "Studs on a Soapbox," Media Burn Independent Video Archive, http://mediaburn.org/video/studs-on-a-soapbox-3/.
27. Bill Ayers, *Fugitive Days* (Boston: Beacon Press, 2001), 53.
28. Author's interview with Bill Ayers, 2015.

7. ENGAGING YOUTH: THE DEMOCRATIC CONVENTION AND CONTINUING PROGRESSIVE POLITICS

1. James Cameron to Studs Terkel, 1968.
2. Studs Terkel, *Talking to Myself* (New York: Pantheon Books, 1973), 197.
3. James Cameron interview, WFMT, May 1969.
4. Terkel, *Talking to Myself*, 200.
5. People who lived in Uptown were featured in Terkel's *Division Street: America*. Studs reviewed Todd Gitlin's and Nancy Hollander's *Uptown: Poor Whites in Chicago* in "Exile from the Mountains," *The Nation*, September 28, 1970, 280.
6. Arnie Bernstein, *Hollywood on Lake Michigan* (Chicago: Lake Claremont Press, 1998), 156.
7. Denis Brian, *Murderers and Other Friendly People* (New York: McGraw Hill, 1973), 309, 310.
8. Author's interview with Rick Ayers, 2014.
9. Author's interview with George Drury, 2014.
10. Author's interview with Tom Engelhardt, 2014.
11. Garry Wills, *Outside Looking In* (New York: Penguin, 2010), 13.
12. Ibid.
13. Studs Terkel, *Touch and Go* (New York: The New Press, 2007), 108.
14. Author's interview with Jo Friedman, 2015.
15. Guests included Saul Alinsky, Maya Angelou, Uri Avnery, Daniel Berrigan, Prexy Nesbit and Urie Bronfenbrenner, Gwendolyn Brooks, Mel Brooks, Art Buchwald, James Cameron, Marc Chagall, John Cheever, Noam Chomsky, Ramsey Clark, Judy Collins, Emile DeAntonio, Ralph Ellison, Naomi Weisnstein, Nadine Gordimer, Dick Gregory, David Halberstam, Janice Ian, C. L. R. James, P. D. James, Doris Kearns, Janis Joplin, Harry Kalven, Louis Malle, Marcel Marceau, Bernadette Devlin, Dave Van Ronk, Arthur Miller, Anais Nin, Scott and Helen Nearing, Tom Paxton, Utah Phillips, John Prine, Mike Royko, William Saroyan, Pete Seeger, Hunter Thompson, Dalton Trumbo, Steve Goodman, Hugo Black, Barry Commoner, Merce Cunningham, John Cage, Ernest Gaines, Tito Gobbi, Thich Nat Hanh,

Arlo Guthrie, John Lee Hooker, Norman Mailer, Charlie Mingus, Victor Navasky, Barbara Tuchman, Tom Wolfe, Dave Bromberg, William Sloane Coffin, Jonathan Kozol, Daniel Ellsberg, R.D. Laing, Anthony Quinn, Eubie Blake, Jimmy Breslin, Joseph Campbell, Gunter Grass, Lillian Hellman, Alger Hiss, Eric Hobsbawm, Herman Kogan, Robert Jay Lifton, Gary Hart, Jessica Mitford, Olaf Palme, Rosa Parks, Myles Horton, Florence Scala, Peggy Terry, Fred Wiseman, Diane Arbus, Nelson Algren, Cornell Capa, Robert Caro, Dick Cavett, Alistair Cooke, Dave Garroway, Geraldine Page, Erica Jong, Maggie Smith, Alison Lurie, Toni Morrison, Jules Feiffer, Ed Sadlowski, Bobby Short, Gore Vidal, Quentin Young, Bernstein and Woodward, Bruno Bettelheim, Dave Dellinger, Vine Deloria, Leon Despres, Nora Ephron, John Kenneth Galbraith, Brendan Gill, Allen Ginsberg, William Burroughs, Fred and LaDonna Harris, Joseph Heller, John Houseman, Delores Huerta, Bernie Jacobs Memorial, Elia Kazan, Shirley MacLaine, Eugene McCarthy, Michael Meeropol.

16. Topics included Pakistan, Vietnam, Chicago schools, gays and lesbians, feminism, environmentalism, truckers, drug addiction, Waldorf School education, the Young Lords, school integration, civil rights, baseball, the Depression, Bastille Day, Frederick Douglass and the abolitionists, Cambodia, political activism, Hispanic Americans, community organizing, Kent State, political prisoners, capital punishment, China, special education, infidelity, and six shows on Chicago neighborhood activism that corresponded to Studs' attempts to help save the Hull House community from urban removal.

17. Author's interview with Lois Baum, 2014.

18. Andi Lamoreaux, "Let's Get Working," A Celebration of Studs Terkel, May 10, 2014.

19. Author's interview with George Drury, 2014; and interview with Donald Tait, 2015.

20. Brian, *Murderers and Other Friendly People*, 300.

21. Noam Chomsky interview, WFMT, January 1970 (https://archive.org/details/popuparchive-1950324).

22. Ibid.

23. Mrs. Herb Gottlieb to Studs Terkel, 1968.

24. Elizabeth Eddy to Studs Terkel, 1968.

25. Donald Palmer to Studs Terkel, 1970.

26. Harrison Salisbury to Studs Terkel, 1969.

27. Studs Terkel, *Hope Dies Last: Keeping the Faith in Difficult Times* (New York: The New Press, 2003), 142.

28. Haki Madhubuti, National Literary Hall of Fame for Writers of African Descent, Chicago, 1999.

29. Studs Terkel, *Race* (New York: The New Press, 1992), 6.

30. Studs Terkel, "Frank," *Chicago Magazine*, July 1975, 86, 87.

31. Author's interview with Bernardine Dohrn, 2015.

32. Raymond Nelson to Studs Terkel, 1968.

33. Author's interview with Hank DeZutter, 2014.

34. Senator Paul Simon to Studs Terkel, 1971.

35. Brian, *Murderers and Other Friendly People*, 304.

36. Andi Lamoreaux, "Let's Get Working," A Celebration of Studs Terkel at the University of Chicago, May 10, 2014.

37. Brian, *Murderers and Other Friendly People*, 296.

8. *HARD TIMES* AND *WORKING*: BOOKS AND LIFE

1. Tony Parker, *Studs Terkel: A Life in*

Words (New York: Henry Holt and Company, 1996), 223.

2. Studs Terkel, *Hard Times* (New York: Avon Books, 1979), 3.

3. Studs Terkel, "Notes on the Big D," Chicago History Museum, unpublished ms.

4. Ibid., 310.

5. Ibid., 310, 311.

6. Ibid., 462.

7. Ibid., 420.

8. Ibid., 113.

9. Ibid., 109, 110.

10. Ibid., 48, 49.

11. Henry Resnick, "America Was Singing, 'Brother Can You Spare a Dime,'" *Saturday Review*, 27.

12. Michael Frisch, "Oral History and Hard Times," in Robert Perks and Alistair Thomson, *The Oral History Reader* (London: Routledge, 1998), 31.

13. Resnick, "America Was Singing," 27.

14. Michael Frisch, *A Shared Authority: Essays on the Craft and Meaning of Oral and Public History* (Albany, NY: SUNY Press, 1990), 9.

15. Studs Terkel, *Working: People Talk About What They Do All Day and How They Feel About What They Do* (New York: Avon Books, 1972), xiii.

16. Ibid.

17. Ibid., xiv.

18. Ibid.

19. This became one of the stories that Studs often told, including in his 2003 appearance on *The Daily Show*.

20. Terkel, *Working*, xxi.

21. Ibid., xxii.

22. Gus Tyler, *Industrial Labor Relations Review* 28/2 (January 1975): 324.

23. Ibid.

24. Studs Terkel to Jack Egan, 1972.

25. Author's interview with Haki Madhubuti, 2014.

26. Calvin Trillin, "Interview with Studs Terkel," San Francisco City Arts and Lecture Series, 2002.

27. Tom Weinberg, Media Burn Independent Video Archive, http://

mediaburn.org/blog/the-story-of-studs-terkel-and-nelson-algren/.

28. Author's interview with Lois Baum, 2014.

29. H. E. F. Donohue and Nelson Algren, *Conversations with Nelson Algren*, (Chicago: University of Chicago Press, 1963), 308.

9. MEMOIR MEETS ORAL HISTORY

1. Muhammed Ali, WFMT interview, 1975, https://www.popuparchive.com/collections/938/items/6950

2. Ibid.

3. Ibid.

4. Phillip Levine, WFMT interview, 1977. The book under discussion was Phillip Levine, *Don't Ask: Poets on Poetry* (Ann Arbor: University of Michigan Press, 1981).

5. Ibid.

6. Author's interview with Calvin Trillin, 2014.

7. Nadine Gordimer, WFMT interview, 1978.

8. John Nichols, "Studs Terkel, You Will Be Missed," *The Nation*, October 31, 2008.

9. John R. MacArthur, *Harper's*, February 13, 2009, http://harpers.org/blog/2009/02/studs-terkel-radical-conservative/.

10. Studs Terkel, "For 21 Years, He Was the Boss, the Ultimate Clout," *New York Times*, December 22, 1976, https://www.nytimes.com/books/99/09/26/specials/terkel-boss.html.

11. Studs Terkel, *Working: People Talk About What They Do All Day and How They Feel About What They Do* (New York: Avon Books, 1972), xxiv.

12. Nora Ephron, "A Higgledy-Piggledy Life," *New York Times*, April 10, 1977.

13. Terkel, *Talking to Myself* (New York: Pantheon Books, 1973) NP.

14. Carol deGiere, *Defying Gravity: The Creative Career of Stephen Schwartz from Godspell to Wicked* (New York: Applause Books, 2014), 148.

15. Ibid., 147.
16. Author's interview with Stephen Schwartz, 2014.
17. Ibid.
18. DeGiere, *Defying Gravity*, 163.
19. Clifford Terry, "The Wide World of Studs," *Chicago Tribune Magazine*, July 2, 1978, http://archives.chicago-tribune.com/1978/07/02/page/149/article/display-ad-122-no-title.
20. Ibid.
21. Ibid.
22. Ibid.
23. Author's interview with Steve Robinson, 2015.
24. Ibid.
25. Dan Eastman, "The MoJo Interview: Studs Terkel," *Mother Jones*, September/October 1995, http://www.mother-jones.com/media/1995/09/mojo-interview-studs-terkel.
26. Author's interview with David Royko, 2015.
27. Mike Royko, *Sez Who? Sez Me* (New York: Warner Books, 1973), 1, 2.
28. Dan LaBotz, "Barry Commoner, a Great Presidential Candidate (1917–2012)," *New Solutions* 22/4 (February 2013): 419–21.
29. Studs Terkel, Citizen's Party Convention, Cleveland, 1980.
30. Author's interview with Sandy McCall, 2015.
31. Ibid.
32. Ibid.
33. Ibid.
34. Author's interview with Elizabeth Furse, 2015.
35. Studs Terkel, *American Dreams Lost and Found* (New York: Ballantine Books, 1981), xx, xxi.
36. Author's interview with Furse.
37. In the book Amanda Jones is Emma Knight.
38. Terkel, *American Dreams*, 6.
39. Ibid.
40. Ibid., 226.
41. Dan Rather, "Interview with Studs Terkel," *60 Minutes*, December 28, 1980, http://mediaburn.org/video/60-minutes-studs-terkel/.
42. Terkel, *American Dreams*, 232, 233.

10. CHICAGO AND BEYOND: THE FIRST HALF OF THE 1980s

1. Joe Pintauro, "Nelson Algren's Last Year: Algren in Exile," *Chicago Magazine*, February 1, 1988, http://www.chicagomag.com/Chicago-Magazine/February-1988/Nelson-Algrens-Last-Year-Algren-in-Exile/.
2. Ibid.
3. "Come In at the Door," *Studs Terkel Show*, WFMT, 1981.https://www.popuparchive.com/collections/938/items/36581.
4. Frank Walsh to Studs Terkel, 1981.
5. Author's interview with David Royko, 2014.
6. Author's interview with Hamilton Fish, 2014.
7. Studs Terkel and Calvin Trillin, *Nightcap*, https://www.youtube.com/watch?v=RZvcKB9vQO0.
8. Calvin Trillin, "Interview with Studs Terkel," San Francisco City Arts and Lecture Series, 2002.
9. Author's interview with Kay Nichols, 2014.
10. Ibid.
11. Ibid.
12. Ibid.
13. Gwendolyn Brooks, "Black Woman in Russia," in Elaine Lee, *Go Girl! The Black Woman's Book of Travel and Adventure* (Portland, OR: Eighth Mountain Press, 1997), 237.
14. Ibid.
15. Yassen Zassoursky interview, WFMT, https://www.popuparchive.com/collections/938/items/9078.
16. Studs Terkel, *"The Good War"* (New York: Pantheon, 1984), 435.
17. Author's interview with Don Rose, 2014.
18. Bill Stamets, *Chicago Politics: A Theatre of Power*, Chicago, Media Burn, April 15, 1987.http://

mediaburn.org/video/chicago-politics-a -theatre-of-power-4/.

19. Robert Davis, "The Election of Harold Washington the First Black Mayor of Chicago," *Chicago Tribune* http://www.chicagotribune.com/news/nationworld/politics/chi-chicagodays-haroldwashington-story-story.html.

20. Kurt Jacobsen, "A Conversation with Studs Terkel," *Logos* 3/2 (Spring 2004), available at http://www.logosjournal.com/terkel.pdf.

11. "THE GOOD WAR"

1. Author's interview with Tony Judge, 2014.

2. Ibid.

3. Stewart McBride, "Studs Terkel," *Christian Science Monitor*, September 1, 1983, http://www.csmonitor.com /1983/0901/090144.html.

4. Ibid.

5. Ibid.

6. Ibid.

7. Author's interview with Mike Edgerly, 2014.

8. Ibid.

9. Ibid.

10. Author's interview with Rick Ayers, 2014.

11. Studs Terkel, "*The Good War*" (New York: Pantheon Books, 1984), 404.

12. Calvin Trillin, "Interview with Studs Terkel," San Francisco City Arts and Lecture Series, 2002.

13. Terkel, "*The Good War*," 5.

14. Ibid.

15. Ibid., 201.

16. Ibid., 335.

17. Ibid., 497, 498.

18. Ibid., 28.

19. A survivor of the bombings of Hiroshima and Nagasaki.

20. Terkel, "*The Good War*," 39.

21. Ibid., 59.

22. Ibid., 121.

23. Carol Brightman, " 'The Good War': An Oral History of World War II," *The Nation*, December 8, 1984.

24. Loudon Wainwright, "I Can Remember Every Hour," *New York Times*, October 7, 1984, https://www.nytimes.com/books/99/09/26/specials/terkel-goodwar.html.

25. Maureen Dowd, "Sunday in the Park among Winners of Pulitzers," *New York Times*, April 25, 1985, https://www.nytimes.com/books/98/07/19/specials/sondheim-pulitzer.html.

26. John Blades, "Prize Winner: Studs Terkel's Pulitzer a Popular Choice but Controversial to His Critics," *Chicago Tribune*, April 26, 1985, http://articles.chicagotribune.com/1985-04-26/features/8501250462_1_oral-histories -studs-terkel-critics.

27. Mike Royko, "Vintage Whines from Professors," *Chicago Tribune*, May 20, 1985, http://articles.chicagotribune.com/1985-05-20/news/8501310946_1_english-professor-oral-history-studs-terkel.

28. Norman Corwin to Studs Terkel, 1985/6.

12. CONTROVERSY AT WORK: BUT LIFE GOES ON

1. Studs Terkel to the WTTW Board, February 17, 1987.

2. Eric Zorn, "Volume Turned Up in WFMT Battle," *Chicago Tribune*, April 15, 1985, http://articles.chicagotribune.com/1985-08-15/features/8502230355_1_studs-terkel-station-tribune-broadcasting.

3. Author's interview with Sydney Lewis, 2014.

4. Studs Terkel, "McCarter and His Board," *Chicago Reader*, September 17, 1992, http://www.chicagoreader.com/chicago/terkel-on-mccarter/Content?oid=880471.

5. Michael Miner, "WFMT Takes a Turn," *Chicago Reader*, http://www.chicagoreader.com/chicago/wfmt-takes-a-turn/Content?oid=875087.

6. Author's interview with Tony Judge,

2014.
7. Kay Richards to WFMT Board, 1990.
8. Studs Terkel, "McCarter and His Board," *Chicago Reader*, September 17, 1992, http://www.chicagoreader.com/chicago/terkel-on-mccarter/Content?oid=880471.
9. Mike Royko, "A TV Masterpiece of Sneaking Around," *Chicago Tribune*, June 26, 1990, http://articles.chicagotribune.com/1990-06-26/news/9002210535_1_studs-place-studs-terkel-oral-histories.
10. Author's interview with Ed Sadlowski, 2014.
11. John Madigan, WBBM Radio, November 20, 1986.
12. Author's interview with Don Rose, 2014.
13. Author's interview with Penelope Rosemont, 2015.
14. Alice McGrath to Studs Terkel, November 30, 1994.
15. Studs Terkel, *The Great Divide: Second Thoughts on the American Dream* (New York: Avon Books, 1988), 10.
16. Ibid., 2.
17. Scott Craig, *Documentary on Studs Terkel*, June 15, 1989, http://mediaburn.org/video/studs-2/.
18. Jim Stull, *Oral History Review* 17/2 (Autumn 1989): 186.
19. Ibid.
20. Mel Elfin, "The Haves, the Have-Nots and the Have-Somewhats," *New York Times*, October 9, 1988. Available at https://www.nytimes.com/books/99/09/26/specials/terkel-divide.html.
21. After appearing in *Eight Men Out*, a Studs Terkel baseball card was issued and numerous people sent them to Studs for his signature.
22. Media Burn Independent Video Archive, http://mediaburn.org/?s=john+sayles.
23. Ibid.
24. Media Burn Independent Video Archive, http://mediaburn.org/video/studs-2/.
25. Alexander Tchachenko to Studs Terkel.
26. Studs Terkel, "A Couple of Guys Talk Peace," *The Nation*, July 30–August 6, 1990, 1.
27. Ibid., 130.
28. "350 at Rally Accuse Random House of Killing Subsidiary," *Los Angeles Times*, March 6, 1990, http://articles.latimes.com/1990-03-06/news/mn-1942_1_random-house.
29. Blades, John, "Notes Uprooted Legend: Studs Terkel Cries Foul at 'Bean Counters and Hit Men,'" *Chicago Tribune*, June 13, 1990 (file:///Users/awieder/Desktop/studs/studsmarch/Tribune/Uprooted%20Legend%20-%20tribunedigital-chicagotribune.html).

13. 80th BIRTHDAY AND OTHER MILESTONES

1. Minsa Craig to Ida and Studs Terkel.
2. Author's interview with Laura Watson, 2014.
3. Rick Kogan, "Studs Terkel: 1912–2008, *Chicago Tribune*, November 1, 2008, http://articles.chicagotribune.com/2008-11-01/news/0810310493_1_louis-studs-terkel-radio-chicago/3.
4. Tom Buckley, Bob Saldeen, and Bernard Van Marm, "Studs Terkel Toast," Chicago, Media Burn, http://mediaburn.org/video/studs-terkel-toast/.
5. Mike Royko interview, June 17, 1996, WFMT, https://www.popuparchive.com/collections/938/items/22277.
6. Jacques Testard and Gwenael Pouliquen, "Interview with Andre Schiffrin," January 2011, http://www.thewhitereview.org/interviews/interview-with-andre-schiffrin/.
7. Sydney Lewis, "Working w ith Studs," http://transom.org/2010/working-with-studs/.

8. Author's interview with Sydney Lewis, 2014.

9. Dick Gordon's interview with Mark Larson, WBEZ, 2008, http://www.thestory.org/stories/kenyan-connection-1172008.

10. Ibid.

11. Author's interview with Hank DeZutter, 2014.

12. Studs Terkel, *Race: How Blacks and Whites Think and Feel About the American Obsession* (New York: The New Press, 1992), 198.

13. Ibid., 288, 289.

14. Ibid., 9, 10.

15. Ibid., 236.

16. Ibid., 103.

17. Ibid., 98.

18. Ibid., 112.

19. Ibid., 263.

20. Author's interview with Tom Engelhardt, 2014.

21. Author's interview with Ken Burns, 2015.

22. Studs Terkel, in Ken Burns, *Baseball*, Public Broadcasting System, 1994.

23. Author's interview with Ken Burns, 2015.

24. Guests included Mortimer Adler, Bill Ayers, Jim Bailey, Jack Beatty, Leonard Bernstein, Eric Bogosian, Hoagy Carmichael, Robert Coles, Judy Collins, David Dellinger, Louise Erdrich, Jules Feiffer, Shel Silverstein, David Halberstam, Jim Hightower, Molly Ivins, Ella Jenkins, Paul Krasner, Donna Blue Lachman, David Levering Lewis, N. Scott Momaday, Bill Moyers, Sebastiao Salgado, Clancy Sigal, Mona Simpson, Calvin Trillin, Cornel West, Derrick Bell, Norman Corwin, John Egerton, Daniel Ellsberg, Allen Ginsberg, Doris Kearns Goodwin, Lani Guinier, Pete Hamill, Joseph Heller, Alan Lomax, Scott McCloud, Tom Paxton, Nelson Peery, Sister Helen Prejean, Art Spiegelman, Brent Staples, Lily Tomlin, Calvin Trillin, Milton Viorst, Jim Wallis, Garry Wills, Tobias Wolff, Edwin Albee, Shana Alexander, Russell Banks, Guy Carawan, Charlayne Hunter-Gault, Keith Jarrett, Dennis Kucinich, Sydney Lewis, Deborah Meier, Herbert Mitgang, Tony Parker, Charles Payne, Reynolds Price, Jeremy Rifkin, Anna Deavere Smith, Father Daniel Berrigan, Jimmy Breslin, Robert Coover, Roger Ebert, Mary Gordon, Stephen Jay Gould, Arlo Guthrie, Uta Hagen, William Kennedy, Jamaica Kincaid, Eartha Kitt, Lawrence Levine, James McBride, George McGovern, Michael Moore, Lisel Mueller, Victor Navasky, Martha Nussbaum, Conor Cruise O'Brien, Mike Rose, Carl Rowan, Nora Sayre, Ruth Sidel, Daniel Singer, Patricia Sullivan, William Julius Wilson, Margaret Atwood, Ira Berkow, Patricia Bosworth, Robert Coles, Claudia Dreifus, Richard Ford, Leon Forrest, Eduardo Galeano, Daniel Goldhagen, William Greider, Seymour Hersh, Doris Lessing, Staughton Lynd, Marcel Marceau, Oliver Sacks, André Schiffrin, Wallace Shawn, Paul Simon, James Weinstein, Eudora Welty, Quentin Young, and Richard Stern. Besides shows on music and theater, themes included education, nuclear weapons, ACORN, international Brotherhood of Electrical Workers, James Earl Jones, peace activists, Maxwell Street vendors, Cuba, environmentalism, Irish politics, African American journalists, gangs, homelessness, women from Serbia, Bosnia, Croatia, Nicaragua, gay men, neighborhood activists, architects, Schools of America Watch, El Salvador, Cuba, poetry, basketball, Elvis Presley, Mahalia Jackson, Viet Nam, AIDS, Algren, People's Uptown Law Center, political refugees, disarmament, Hoop Dreams, health care reform, nuclear energy, Haymarket, China, Haiti, abortion, and grassroots organizing.

25. John Blades, "Notes Uprooted Legend: Studs Terkel Cries Foul at 'Bean Counters and Hit Men,'" *Chicago Tribune*, June 13, 1990 (file:///Users/awieder/Desktop/studs/studsmarch/Tribune/Uprooted%20 Legend%20-%20tribunedigital-chicagotribune.html).

26. Author's interview with Donald Tait, 2015.

27. Studs Terkel, *Coming of Age: The Story of Our Century by Those Who've Lived It* (New York: St. Martin's Press, 1995), 239.

28. Ibid., 44, 45.

29. Ibid., 47.

30. Author's interview with Sydney Lewis, 2014.

31. Kurt Jacobsen, "A Conversation with Studs Terkel," *Logos*, Spring 2004, http://www.logosjournal.com/terkel.pdf.

32. Author's interview with Sydney Lewis, 2014.

33. Studs Terkel, *The Spectator* (New York: New Press, 1999), 23.

34. Jerry Crimmins and Rick Kogan, "A Tribute to Mike Royko," *Daily Reporter*, May 6, 1997, 4.

35. Robert Coles is known for his book series *Children of Crisis*.

36. Studs Terkel, *My American Century* (New York: The New Press, 1997), xv.

37. Author's interview with Ronald Grele, 2015.

38. "Arts and Humanities Medals Awards," C-SPAN, September, 29, 1997, http://www.c-span.org/video/?92124-1/arts-humanities-medal-awards.

39. Calvin Trillin, "Interview with Studs Terkel," San Francisco City Arts and Lecture Series, 2002.

40. 1997 National Book Foundation Awards, http://www.nationalbook.org/nbaacceptspeech_sterkel_intro.html#.VubpXBiQO-k.

41. Ibid.

42. Tom Weinberg, "Studs on a Soapbox," Chicago, Media Burn, http://mediaburn.org/video/studs-on-a-soapbox-3/.

43. Haki Madhubuti, National Literary Hall of Fame for Writers of African Descent, Chicago, 1999.

44. Author's interview with Haki Madhubuti, 2014.

45. Terkel, *The Spectator*, xiv.

46. Ibid., 3.

47. Ibid., 80.

48. Ibid.

14. GRIEF, AND THEN AGAIN LIFE

1. Rick Kogan, "Studs Terkel Dies," *Chicago Tribune*, October 31, 2008, http://www.chicagotribune.com/news/chi-studs-terkel-dead-story.html.

2. Sydney Lewis, "Ida Terkel Memorial," Chicago, 1999, Media Burn Independent Video Archive, http://mediaburn.org/video/ida-terkels-memorial-service-2/.

3. Author's interview with Quentin Young, 2014.

4. Ibid.

5. Lewis, "Ida Terkel Memorial."

6. Garry Wills, "Ida Terkel Memorial."

7. Ibid.

8. Studs Terkel, Chicago City Council, 2000, https://www.youtube.com/watch?v=vP5jXEGrKfw.

9. Studs Terkel, "The Nader Factor," panel on *The Nation* cruise, Media Burn Independent Video Archive, http://mediaburn.org/video/the-nation-panel-the-nader-factor/.

10. Author's interview with Katrina vanden Heuvel, 2014.

11. Terkel, "The Nader Factor."

12. Author's interview with Jim Hightower, 2015.

13. Author's interview with Patricia Williams, 2014.

14. Palash Davé, *Hitch Hike* https://www.youtube.com/watch?v=QzSiNOYL-d0.

15. Studs Terkel, Letter to the Editor, December 2002.

16. Author's interview with Danny Postel, 2015.

17. Steve Neal, "Falwell, Terkel Fill the Air with Nonsense," *Chicago Sun Times*, September 21, 2001, http://work.colum.edu/~amiller/nealattacksstuds.htm.

18. Studs Terkel, blurb for Bill Ayers's *Fugitive Days* (Boston: Beacon, 2001).

19. Author's interview with Bill Ayers, 2015.

20. Michael Miner, "The Knife in Studs' Back/With New Teflon Coating," *Chicago Reader,* http://www.chicagoreader.com/chicago/the-knife-in-studss-backws-new-teflon-coating/Content?oid=906557.

21. Ibid.

22. Ibid.

23. Rick Ayers, *Studs Terkel's Working: A Teaching Guide* (New York: New Press, 2001), 142.

24. Author's interview with Ken Burns, 2015.

25. Author's interview with Steve Robinson, 2015.

26. Studs Terkel on *60 Minutes*, CBS, 2001.

27. Author's interview with Carol Marin, 2015.

28. Author's interview with Eric Simonson, 2015.

29. Studs Terkel, "The Importance of Remembering History," Pennsylvania State Legislature, 2001, Media Burn Independent Video Archive, http://mediaburn.org/video/the-speakers-millennium-lecture-with-studs-terkel/.

30. Ibid.

31. Ibid.

32. "Harry Kreisler Interview with Studs Terkel," University of California-Berkeley, 2003, Media Burn Independent Video Archive, http://mediaburn.org/video/keeping-the-faith-in-difficult-times-an-evening-with-studs-terkel/.

33. Author's interview with Bill Ayers, 2015.

34. Studs Terkel in Conversation with Craig Kridel, Bill Ayers, and Rick Ayers, American Educational Research Association Conference, Chicago, 2003.

35. Author's interview with Rick Ayers, 2013.

36. Author's interview with Joy Gregory, 2015.

37. Ibid.

38. Author's interview with David Schwimmer, 2015.

39. Ibid.

40. Author's interview with Joy Gregory, 2015.

41. Studs Terkel, "Kucinich Is the One," *The Nation*, May 6, 2002.

14. WILL THE CIRCLE BE BROKEN? AND HOPE DIES LAST

1. Author's interview with Tom Engelhardt, 2014.

2. Ibid.

3. Studs Terkel, *Will the Circle Be Unbroken? Reflections on Death, Rebirth, and Hunger for Faith* (New York: Ballantine Books, 2001), xx.

4. Ibid., 21.

5. Ibid., 399.

6. Ibid., 216.

7. Ibid., 227.

8. "Bob Edwards' Interview with Studs Terkel," National Public Radio, November 8, 2001, http://www.npr.org/templates/story/story.php?storyId=1132885.

9. Barry Miles, *Mother Jones*, November–December 2001, v26, i6, 80, 81.

10. Ibid.

11. Ibid.

12. Ibid.

13. Rick Kogan, "Conversations With Studs," *Chicago Tribune Magazine*, October 28, 2001, 10.

14. Ibid.

15. Herbert Mitgang, "A Microphone for Eternity," *The Nation*, December 3, 2001, 32.

16. Ibid., 34.

17. Ibid.
18. Author's interview with Engelhardt.
19. Studs Terkel, *Hope Dies Last: Keeping the Faith in Difficult Times* (New York: New Press, 2003), xvii.
20. Ibid., 115.
21. Ibid., 123.
22. Ibid., 128.
23. Margaret Atwood, "He Springs Eternal," *New York Review of Books,* http://www.nybooks.com/articles/archives/2003/nov/06/he-springs-eternal/.
24. "Ray Suarez Interview with Studs Terkel," *PBS News Hour*, December 1, 2003.
25. Studs Terkel Interview, *Religion and Ethics Weekly*, December 19, 2003, http://www.pbs.org/wnet/religionandethics/2003/12/19/december-19-2003-interview-studs-terkel/11022/.
26. Ibid.
27. Author's interview with David Isay, 2015.

16. COMPLETING THE CIRCLE

1. Author's interview with Katrina vanden Heuvel, 2015.
2. Author's interview with Steve Robinson, 2015.
3. Author's interview with J. R. Millares, 2015.
4. Ibid.
5. Author's interview with Sydney Lewis, 2014.
6. Ibid.
7. Author's interview with Jackie Rivers-Rivet, 2014.
8. Author's interview with Kathy Kelly, 2014.
9. See http://storycorps.org/animation/the-human-voice/.
10. Ibid.
11. Carol Marin, "Interview with Studs Terkel," *Chicago Tonight*, 2006, http://chicagotonight.wttw.com/2014/05/08/celebrating-studs-terkel.
12. Ibid.
13. Author's interview with Steve Robinson, 2015.

14. Roger Ebert, *Life Itself* (New York: Grand Central Publishing, 2011), 399.
15. Studs Terkel, *And They All Sang* (New York: New Press, 2005), xvi.
16. Ibid., 8. ttp://muse.jhu.edu/journalshtmloans the city' then giggles, "y the silence except for the computer generated ttp://muse.jhu.edu/journals.html.
17. Ibid., 18.
18. Ibid., 78.
19. Jon Stewart's interview with Studs Terkel, *The Daily Show*, Comedy Central, April 4, 2006, http://thedailyshow.cc.com/videos/yth8q7/studs-terkel.
20. Ibid.
21. Ibid.
22. Mary Beth Hamilton, *Belfast Telegraph,*
23. Anthony DeCurtis, "Maestro of Chat," *Chicago Tribune*, October 2, 2005, http://articles.chicagotribune.com/keyword/studs-terkel/featured/4.
24. Studs mentioned a second memoir to Roger Ebert just before his heart surgery. He said that the title might be *The Great American Lobotomy*, referring to his view that we collectively suffered from Alzheimer's disease.
25. I owe this insight to Michael Frisch.
26. See http://wttw.vo.llnwd.net/o16/wfmt/specials/studs_bday2.mp3.
27. Amy Goodman interview with Studs Terkel, *Democracy Now!*, May 16, 2007, http://www.democracynow.org/2007/5/16/studs_terkel_at_95_ordinary_people.
28. Ibid.
29. See https://www.aclu.org/news/author-studs-terkel-other-prominent-chicagoans-join-challenge-att-sharing-telephone-records.
30. See https://zcomm.org/zmagazine/studs-terkel-1912-2008-by-various-contributors/.
31. See http://www.nytimes.com/2007/10/29/opinion/29terkel.html.

32. *The Elder Studs Terkel: Activist for Labor* (https://www.youtube.com/watch?v=vP5jXEGrKfw).
33. Studs Terkel with Sydney Lewis, *Touch and Go* (New York: The New Press, 2007), xii.
34. Jacqueline Lazu, "*Touch and Go* (Review)," *Oral History Review* (Winter/Spring 2009), (http://muse.jhu.edu/journals/ohr/summary/v036/36.1.lazu.html).
35. Ibid.
36. Author's interview with Sydney Lewis, 2014.
37. Author's interview with Carol Marin, 2015.
38. Ibid.
39. Ebert, *Life Itself*, 401.
40. Ibid.
41. Ibid.

EPILOGUE
1. Laura Flanders, "Memorial Service for Studs Terkel," http://www.c-span.org/video/?282901-1/memorial-service-studs-terkel.
2. Katrina vanden Heuvel, ibid.
3. André Schiffrin, ibid.
4. Dan Terkell, ibid.
5. Rick Kogan, "A Celebration of the Life of Studs Terkel," http://mediaburn.org/video/a-celebration-of-the-life-of-studs-terkel/.
6. Chaz Ebert, ibid.
7. Timuel Black, ibid.
8. Garry Wills, ibid.
9. Edward Rothstein, "He Gave Voice to Many," *New York Times*, November 1, 2008, http://www.nytimes.com/2008/11/03/books/03terk.html.
10. Victor Navasky, "Memorial Service for Studs Terkel."
11. André Schiffrin, "A Celebration of the Life of Studs Terkel."
12. Michael Frisch, "Studs Terkel Historian," *History Workshop Journal* 69 (Spring 2010), 197.
13. Ibid.

Index